The Wiles of Women/ The Wiles of Men

The Wiles of Women/ The Wiles of Men

Joseph and Potiphar's Wife in Ancient Near Eastern, Jewish, and Islamic Folklore

Shalom Goldman

State University of New York Press

The author gratefully acknowledges the following for granting permission to quote from previously published material:

The Jewish Publication Society for excerpts from *Tanakh: The Holy Scriptures*. Used by Permission.

Princeton University Press for excerpts from James Pritchard, *Ancient Near Eastern Texts Relating to the Old Testament*. Used by Permission.

Simon and Schuster, Inc. for excerpts from *The Koran Interpreted* by A. J. Arberry, translator. Copyright by George Allen and Unwin, Ltd. Used by Permission.

The University of Chicago Press for excerpts from *The Iliad of Homer*, R. Lattimore, translator. Used by Permission.

The illustrations are from a seventeenth-century Persian manuscript of Firdawsi's *Yūsuf and Zuleikha* (Dartmouth College LIbrary, Special Collections, Hanover, NH)

Published by
State University of New York Press, Albany

For information, address State University of New York Press,
State University Plaza, Albany, NY 12246

Production by Cynthia Tenace Lassonde
Marketing by Bernadette LaManna

Library of Congress Cataloging-in-Publication Data

Goldman, Shalom.
    The wiles of women/the wiles of men : Joseph and Potiphar's wife in ancient Near Eastern, Jewish, and Islamic folklore / Shalom Goldman.
        p.   cm.
    Includes bibliographical references and index.
    ISBN 0-7914-2683-1 (hc : alk. paper). — ISBN 0-7914-2684-X (pb : alk. paper)
    1. Joseph (Son of Jacob)—Legends. 2. Potiphar's wife (Biblical figure)—Legends. 3. Legends, Jewish—History and criticism. 4. Legends—Middle East—History and criticism. 5. Middle Eastern literature—Relation to the Hebrew Bible. I. Title.
BS580.J6G55 1995
398'.35—dc20   95-17220
                                                       CIP

10 9 8 7 6 5 4 3 2 1

In memory of my mother
Judith Goldman
1924–1995

Contents

Illustrations

Acknowledgments

I am indebted to colleagues who read and commented upon the manuscript, among them Alan Tansman and Barbara Kreiger of Dartmouth College, Michael Cooperson of UCLA, Harvey Goldberg of the Hebrew University, and Ktziah Spanier of The New School for Social Research. Adel Allouche provided valuable information on the Arabic sources, and Charles Stinson of Dartmouth provided guidance in the use of Christian sources. My brother Ari Goldman brought his usual good judgment to bear on questions of style and the use of Rabbinic texts. For all errors, I alone bear full responsibility.

My students at Dartmouth College, The New School for Social Research, and the 92nd St. Y Jewish Omnibus Program provided me with feedback and inspiration. My teacher Cyrus Gordon and his wife Connie Gordon encouraged me to complete this long-term project. Ted and Cynthia Arenson of Sunny Oaks provided me with a "summer world" in which I could write and pursue my research. My wife, Liora Alschuler, and my son Daniel Goldman, were my first and best readers and editors, and it is to them that I owe the greatest *todah mikerev halev*.

Joseph with His Father and His Brothers

Introduction:
Joseph, Comparative Folklore, and
Questions of "Influence"

One of the world's oldest recorded folktales tells the story of a handsome young man and the older woman in whose house he resides. Overcome by her feelings for him, the woman attempts to seduce him. When he turns her down, she is enraged. Turning to her husband, she accuses the young man of attacking her. The husband, seemingly convinced of his wife's innocence, has the young man imprisoned or otherwise punished. It is precisely that punishment that leads to the hero's vindication and eventual rise to power and prominence.

In the West we know this tale from its terse and vivid narration in the Hebrew Bible. In the latter part of Genesis we read this episode as part of the adventures of Joseph in Egypt. He rises from his position as servant in the household of the Egyptian nobleman Potiphar to become administrator of all of Egypt. On his appointment to that position he is told by the Pharoah "Only the throne shall be greater than you." The pivotal enabling incident in his rise to power is his earlier precipitous fall from grace while serving in the Egyptian's house. It was there that "his master's wife cast her eyes upon Joseph and said 'lie with me.'" Joseph protests that if he were to do so both his master and God would condemn him. When Potiphar hears from his wife that "the Hebrew slave whom you brought into our house came to dally with me," he is furious and has Joseph put in prison. It is in that prison that Joseph establishes a reputation as an interpreter of dreams, a reputation that leads him to the Pharaoh's court. There he interprets the Pharaoh's dreams, rises in the royal household, and eventually is appointed second to the king.

The Bible's is only one telling of a story that appears in the scriptures and folklore of many peoples. The text of one of these stories, the Ancient Egyptian "Tale of Two Brothers," may ante-date the text of the Bible. In post-Biblical Jewish literature the story of Joseph and his master's wife was richly embellished. In the Qur'ān, the scripture of Islam, a long and detailed narrative is devoted to Joseph. Within that narrative, the story of his encounter with his master's wife is both thematically central and elaborately detailed. At the core of all of these versions is the folklore motif identified by Stith Thompson, pioneer of folklore classification, as "Potiphar's Wife: A woman makes vain overtures to a man and then accuses him of attempting to force her."[1]

Variations of the tale appear in cultures as far flung in place and time as those of the Inuit, Classical Greece, and Ancient Mesopotamia, and one would have to agree with John Yohannan's assessment that "one would be hard put to find a story that has had a wider circulation among more varied audiences over a longer period of time than this story."[2]

As in the Biblical story of Joseph, "Potiphar's Wife" is often one motif, a narrative element, in a larger and more complex story. Thompson defined a motif as "the smallest element in a tale having the power to persist in tradition." In our survey of parallel tales from a number of Near Eastern cultures, the remarkable staying power of this motif will become evident. The relationship between variations on the Potiphar's Wife motif in the Near Eastern cultural sphere is the subject of this study. The episode of Bellerophon in the Iliad, a story with many parallels to the Joseph tale, will also figure in our discussion. While historical context will not be overlooked (we will inquire into the history and provenance of the texts) the focus will be on the *literary aspects* of the story. In Jewish Midrash and in one of its Islamic counterparts, the "Tales of the Prophets," the motif is lavishly embellished, often with an emphasis on the greatness of the temptation that Joseph had to withstand. The more beautiful and seductive Potiphar's wife is in these tales, the more virtuous Joseph is in resisting her. In some tellings, we read of "Joseph the chaste," in others, he is a character more susceptible to passion. And in some late legends and paintings we can see Joseph actively pursuing his master's wife.

The texts analyzed in this comparative study draw on three traditions. 1) Ancient Egyptian Literature: The Tale of Two

Brothers (Papyrus D'Orbiney) and The Romance of Sinuhe. 2)
Biblical and Jewish Literature: The Story of Joseph in the Hebrew
Bible (Genesis 37–50), and its elaboration in Targum, Talmud,
and early and late Midrashim; up to and including the thirteenth
century Midrashic compendium, the Midrash Hagadol.[3] 3) Islamic
Literature: The Twelfth Sūra of the Qur'ān, (Sūrat Yūsuf, The
Chapter of Joseph) and the legends transmitted in *tafsīr* (exegesis), *Ḥadīth* (prophetic traditions), and the *Qiṣaṣ al-anbiyā'*
(Tales of the Prophets), with emphasis on the material presented
in the anthologies of al-Thaʻlabī (eleventh century) and al-Kisāʼi
(early thirteenth century).[4]

Medieval Muslim historians (foremost among them al-Ṭabarī,
838–923) also concerned themselves with the pre-history of the
Islamic Middle East, and their narratives often open with
accounts of Biblical and other ancient peoples. Almost without
exception they include the story of Joseph in their histories, and
I will therefore weave some of the comments of these historians
into the discussion. As al-Ṭabarī wrote both a history and a commentary on the Qur'ān (*tafsīr*) we will have occasion to compare
his treatment of the Joseph story in the different genres. Both
his *History* and his *tafsīr* incorporate and organize a vast body
of law and legend. Al-Thaʻlabī and al-Kisāʼi among other anthologists, often mined al-Ṭabarī's compendia for their own anthologies. In a similar fashion, al-Ṭabarī himself had recourse to
earlier Muslim attempts to link the prehistory of Islam to that of
the Bible and other literatures of the ancient Near East.

While the extant collections of ancient Egyptian literature are
a selection of the writings of a lost (and partially recovered) civilization, both the Torah and the Qur'ān are canonized texts with a
long history of textual transmission, study, and commentary.
Their unity and inviolability are accepted by the respective
believers in each religious tradition. For the believer, the text
originates in the act of divine revelation. While the Enlightenment endeavor of Biblical criticism (and its younger counterpart, source-criticism of the Qur'ān) has shaken the foundations
of belief in the divinely revealed character of scripture, it has not
destroyed those foundations completely. Even for skeptics and
non-believers, a view of scripture as a unified and integral work
prevails. And within scripture, any given narrative, such as the
story of Joseph, has achieved unity in the minds of generations
of readers. Among literary critics and other professional students

of scripture any given narrative within the text may be analyzed into its component parts; but most readers retain a notion of the unity of the text and its distinct narratives. This is not true of the legends that appear in elaborations of scriptural narrative. The community of believers does not affirm their form and authority. The works in which these legends appear are compilations; though a certain sanctity may be attached to them, neither their essential unity nor their revealed character are affirmed.

This flexibility and malleability of "Midrash" (elaboration of scriptural narrative) accounts for its appeal to modern literary sensibilities. Novelists, critics, and literary historians now seem enamored of Midrash as genre and as an analytic tool. A similar, and earlier, appreciation of the genre's creative possibilities accounts for the tendency among the weavers of legend, Jewish, Christian, or Muslim, to borrow legends one from another. Elements of tales that may be traced to an "original" Jewish, Christian, or Muslim source were easily incorporated into the narratives of a sister religion. One of our tasks will be to trace the skeins of this commerce in narrative creativity.

The historical moment when a given story is transmitted from one culture to another is notoriously difficult to pinpoint. There is much scholarly speculation on Jewish-Islamic interaction in this sphere; but let the reader beware, claims about "original versions" and "direct influence" are difficult to substantiate. In the nineteenth century, considerable scholarly energies were expended on proving that the Qur'ān's story of Joseph was "borrowed" or "stolen" from Jewish and Christian narrative traditions. In this century, a more objective view has prevailed, one which recognizes the limitations of our knowledge of the context in which Islam emerged, and at the same time, respects Islam's own claim to originality. The emergence of Islam in seventh century Arabia occurred against a rich and diverse religious background. We know that there were Jewish communities (and Christian monks) in Medina, the heartland of Islam, and in the wider Hijaz. The Qur'ān testifies to the lively interactions and clashes between these communities and nascent Islam, but aside from the Qur'ān, we have little independent material from which we can form a picture of Arabian Judaism and Christianity in the immediate pre-Islamic period. In the Jewish case, aside from what the Qur'ān has to say of the Jews, we have no textual evidence from seventh century Arabia. The first two Islamic centuries (the seventh and eighth Christian centuries) are a blank page so far as Arabian Jewish sources are concerned. In speaking of the history of the Jews of Arabia from antiquity to the early Islamic centuries, Gordon Newby noted that "the majority of the sources available to us were not written or created by these Jews, but are writings or tales from other people who were often hostile to the Jews or indifferent to their activities."[5] S. D. Goitein, an earlier generation's dean of historians of the medieval Mediterranean world, posits the existence in Arabia of a "Bnai Moshe," a pre-Rabbinic group of Jews for whom Moses was the central figure, and then goes on to suggest that the prophet-centered folklore of these Jews may have reached the ears of Muḥammad and his followers. While this is an intriguing theory, it cannot be substantiated. Whatever the mode of transmission might have been, it is clear, as Rueven Firestone has noted, that between Jews and Muslims there was "a shared realm of religious and literary discourse during the early Islamic period."[6]

Despite these difficulties in assigning a date and method to the transmission of tales, Jewish and Muslim legends offer the student of folklore a particularly rich treasure house of tales for comparative study. Narrative elements common to both traditions are embedded in a complex matrix of cultural reciprocity and mutuality. Goitein spoke of the "need" that Muslim readers had for the details omitted from Qur'ānic narratives, a need similar to one that Jewish readers of the Bible had satisfied earlier through the endeavor of Midrash. He described the development of Islamic analogues to Midrash in this way: "There arose in early Islam a class of professional storytellers, whose subject was mainly the "prophets," i.e., the heroes of the Qur'ān. These storytellers freely borrowed from Jews and Christians, and in particular, from the vast literature of the Midrash, the popular exposition of the Bible. Naturally, they added material from other sources and from their own imagination. In their turn, these "Tales of the Prophets" are echoed in some of the later Jewish Midrashim, which may contain some Qur'ānic material."[7]

But we err if we view the "Tales of the Prophets" (Qiṣaṣ al-anbiyā') literature as a mere reflex of a "Midrashic impulse," of the need to elaborate on scripture. From a history of religions standpoint, the compilation of these tales may be seen as one Islamic attempt to "define the place of nubuwwa, or prophecy,

in God's scheme of things."[8] For Muslims, Yūsuf/Joseph is one
of a long series of prophets, a roster which includes figures from
the Hebrew Bible, the New Testament, and prophets of Arabian
provenance. As William Brinner has noted, "the more scholarly
approach to the issue of prophecy in Islam is addressed in theological and philosophical writings. A parallel, and more popular,
attempt to understand prophecy, is a presentation, usually in
chronological order, of the lives of the various prophets whom
Allah has sent to mankind bearing his message, the response of
each one's community to his message, as well as the ultimate
fate of each of these prophets."[9]

The most elaborate and fanciful of these retellings of the
Qur'ān's stories were dubbed Isrā'īlīyāt (Israelite) stories by some
of the more rigorous Muslim scholars. This was not necessarily
an attack on the stories alleged (or actual) Jewish origins, rather
it was an expression of displeasure with the whole endeavor of
fanciful elaboration of the Qur'ān's narratives. When, in the
fourth and fifth Islamic centuries (the tenth and eleventh centuries C.E.) many of the Isrā'īlīyāt were incorporated into the Qiṣaṣ
al-anbiyā', the Tales of the Prophet genre, the genre as a whole
was roundly condemned by the stricter Muslim theologians.

The late Haim Schwarzbaum, an Israeli folklorist who pio-
neered in the comparative study of Jewish and Islamic legends,
pointed out that a similar attitude toward the study of legends
exists in some modern Jewish circles and that he could "still
remember the similar negative attitude towards popular storytelling exhibited by orthodox leaders of Polish Jewry forty years
ago in his native city of Warsaw." While condemnation of the
study of Midrash is unusual in Rabbinic Judaism, it is true that
the study of halakha, Jewish law, was considered a more worthy
endeavor. Louis Ginzberg's comment, that in Judaism, "legends
are the handmaidens of the law," is a reflection of the subordinate
status attached to making the study of Midrash one's primary
endeavor. Midrash often served to encourage adherence to the
law. That Joseph acted appropriately in resisting the advances of
his master's wife, and that his actions should be emulated, is an
obviously halakhic point. Less obvious, and often emphasized in
Jewish lore, is that Joseph kept other traditions of his father
while living in a foreign land. As various Midrashim would have it,
Joseph, in Egypt, ate only kosher food, taught his sons the
Hebrew language, and as noted in Genesis, arranged for his own
burial in the land of Israel.

The historical development of rabbinic literature reflects the greater importance of *Halakhic* texts. For these texts were organized first, in the Mishnah (c. 200 C.E.) and in the Talmuds (c. 500–600 C.E.). Only later were the legends that elaborated scriptural narrative organized into the Aggadic tales of Midrash. As Ginzberg's student Shalom Spiegel noted, "While attempts were repeatedly made to systematize the *Halakhah*, no such efforts were made for the non-legal parts of oral tradition, all the miscellany of literature known as *Aggadah*. Even when the legends were assembled in special books, the principle of their arrangement was purely mechanical: they were strung to the passages of scripture which they employed or elaborated."[10]

Works both scholarly and popular categorize Midrash as "folklore." But to call these collections of tales "folklore" is not to denigrate or undervalue them. In the sense that elaborations of scripture constitute a body of transmitted stories that appear in many variations, they fit one of the many definitions of folklore. That *aggadot* (stories, folktales) are no longer transmitted orally, but are fixed in textual traditions, (compiled by writers we now call *aggadists*), does not exclude them from the folklore rubric and the methodology of folklore studies.[11]

The Joseph stories that we will encounter in this comparative study are replete with tales of jealousy, sibling rivalry, sexual temptation, and magical praxis. It should not surprise us that storytellers of different traditions were tempted to borrow one from another. When stories are this compelling, and when they touch upon the forbidden and the exotic, cultural borders are remarkably fluid. But it is important that we not jump to conclusions about stories that seem at first glance similar, but after a close reading, turn out to be markedly different. This tendency to facile parallel identification is all too evident in the area of translation into English. Because of the Biblical orientation of many translators, the scriptures of other cultures, including that of Islam, often strike the English reader as variants of the Bible. Often this impression is created by the translator; it is not inherent in the text. Recourse to the original language and text yields different results, and may sharpen our appreciation of the differences between traditions.

For these reasons, conclusions concerning mutual influence will be made with caution. To validate any comparisons or contrasts made, I will use the methodologies of folklore studies and comparative philology. The languages of these texts—Ancient

Egyptian, Hebrew, Aramaic, and Arabic—are, since the late eighteenth century, classified as Semitic (or, more recently, Hamito-Semitic). But long before this scientific classification was advanced, the "familial" relationship between these languages was recognized by medieval Jewish and Muslim scholars.

The comparative study of Jewish and Muslim scripture and legend was once a topic reserved for learned dissertations and scholarly monographs. Recently, it has become a controversial topic with political implications. The Arab-Israeli conflict, and the welter of conflicting emotions that it evokes, has intruded into what was once a purely scholarly domain. On both the Israeli and Arab sides, politicians, religious reformers, and social critics, advance territorial and historical claims based upon scripture and the post-scriptural narrative traditions.[12]

In the Western world, and particularly in the United States, political figures often refer to the "Biblical" dimensions of the Arab-Israeli conflict. In the mid-1980s, former President Carter published a book on the Arab-Israeli conflict titled *The Blood of Abraham*. The book's concept demonstrates that a Biblicizing approach to the modern Middle East is not limited to the Christian Right, which tends to see the apocalyptic aspects of the struggle; it is equally present on the Christian left and center, which, in its search for peace and reconciliation appeals to the commonality of the "People of the Book." This biblicizing tendency was evident in President Clinton's speech at the September 1993 White House ceremony at which the Israeli-Palestinian accords were signed. The speech was filled with Biblical allusions, and described the Middle East as "that hallowed piece of earth, that land of light and revelation, the home to the memories of Jews, Muslims, and Christians throughout the world."

Comparative study of Jewish and Muslim legends antedates the now century-old Arab-Israeli conflict. It is part of a Western cultural endeavor in which scholars have been engaged for almost two centuries. Since the Enlightenment, European scholarship, in its restless search for the origins of religions and cultures, focused on the roots of Christianity's "sister religions," Judaism and Islam. The apparent similarities between these two traditions engaged the attention of scholars of comparative religion. In many scholarly tomes, Jewish and Islamic texts were translated, compared, and contrasted. But for the most part, the foundation stories of Christian scripture and history were spared the comparative approach. Even today, in the age of the scientific study of religion, there is a tendency to shy away from *comparative* study of the Gospel narratives. This is not to say that they are not examined and scrutinized in great detail; they are, but they are seldom compared to, and contrasted with, similar tales from non-Christian traditions. As folklorist Alan Dundes noted, one of the classics of late nineteenth century comparative studies was Sir James Frazer's three volume *Folklore of the Old Testament*; there was no parallel study on the folklore of the New Testament. "It was perfectly all right to argue that Old Testament or Jewish heroes were folkloristic rather than historical. But heaven forbid that a proper member of the British House of Lords should apply this reasoning to the life of Jesus! Moses might be folklore but Jesus was history or, to put it another way, Moses was 'false' while Jesus was 'true.'"[13]

For Christians, the scriptures and legends of the Jews and the Muslims were a safer area of inquiry, and from the 1830s onward there was a steady stream of works, in German, English, and French, on the quaint, colorful and *similar* folkways and folk legends of the non-Christian monotheistic faiths. The assumption that the origins of both Judaism and Islam lie in an imagined "Semitic" religion (very much on the model of "Semitic languages," the philological model advanced in the 1780s), was exemplified in the title and text of the most influential work of the genre, William Robertson Smith's *Lectures on the Religion of the Semites: The Fundamental Institutions* (1901). While Robertson Smith's examples of cultic parallels to Biblical law were drawn from the then quite limited knowledge of pre-Israelite Canaanite religion, he does make reference to pre-Islamic and Islamic cultic practices, and sees them as the manifestation of the religious impulse in one "Semitic" cultural sphere.

Many late nineteenth and early twentieth century comparative studies of Islam and its "sister religion," Judaism, attempted to prove that Qur'ānic narrative, and later Muslim elaborations on it, were directly influenced by Jewish or Christian legends circulating in seventh century Arabia. More recent studies, in whose spirit I proceed, have moved beyond arguments about influence, with their emphasis on "who was there first," to a model in which mutuality is acknowledged. Yes, historically, Judaism and Christianity preceded Islam, and elements from the earlier traditions may appear, in transmuted form, in Islamic texts. But it is equally demonstrable that Islamic legends repaid this cultural debt by leaving their distinctive mark on Jewish and

Christian stories that were told and written after the emergence
of Islam. And it is important to take into account the classical
Muslim view that Islam offers us a pure, original, unsullied
"version" of each of the "Stories of the Prophets." For Muslims,
Jewish, and Christian retellings of stories that appear in the
Qur'ān are distortions, deliberate or otherwise, of what Islam
claims is the original tale.[14]

We have seen that the study of Jewish and Muslim texts,
and of the Joseph story in particular, touches on the question of
Christian perception of the other monotheistic faiths and upon
contemporary Middle Eastern politics. The variant readings of
the Joseph story also have implications for the study of sexual
politics. One common reading of the Potiphar's Wife episode
assigns all blame to the woman; the younger man is exonerated.
She tempted the young man, and, in many of the retellings of
the seduction attempt, this occurred on more than one occasion.
The wife's behavior, and the young servant's reactions, were
understood in the context of assumptions about male and
female roles in the social order. This was true in Ancient Egypt,
Ancient Israel, and post-Biblical Jewish societies. In the Qur'ān
this is explicitly spelled out: when her husband doubts the
truth of his wife's version of the encounter with Joseph, he
generalizes from her behavior to the behavior of all women.
"This is of your women's guile, surely your guile is great." And
when his wife's companions are also smitten with Joseph, we
read that "God turned away from him their guile."

A simplistic reading of "women's guile," one that brands this
phrase as an illustration of patriarchal misogyny, overlooks a
parallel theme, that of "the wiles of men." Genesis abounds in
tales of trickery both female *and* male. Whether gender is a
primary factor in the construction and depiction of the trickster
character is an issue that we will deal with at a number of
points in this study. In many Islamic and Jewish legends
Joseph does not lack guile, he is not innocent of complicity in
his situation; he too is susceptible to passion and capable of
trickery. In some of our versions Joseph is sorely tempted by
the older woman, a woman he has tempted by his provocative
behavior, and he is about to act on his impulses when stopped
by divine intervention. The Qur'ān states: "For she desired him;
and he would have taken her, but that he saw the proof of his
Lord." Though for cultural reasons, "the wiles of women" are

often highlighted in our texts, I will argue that in the depictions of the heroes and villains in our tale neither gender is spared. The acerbic wit and social commentary often embedded in folkloric accounts is at its sharpest in its critique of gender relations, and we may find that Joseph is not as saintly, nor Potiphar's wife as villainous, as first impressions of tradition would have it. In some versions the young Joseph is arrogant and vain. Other stories paint Potiphar's wife in a sympathetic light.

Gender issues, which inform our discussions of the cultures from which the respective Joseph stories emerged, must be viewed within a larger cultural matrix. Gender is constructed differently in each culture, though one culture may have considerable influence on another. In Middle Eastern societies there was a degree of cultural continuity remarkable for its strength and longevity. But continuity does not imply *identity* across vast spans of time. The norms of acceptable social behavior were vastly different in Biblical Israel, Talmudic Babylonia, and early Islamic Arabia. On reflection, this may seem obvious, but a tendency to think of the Middle East as the "eternal orient" or "unchanging East" may obscure this obvious point. The status of women in Biblical Israel and the reflection of that status in Genesis will be our departure point. But from that historical point onward, women's status, along with other social norms, changed. How it changed is, to some extent, reflected in narrative traditions.[15]

Linked to our awareness of mutual and reciprocal influence between the folklores of Judaism and Islam is a parallel awareness that the traditions of Judaism, Christianity, and Islam, were themselves heir to the Ancient Near Eastern and Hellenistic cultural worlds from which they emerged. As a scholar of the Muslim-Jewish cultural symbiosis recently remarked, "One should not think in terms of influences or cultural borrowing only, however. It has been said that the Near East resembles a palimpsest, layer upon layer, tradition upon tradition, intertwined to the extent that one cannot really grasp one without the other, certainly not the later without the earlier, but often also not the earlier without considering the shapes it took later."[16] A half century earlier Gustav von Grunebaum, in an essay on the interplay between the Islamic and the Greek cultural spheres, bemoaned the "all too strict separation between oriental and classical studies." Such artificial distinctions between disciplines, von Grunebaum felt, accounted for "the relative backwardness of our knowledge in this field."[17]

The mutual interconnectedness of Jewish and Muslim folklore, and the relationship between these traditions and their Near Eastern antecedents, is at the core of this study. These connections have been explored in the last decade in the work of Marilyn Waldman, William Brinner, Gordon Newby, and Reuben Firestone; lengthier treatments of individual tales appear in James Kugel's *In Potiphar's House* (1990) and Jacob Lassner's *Demonizing the Queen of Sheba* (1993). This book will focus on what may be the most often told and retold of these tales, Joseph and Potiphar's wife. In order to study the development of the Potiphar's Wife motif, we must view this part of the Joseph tale in its scriptural context. Therefore, I often will make reference to the Biblical Joseph narratives (Genesis 37– 50) in their entirety. Similarly, the Ancient Egyptian Tale of Two Brothers, and Sūrat Yūsuf in the Qur'ān, though both centered on our motif, situate that motif within a much wider context. In addition to The Potiphar's Wife Motif, folklorists see a number of other motifs at work in these narratives from Ancient Egypt, Ancient Israel, and seventh century Arabia. These include the motif of "The Wise Man as Saviour"[18] in which a man, "through his god-given ability to interpret dreams, sees into the future and saves the nation from disaster." Also present in the Joseph narratives is "The Motif of the Young Man Triumphant"[19] in which a younger man triumphs over adversity and reaches a high station.

These motifs may all be present in the "versions" of Joseph, but with differing degrees of emphasis in each retelling. The Genesis narrative, in which these three motifs are strongly represented, will remain our center of reference throughout this study. This is not to imply that the Biblical version is somehow superior, nor to indulge in what one prominent critic has called "cultural imperialism." Nor do I mean to assert that the Biblical version is an "original" from which all other versions have borrowed. We shall see that the situation is much more complex than that. But I begin with the Bible to assert its centrality in Western culture, and use it as a point of departure for discussion of the scriptures and legends of other cultures.

A study of the structure and content of the Joseph narratives in Genesis 37–50 will be the focus of my first chapter. Within that chapter, I proceed to a comparative discussion of the parallel Islamic material and show how the Joseph stories were used in disputations between Muslims and Jews, as well as between competing Islamic sectarian groups. Chapter Two is dedicated to Joseph's fateful encounter with Potiphar's wife, and it is in this part of the tale that the Egyptian background is most elaborately delineated, and the Jewish-Islamic cultural interaction is at its liveliest. In Chapter Three, I address a question that has long occupied Egyptologists and Biblical scholars—how "authentically Egyptian" is the milieu described in Genesis? Do the names, places, and events of the story reflect an historically-based Egyptian reality? Or are they simply anachronistic details provided by a late author to authenticate his or her tale?

In Chapter Four, I draw a portrait of the young Joseph. Constructing this portrait enables us to compare and contrast descriptive elements from the Egyptian, Biblical and Qur'ānic sources. Chapter Five is devoted to the depiction of women in the narratives. These include Joseph's mother Rachel, his brother Judah's daughter-in-law Tamar, the elusive and legendary Seraḥ bat Asher, Joseph's wife Asenath, and the companions of Potiphar's wife, "the women of the city." Feminist readings of our texts, readings that call into question the validity of earlier scholarly evaluations of women's roles in Biblical Israel, Rabbinic Judaism, and Islam, will enable us to view the stories of these women in a fresh light. Chapter Six, "Joseph's Bones, Linking Canaan and Egypt," demonstrates that even in death Joseph remained a compelling figure in folklore, particularly in the realm of popular religious practices. For the Jewish and Muslim fascination with Joseph extended to his mortal remains, and Joseph's name came to be a charm against malevolence and evil magic.

The text of the Potiphar's Wife episode in Genesis, and parallel accounts in Ancient Egyptian literature, Homeric Epic, and the Qur'ān, are presented following this introduction. The post-scriptural elaborations of the motif, elaborations that appear in fragmentary form in the written folklore and histories of Jews and Muslims, are cited and quoted throughout this book.

This foray into comparative Ancient Near Eastern, Jewish, and Islamic lore, will, I trust, be both stimulating and rewarding. Like the situation of Joseph in his master's house, the endeavor of comparative study is strewn with pitfalls. But with some wisdom and prudence, we may emerge enriched and enlightened by the experience.

The Women of the City at Zuleikha's Banquet

The Texts: The Hebrew Bible, The Qur'ān, Ancient Egyptian Literature, and The Iliad

1. Genesis 39, The Hebrew Bible
   (New J. P. S. Translation)

2. Sura 12, The Qur'ān
   (A. J. Arberry Translation)

3. Ancient Egyptian Literature: The Story of Two Brothers
   (J. Wilson Translation in ANET)

4. Book VI of the Iliad, The Tale of Bellerophon
   (R. Lattimore Translation)

The Hebrew Bible: Genesis 39:1-23

When Joseph was taken down to Egypt, a certain Egyptian, Potiphar, a courtier of Pharaoh and his chief steward, bought him from the Ishmaelites who had brought him there. The Lord was with Joseph, and he was a successful man, and he stayed in the house of his Egyptian master. And when his master saw that the Lord was with him and that the Lord lent success to everything he undertook, he took a liking to Joseph. He made him his personal attendant and put him in charge of his household, placing in his hands all that he owned. And from the time that the Egyptian put him in charge of his household and of all that he owned, the Lord blessed his house for Joseph's sake, so that the blessing of the Lord was upon everything that he owned, in the house and outside. He left all that he had in Joseph's hands and, with him there, he paid attention to nothing save the food that he ate. Now Joseph was well built and handsome.

After a time, his master's wife cast her eyes upon Joseph and said, "Lie with me." But he refused. He said to his master's wife, "Look, with me here, my master gives no thought to anything in this house, and all that he owns he has placed in my hands. He wields no more authority in this house than I, and he has withheld nothing from me except yourself, since you are his wife. How then could I do this most wicked thing, and sin before God?" And much as she coaxed Joseph day after day, he did not yield to her request to lie beside her, to be with her.

One such day, he came into the house to do his work. None of the household being there inside, she caught hold of him by his garment and said, "Lie with me!" But he left his garment in her hand and got away and fled outside. When she saw that he had left it in her hand and had fled outside, she called out to her servants and said to them, "Look, he had to bring us a Hebrew to dally with us! This one came to lie with me; but I screamed loud. And when he heard me screaming at the top of my voice, he left his garment with me and got away and fled outside." She kept his garment beside her, until his master came home. Then she told him the same story, saying, "The Hebrew slave whom you brought into our house came to me to dally with me; but when I screamed at the top of my voice, he left his garment with me and fled outside."

When his master heard the story that his wife told him, namely, "Thus and so your slave did to me," he was furious. So Joseph's master had him put in prison, where the king's prisoners were confined. But even while he was there in prison, the Lord was with Joseph: He extended kindness to him and disposed the chief jailer favorably toward him. The chief jailer put in Joseph's charge all the prisoners who were in that prison, and he was the one to carry out everything that was done there. The chief jailer did not supervise anything that was in Joseph's charge, because the Lord was with him, and whatever he did the Lord made successful.

The Qur'ān: Sura 12: 23-35

Now the woman in whose house he was
solicited him, and closed the doors on them.
"Come," she said, "take me!" "God be my refuge,"
he said. "Surely my lord has given me
a goodly lodging. Surely the evildoers
    do not prosper."
For she desired him; and he would have taken her,
but that he saw the proof of his Lord.
So was it, that We might turn away from him
evil and abomination; he was one of
    Our devoted servants.
They raced to the door; and she tore his shirt
from behind. They encountered her master
by the door. She said, "What is the recompense
of him who purposes evil against thy folk,
but that he should be imprisoned, or
    a painful chastisement?"
Said he, "It was she that solicited me";
and a witness of her folk bore witness,
"If his shirt has been torn from before
then she has spoken truly, and he is
    one of the liars;
but if it be that his shirt has been torn
from behind, then she has lied, and he is
    one of the truthful."
When he saw his shirt was torn from behind
he said, "This is of your women's guile; surely
    your guile is great.
Joseph, turn away from this; and thou, woman,
ask forgiveness of thy crime; surely thou art
    one of the sinners."
Certain women that were in the city said,
"The Governor's wife has been soliciting her
page; he smote her heart with love; we see her
    in manifest error."

When she heard their sly whispers, she sent
to them, and made ready for them a repast,
then she gave to each one of them a knife.
"Come forth, attend to them," she said.
And when they saw him, they so admired him
that they cut their hands, saying, "God save us!
This is no mortal; he is no other
      but a noble angel."
"So now you see," she said. "This is he you
blamed me for. Yes, I solicited him, but
he abstained. Yet if he will not do what I
command him, he shall be imprisoned, and be
      one of the humbled."
He said, "My Lord, prison is dearer to me
than that they call me to; yet if Thou
turnest not from me their guile, then I
shall yearn towards them, and so become
      one of the ignorant."
So his Lord answered him, and He turned
away from him their guile; surely He is
      the All-hearing, the All-knowing.
Then it seemed good to them, after they had
seen the signs, that they should imprison
      him for a while.

Ancient Egyptian Literature:
"The Story of Two Brothers"

Now they say that once there were two brothers of
one mother and one father. Anubis was the name of the
elder, and Bata was the name of the younger. Now, as for
Anubis, he had a house and had a wife, and his younger
brother lived with him as a sort of minor. He was the one
who made clothes for him and went to the fields driving
his cattle. He was the one who did the plowing and who
harvested for him. He was the one who did all kinds of
work for him which are in the fields. Really, his younger
brother was a good grown man. There was no one like
him in the entire land. Why, the strength of a god was in
him.

Now after many days after this, they were in the
fields and ran short of seed. Then he sent his younger

brother, saying: "Go and fetch us seed from the village."
And his younger brother found the wife of his elder
brother sitting and doing her hair. Then he said to her:
"Get up and give me some seed, for my older brother is
waiting for me. Don't delay!" Then she said to him: "Go
and open the bin and take what you want! Don't make
me leave my combing unfinished!" Then the lad went
into his stable, and he took a big jar, for he wanted to
carry off a lot of seed. So he loaded himself with barley
and emmer and came out carrying them.

Then she said to him: "How much is it that is on
your shoulder?" And he said to her: "three sacks of
emmer, two sacks of barley, five in all, is what is on my
shoulder." So he spoke to her. Then she talked with him,
saying "There is great strength in you! Now I see your
energies every day!" And she wanted to know him as one
knows a man.

Then she stood up and took hold of him and said to
him: "Come, let's spend an hour sleeping together! This
will do you good, because I shall make fine clothes for
you!" Then the lad became like a leopard with great rage
at the wicked suggestion which she had made to him,
and she was very, very much frightened. Then he argued
with her, saying: "See here—you are like a mother to me,
and your husband is like a father to me! Because—being
older than I—he was the one who brought me up. What is
this great crime which you have said to me? Don't say it
to me again! And I won't tell it to a single person, now will
I let it out of my mouth to any man!" And he lifted up his
load, and he went to the fields. Then he reached his elder
brother, and they were busy with activity at their work.

Now at the time of evening, then his elder brother left
off to go to his house. And his younger brother tended
his cattle, and he loaded himself with everything of the
fields, and he took his cattle in front of him, to let them
sleep in their stable which was in the village.

But the wife of his elder brother was afraid because
of the suggestion which she had made. Then she took fat
and grease, and she became like one who has been
criminally beaten, wanting to tell her husband: "It was
your younger brother who did the beating!" And her

husband left off in the evening, after his custom of every day, and he reached his house, and he found his wife lying down, terribly sick. She did not put water on his hands, after his custom, nor had she lit a light before him, and his house was in darkness, and she lay there vomiting. So her husband said to her: "Who has been talking with you?" Then she said to him: "Not one person has been talking with me except your younger brother. But when he came to take the seed to you he found me sitting alone, and he said to me: 'Come, let's spend an hour sleeping together! Put on your curls!' So he spoke to me. But I wouldn't listen to him: 'Aren't I your mother?—for your elder brother is like a father to you!' So I spoke to him. But he was afraid, and he beat me, so as not to let me tell you. Now, if you let him live, I'll kill myself! Look, when he comes, *don't let him speak*, for, if I accuse him of this wicked suggestion, he will be ready to do it *tomorrow again!*"

Then his elder brother became like a leopard, and he made his lance sharp, and he put it in his hand. Then his elder brother stood behind the door of his stable to kill his younger brother when he came back in the evening to put his cattle in the stable.

Now when the sun was setting, he loaded himself with all plants of the fields, according to his custom of every day, and he came back. When the first cow came into the stable, she said to her herdsman: "Here's your elder brother waiting before you, carrying his lance to kill you! Run away from him!" Then he understood what his first cow had said. And another went in, and she said the same. So he looked under the door of his stable, and he saw the feet of his elder brother, as he was waiting behind the door, with his lance in his hand. So he laid his load on the ground, and he started to run away and escape. And his elder brother went after him, carrying his lance.

Then his younger brother prayed to the Re-Har-akhti (the sun disc), saying: "O my good lord, thou art he who judges the wicked from the just!" Thereupon the Re heard all his pleas, and the Re made a great body of water appear between him and his elder brother, and it was full of crocodiles. So one of them came to be on one side and the other on the other. And his elder brother struck his hand twice because of his not killing him. Then his younger brother called to him from the other side, saying: "Wait here until dawn. When the sun disc rises, I shall be judged with you in his presence, and he will turn the wicked over to the just, for I won't be with you ever *again*; I won't be in a place where you are—I shall go to the Valley of the Cedar!"

Now when it was dawn and a second day had come, the Re-Har-akhti arose, and one of them saw the other. Then the lad argued with his elder brother, saying: "What do you mean by coming after me to kill me falsely, when you wouldn't listen to what I had to say? Now I am still your younger brother, and you are like a father to me, and your wife is like a mother to me! Isn't it so? When I was sent to fetch us some seed, your wife said to me: 'Come, let's spend an hour sleeping together!' But, look, it is twisted for you into something else!" Then he let him know all that had happened to him and his wife. Then he swore to the Re-Har-akhti, saying "As for your killing me falsely, you carried your lance on the word of a filthy whore!" And he took a reed-knife, and he cut off his phallus, and he threw it into the water. And the shad swallowed it. And he was faint and became weak. And his elder brother's heart was very, very sad, and he stood weeping aloud for him. He could not cross over to where his younger brother was because of the crocodiles....

Then the younger brother went off to the Valley of the Cedar, and his elder brother went off to his house, with his hand laid upon his head, and he was smeared with dust. So he reached his house, and he killed his wife, and he threw her out to the dogs. And he sat in mourning for his younger brother....

(In the continuation of the story the younger brother, Bata, undergoes a series of magical transformations after death. Eventually he is elevated to the ranks of the God-Kings.)

The Iliad, Book VI, 155–205

To Bellerophontes the gods granted beauty and desirable manhood; but Proitos in anger devised evil

things against him, and drove him out of his own
domain, since he was far greater, from the Argive country
Zeus had broken to the sway of his sceptre. Beautiful
Anteia the wife of Proitos was stricken with passion to lie
in love with him, and yet she could not beguile valiant
Bellerophontes, whose will was virtuous. So she went to
Proitos the king and uttered her falsehood: "Would you
be killed, o Proitos? Then murder Bellerophontes who
tried to lie with me in love, though I was unwilling." So
she spoke, and anger took hold of the king at her story.
He shrank from killing him, since his heart was awed by
such action, but sent him away to Lykia, and handed
him murderous symbols, which he inscribed in a folding
tablet, enough to destroy life, and told him to show it to
his wife's father, that he might perish. Bellerophontes
went to Lykia in the blameless convoy of the gods; when
he came to the running stream of Xanthos, and Lykia,
the lord of wide Lykia tendered him full-hearted honour.
Nine days he entertained them with sacrifice of nine
oxen, but afterwards when the rose fingers of the tenth
dawn showed, then he began to question him, and asked
to be showed the symbols, whatever he might be carrying
from his son-in-law, Proitos. Then after he had been
given his son-in-law's wicked symbols first he sent him
away with orders to kill the Chimaira none might
approach; a thing of immortal make, not human, lion-
fronted and snake behind, a goat in the middle, and
snorting out the breath of the terrible flame of bright fire.
He killed the Chimaira, obeying the portents of the immortals. Next after this he fought against the glorious
Solymoi, and this he thought was the strongest battle
with men that he entered; but third he slaughtered the
Amazons, who fight men in battle. Now as he came back
the king spun another entangling treachery; for choosing
the bravest men in wide Lykia he laid a trap, but these
men never came home thereafter since all of them were
killed by blameless Bellerophontes. Then when the king
knew him for the powerful stock of the god, he detained
him there, and offered him the hand of his daughter, and
gave him half of all the kingly privilege. Thereto the men
of Lykia cut out a piece of land, surpassing all others,
fine ploughland and orchard for him to administer. His

bride bore three children to valiant Bellerophontes,
Isandros and Hippolochos and Laodameia. Laodameia
lay in love beside Zeus of the counsels and bore him god-
like Sarpedon of the brazen helmet. But after Bellerophontes was hated by all the immortals, he wandered
alone about the plain of Aleios, eating his heart out,
skulking aside from the trodden track of humanity. As
for Isandros his son, Ares the insatiate of fighting killed
him in close battle against the glorious Solymoi, while
Artemis of the golden reins killed the daughter in anger.

The Pharaoh's Dream

The Centrality and Significance of the Joseph Narratives

> So perfect a story as the Romance of Joseph, dating
> moreover from hoary antiquity, can, strictly speaking, be
> neither history nor fiction. Like most of the ever-
> enchanting tales of the past, it is likely to be the product
> of long evolution. This may be said without eliminating
> the hand of dramatic genius, which makes itself felt in
> style and development.[1]
>
> —W. F. Albright (1918)

The Nature of the Biblical Narratives

The Joseph narratives (Genesis 37–50) are the Hebrew Bible's
longest continuous text devoted to one person. Though their style
is elliptical, their length is considerable, thirteen chapters with a
total of 391 verses.[2] While the narratives in which Moses appears
are more extensive, occupying much of the subsequent books of
the Pentateuch, they incorporate within them the history and law
of the developing Hebrew nation. In those narratives, it is not
always Moses who dominates the story. In contrast, throughout
the last quarter of Genesis we never lose sight of Joseph as the
central figure in the text. It is in this spirit that Genesis Rabbah,
the sixth century C.E. compilation of Jewish legends, interprets
the opening of the story in Genesis 37:2, "Such then is the line of
Jacob, Joseph" as follows: "the following events transpired only
on Joseph's merit." For the Rabbinic exegetes, this verse opens a
new epoch in Hebrew history, the epoch of Joseph.[3]

Within the wider Joseph narratives, one section, Genesis 39–41, demonstrates an independent, internal unity. This section tells of the failed attempt by Potiphar's wife to seduce Joseph, his subsequent imprisonment, his success as interpreter of dreams, and his rise to power as administrator of Egypt. In this study in comparative folklore our focus will be on Genesis 39, the tale of Joseph and Potiphar's Wife, but we will often widen the focus to include Genesis 39–41, and from these chapters expand the discussion to the Joseph narratives as a whole. These narratives tell the story of Joseph and his brothers from the time that Joseph was seventeen until his demise at the age of 110. At the point where Potiphar's wife enters the story he no longer has contact with his brothers. Acting out of jealousy and resentment, they have sold Joseph into slavery. Joseph's adventures and misadventures in Egypt, which culminate in his rise to stewardship over the country and its food supply, will bring his brothers to him. Their tribulations in Egypt, told in Genesis 42–45, culminate in Joseph's reunion with his father Jacob and the settlement of all of Jacob's family in the Land of Goshen (46–48). Jacob's deathbed blessings to his children and grandchildren signal the closure of the Patriarchal period. Genesis ends with Jacob's burial in Canaan and Joseph's death and burial in Egypt (49–50).

Nineteenth and early twentieth century Biblical scholarship focused on the source analysis of these narratives; contemporary scholarship has paid more attention to the literary and folkloric aspects of the tale. In 1970, Donald Redford offered a synthesis of earlier critical opinion concerning the narratives:

> All commentators, no matter how far they diverge on the subject of its origins, are unanimous in their judgment that the Joseph story is a masterpiece of storytelling, perhaps unequalled in Biblical literature.[4]

In the twenty-five years since this was written, interest in the application of literary theory to Biblical texts, and the parallel refinement of narratology, has focused further attention on the Joseph Story. Modern Biblical and literary critics were not the first readers to comment on the unique qualities of the Joseph narratives. For the elaboration and embellishment that the tale elicited, both in Jewish and non-Jewish works, are but earlier forms of testimony to the story's unity and uniqueness:

One need only investigate the extent to which the Joseph story itself (and not simply the motifs on which it draws) occurs in Midrash and paraphrase in the later literature of the East to learn that it rapidly became one of the most popular of all Biblical tales.[5]

Also adding to the tale's appeal was its lack of didactic or moralizing expression. Although we are reminded that there is a divine plan behind the unfolding events (Genesis 45:5–8) the story can be read and enjoyed without paying full attention to this theological element:

> Most striking and, in fact unique, is the secularistic complexion of the narrative. There are no miraculous or supernatural elements; no divine revelations are experienced by Joseph, who also had no associations with altars or cultic sites.[6]

This "secularistic complexion" provides a sharp contrast to the tales of Jacob, and makes the Joseph story eligible for cultural borrowing on a grand scale. The universal aspects of the tale—a father's love for the son of his late beloved wife, his brothers' jealousy, his descent into slavery and triumph over it and, of course, the temptation offered by the master's wife—had broad appeal. Cultures that did not share the theology and history of Ancient Israel could share in the richness inherent in these stories.

Some contend that this lack of association between Joseph and cultic practices was later compensated for by the veneration of Joseph's bones and tomb, and that in this veneration we may find assimilated elements of the cult of the dead. I will examine this theory at the end of this study. For our present purposes, it should be emphasized that the Joseph narratives are remarkably free of both direct theological statement, and the expression of theological truths in ritual acts. It is this non-theological bent, combined with the timelessness of the story, that ties it to analogous literary forms in Middle Egyptian literature. Stories like "The Tale of Two Brothers," "The Shipwrecked Sailor" and the "Romance of Sinuhe," stories with affinities to the Joseph narratives, "are literature composed for enjoyment, without any religious or political motive. Magical and religious compositions such as the Book of the Dead were for the grim business of securing salvation."[7]

Estimates of the tale's high literary quality, and evaluations of its popularity, are directly related to the reader's recognition of the *unity* of the Joseph narratives; for the long section of Genesis that is devoted to Joseph's adventures struck many an observer as a unified tale. "They are not a collection of isolated and fragmentary incidents."[8]

As a unified tale, the Joseph narratives thus pose a methodological problem to proponents of the Documentary Hypothesis, the nineteenth century theory that posits four textual sources (J, E, P, D) for the later "redacted" text of the Hebrew Bible. E. A. Speiser, in his comments on Genesis 38 praises the "sustained dramatic effort of the narrative, unsurpassed in the whole Pentateuch."[9] He then proceeds to qualify this statement by assigning various strands of the narrative to different authors.

An achievement of such literary excellence should be, one would naturally expect, the work of a single author. Yet such is definitely not the case. While P's part in the story of Joseph is secondary and marginal, J and E are prominently represented throughout, each in his own distinctive way. The casual reader is hardly aware that he has a composite story before him; and even the trained analyst is sometimes baffled when it comes to separating the parallel accounts.[10]

In this statement, Speiser is echoing the classical analysis advanced by proponents of the Documentary Hypothesis. This view is exemplified in the remarks of G. Von Rad in *Genesis: A Commentary*:

The story of Joseph...apart from unimportant sections from the Priestly source, is an artful composition from the representations of the sources J and E. Apparently, both documents contained a story of Joseph. The redactor combined them with each other in such a way that he inserted extensive sections of the Elohistic parallel version into the Yahwistic story of Joseph and thus created an even richer narrative. In any case, the gain from this combination of sources is incomparably greater than the loss.[11]

In his more technical "notes" to Chapter 38, Speiser endorses the "documentary" view of the story and cites one element in it, the references to both Ishmaelites and Midianites as the purchasers of Joseph (Chapter 37, verses 25–28), as the proof text for the validity of the Documentary Hypothesis:

> This single verse alone provides a good basis for a constructive documentary analysis of the Pentateuch; it goes a long way, moreover, to demonstrate that E was not just a supplement to J, but an independent and often conflicting source.[12]

That this view has exerted great influence on contemporary Biblical scholarship is clear from the statement of. O. S. Wintermute in *The Interpreter's Dictionary of the Bible*.

> Genesis 37 is one of the most convincing illustrations of the documentary hypothesis. One ought to be warned, however, of the constant need for reappraisal of this kind of approach. An excellent example of its shortcomings is the case of the double allusion to Midianites and Ishmaelites which may have its origin in poetic parallelism.[13]

In the last two decades, this emphasis on the analysis of the sources of the story has shifted. A 1992 review of the literature noted that, "recent examination of the story softens the argument for two sources by suggesting that one author can use repetition as a narrative technique for emphasis, perhaps simply for variety."[14] With this shift from a "higher criticism" model to a literary criticism mode, and with the application of this model to Genesis, scholars have highlighted the redactional unity of the text. For these scholars, structural and linguistic analysis of Genesis reveals that the strong editorial hand at work in the book's final redaction was striving for artistic and thematic unity. As Gary Rendsburg noted in *The Redaction of Genesis*, "The Joseph story is, by all accounts, the most unified story in Genesis, perhaps in the entire Pentateuch, and indeed in the whole Hebrew Bible."[15]

Whatever an individual scholar's view of the sources of the narrative, the pivotal role of the Joseph story in the unfolding history of Israel is recognized by both the early Rabbinic texts and the modern critics:

> Joseph is the link between Canaan and Egypt, responsible in some manner for the descent into Egypt... When we reflect upon the fact that Genesis ends with the death of Joseph, and that Exodus enters with the reminder that it was the small Jacob clan of "seventy souls...that entered Egypt...Joseph being already in Egypt" (Exodus 1:1, 5), we begin to see Joseph as the bridge between the Patriarchs and Moses.[16]

Genesis Rabbah highlights this centrality and sees Joseph's merit as pivotal in Hebrew history, and as pitotal in accounting for miraculous events in that history:

> These events waited until Joseph was born: as it is written (Genesis 30:25), "After Rachel had borne Joseph..." "Jacob said unto Laban, Give me leave to go to my own homeland." Who brought them down into Egypt? —Joseph: and who provided for them:—Joseph. The sea was divided for Joseph's sake alone, as it is written (Psalms 77:17), "The waters saw you, O God, the very deep quaked as well"—which is preceded by "By your arm you redeemed your people, the children of Jacob and Joseph." Rabbi Judan son of Rabbi Simon said, "The Jordan too was divided for Joseph's sake alone."[17]

From the perspective of this Midrash, it is as if history was held in abeyance, awaiting Joseph's appearance. And it is not only human history that this could be said of, but also the intervention of God in the natural order. Both the splitting of the Red Sea and the dividing of the Jordan River are here attributed to Joseph's merit. Elsewhere in Jewish legend Joseph is linked to each of these miracles on an individual basis. It is through the power of Joseph's coffin that the miracle is effected at the Red Sea. Joshua's own miracle at the Jordan is also tied to the merit of his ancestor Joseph.[18] In later Midrashim, two aspects of the Joseph legend loom large: his beauty and wisdom, and these attributes assure his place in the development of a Joseph motif in Jewish popular religion and magic. Following our survey of

Joseph in Genesis and Jewish Biblical elaboration we will move to the depiction of Joseph in the Qur'ān, and in the commentaries and histories later woven around the Qur'ān's story of Yūsuf. In these distinct tellings of the tale, some of the same themes and depictions seem to repeat themselves. But often the Qur'ān, and its commentators, assert the uniqueness of their interpretations by offering us a markedly different story. The Yūsuf of the Qur'ān is not identical with the Joseph of Hebrew scripture. The hero's names are, of course, cognate Arabic and Hebrew words, and the broad outlines of the Biblical and Qur'ānic stories are similar. How each story diverges from the other will be the subject of much of our inquiry.

Joseph's beauty and wisdom, highlighted in all of our texts, are both an asset and a liability to our hero. As we read both Jewish and Islamic descriptions of Rachel's son it will become apparent that both his triumphs and failures are linked to these attributes. He is a hero who is constantly in and out of trouble. Though scripture and legend remind us that God's hand directs the course of his life, the purely human drama of the beautiful young servant in a foreign land keeps the reader fully engaged and eagerly awaiting the outcome of his tale.

The Narrative in the Qur'ān and Islamic Legend

The twelfth sura of the Qur'ān is unique. It is the only one of the lengthy chapters which develops a single theme. The unity of the theme's treatment indicates, moreover, that, unlike the other chapters of any length, this one is not, for the most part, a composite. It is, therefore, the Qur'ān's longest continuous narrative.[19]

In these remarks by a contemporary student of Islam we find striking similarities to modern critical evaluations of Genesis 37–50. As we have seen earlier, those chapters of Genesis constitute the Bible's longest narrative devoted to one figure. Thus both the length and unity of the two Joseph stories—the Biblical and the Qur'ānic—are unusual within their respective scriptural canons. The question of the relationship between the two treatments is a complex and much-debated one, and it will be dealt with in a separate discussion. What is of interest to us here is the function of Sūra 12 within the Qur'ān.

The uniqueness of this Sūra of the Qur'ān is highlighted by its name, Sūrat Yūsuf (the chapter on Joseph). Most often a Sūra is named after a key word in its opening verses. This Sūra is devoted to only one personage, and it is one of the few Sūras named after an individual or tribe. Other Sūra names that are named after individuals and reflect "Biblicist" traditions are Yūnus (Jonah), Ibrāhīm (Abraham), and Nūh (Noah).

As the nature of Qur'ānic narrative is not chronological, we cannot assign Sūra 12 the pivotal *historical* position that the Joseph narratives command in the Bible. In the Bible, Joseph's story has narrative theological and historical import. Within its layers of law, myth, and poetry, the Bible offers a chronology of human events. Often this chronology is linked to genealogies or to annals, both of which were features of Ancient Near Eastern historiography.[20] The Qur'ān does not attempt to duplicate or improve upon these earlier histories; rather, it seems to assume a prior knowledge of the basics of sacred history. It also extends its own presentation of ancient history to the immediate pre-Islamic and early Islamic periods. But imparting this knowledge, and placing events within the context of history, is not the Qur'ān's prime concern. It comes rather as an "Arabic Qur'ān" and a "warning." As M. G. S. Hodgson noted:

> Because of its intimate interaction with the day-to-day destinies of the community, the Qur'ān cannot be read as a discursive book, for abstract information or even, in the first instance for inspiration. The sequence of its bits and pieces is notoriously often lacking in logical order or development. Even the stories it recounts come not as consecutive narratives but rather in the form of reminders of episodes which are often presumed to be known to the audience—reminders which point up the implications of the episode for faith with little concern otherwise for continuity—as if he who did not know the story should ask someone to tell it to him before approaching the Qur'ān's commentary on it.[21]

In his traditional translation and commentary on Sūrat Yūsuf, Abdullah Yūsuf Ali, a modern Muslim commentator on the Qur'ān, echoes Hodgson's remarks. In his introductory remarks to the Sūra he notes: "For the parable all that is necessary to know about Joseph is that he was one of the chosen ones of God. For the story it is necessary to set down a few more details. His father was Jacob..."[22] Both Hodgson from a secular viewpoint, and Yūsuf Ali from the viewpoint of a believer, affirm that the Sūra presupposes a knowledge of pre-existing materials, materials which it then uses to make its own didactic points. It makes these points in a number of ways: they are stated directly or implied by the speech or action of one of the protagonists. As a "teaching narrative" Sūrat Yūsuf has a unique function in the Qur'ān:

> Even when the narrative predominates, the story is hardly ever told in a straightforward manner, but tends to fall into a series of short word-pictures; the action advances incident by incident discontinuously, and the intervening links are left to the imagination of the hearers...In the relatively few narrative passages in the Qur'ān, the homiletic element is again apt to intrude. The longest narrative is the story of Joseph in Sūra 12, and there every now and then the account of events is interrupted by a parenthesis to make clear the purpose of God in what happened.[23]

This purposefulness is central to an understanding of the nature of Sūrat Yūsuf. Comparing the Biblical and Qur'ānic narratives, M. Waldman noted that:

> When one looks at the place of each story within its entire work, the differences...are striking. Joseph is the subject of one of many teaching stories, albeit one of the longest, most detailed, and most colorful. Without it, however, the Qur'ān would still make sense. And without the Qur'ān, the Sūra of Joseph could still be read on its own, decontextualized as it is. For the Bible, however, the story of Joseph is essential...In the Bible, the telling of the Joseph story is an indispensable step in the unfolding of God's divine plan and manipulation of history to ensure the future of the Hebrews. Consequently, the figure of God seems somewhat more distant in the Biblical story, less concentrated on a relationship with Joseph and more

involved with the lives of all the many characters, whereas in the Qur'ān, God interferes with and guides His messenger constantly, the other characters remaining more shadowy and less clearly defined.[24]

According to the Qur'ānic commentaries, this sense of divine guidance is one of the reasons that Sūrat Yūsuf is considered the best of all tales. For the sūra identifies itself as *aḥsan al-qaṣaṣ* (12:3), "the best of all tales." That is to say that, of all stories told, that of Yūsuf is the best. This interpretation is expanded upon by the eleventh century commentator al-Thaʿlabī:

> It is the most beautiful because of the lessons concealed in it, on account of Yūsuf's generosity and its wealth of matter—in which prophets, angels, devils, jinn, men, animals, birds, rulers, and subjects play a part.[25]

While not questioning the Sūra's qualities or popularity, some of the classical commentaries are more circumspect in their interpretation of the phrase *aḥsan al-qaṣaṣ*. They see it as referring to the manner in which the story is told, and not necessarily to its content:

> *Aḥsan al-qaṣaṣ*..."with the best explanation." This rendering is very close to the interpretation given by Zamakhshari: "We set forth this Qur'an unto thee in the best way in which it could be set forth." According to Razi, it may be safely assumed that *the adjective "best" refers not to the contents of "that which is set forth"—i.e., the particular story narrated in this surah—but rather to the manner in which the Qur'ān (or this particular surah) is set forth.*[26]

For one contemporary Western critic, Yūsuf's lengthy and finely drawn portrayal in the Qur'ān serves as a teaching parable with which Muḥammad illustrates his triumph over opposition to his mission and message. Like Joseph:

> Muḥammad has to leave his home to fulfill his destiny elsewhere. The situations of revelation [*asbāb al-nuzūl*], those traditions that identify the time and place

of each Qur'ānic revelation, place Sūrat Yūsuf in the
Meccan period, before [the Battle of] 'Aqaba, and accord-
ing to tradition it was recited to the first converts from
Medina.[27]

In this reading, Muḥammad, in the process of deciding upon
the future of his mission, is inspired by the figure of Joseph to
leave Mecca and establish his base in Medina. S. M. Stern points
out that the phrase used by the Egyptian King's advisors to describe his dreams (Qur'ān 12:44), *adghāthu aḥlāmin* (a hodge-
podge of nightmares), appears in one other verse of the Qur'ān:

It is used by Muḥammad's opponents to denigrate
his revelations (Sura 21:5). Just as the Egyptian council's failure to recognize a divine message led to their
being replaced in power, so would Muḥammad overcome
the blind and ignorant men of Mecca.[28]

Whatever interpretation may be given to *aḥsan al-Qaṣaṣ*, and
whatever importance is assigned to the didactic import of the
tale, the Joseph story's popularity in the Islamic world seemed
assured. Throughout the Middle Ages the story appeared in
Arabic, Turkish, and Persian, and it became a mainstay of the
anthologies of *Tales of the Prophets*—the *Qiṣaṣ al-anbiyā'*
literature. As M. J. Kister noted "the transmitters of these tales
aimed at widening the scope of these Qur'ānic stories; they
availed themselves of the lore contained in local traditions
current in the Arab peninsula in the period of the Jahiliya, in the
Christian narrative concerning the life of Jesus, the Apostles, the
martyrs, and the monks, in Jewish Biblical legends, and in the
utterances of sages and ascetics."[29]

In the collections of this genre, Yūsuf was a great favorite.
"The Muslim community was eager to learn of the biographies of
the prophets of the past because Muḥammad was identified in
certain passages of the Qur'ān with their mission and vocation,
and especially with the sufferings and persecution which they
had undergone."[30] We have cited al-Tha'labī's excursus on the
reasons for the superiority of Joseph's story. The story also
appears in folk poetry:

Side by side with the literary manifestations of the
genre, there was a long tradition of oral recitations on

these themes by professional *qussas*, which range along with popular epics like the *sirat 'Antar*, etc. all of these have a "Homeric" quality, in that there was a rough approximation to an "established" text, no one author can be pinned down; they are the end product of innumerable recitations over the centuries each of which may have contributed something to them.[31]

A medieval Arabic manuscript, the Leeds ms. 347 (ca. thirteenth-fourteenth centuries), retells the Yūsuf story using the text of Sūrat Yūsuf as its point of departure. Its editors note that:

> The general arrangement of the story narrated in the poem is that of the Qur'ānic story. At some points the Qur'ānic text is quoted directly, while many other phrases used by the poet are adaptations of Qur'ānic phraseology...In all, one sixth of the 469 surviving verses of this poem contain direct quotations or reminiscences of the text of Sūra 12.[32]

On linguistic evidence, the editors of this text have taken the manuscript to be of Egyptian provenance. They note the obvious pleasure the poet takes in allusions to the "blessed Nile."[33] In the poem, Joseph is fetched from his cell by the butler whose dream Joseph had interpreted years before. The butler, sent by the King, knocks on Joseph's door:

> When he knocked upon his door he came with haste, and a smile appeared on his lips when he saw him. Joseph said to him: "Hearty welcome to one who has come to ask me about the seven fat kine..."

Here Joseph knows the king's dream even before it is told to him. He can provide the king with both the dream and its interpretation—a true sign of divine inspiration. This embellishes the Qur'ānic account (12:47) in which Joseph is first told the dream and then asked to interpret it. And this, in turn, echoes the Biblical account in Genesis 41:17. This ability of Joseph's hearkens back to a Biblical and other Ancient Near Eastern tales in which the interpreter knows the dream before it is told to him. In the Book of Daniel, Nebuchadnezzer insists that his wise men and "Chaldeans" be summoned to "tell him" his dreams. They ask that the king relate the dreams that he wishes them to interpret. But Nebuchadnezzer is adamant, he wants them to tell *him* the dream. Finally, in frustration, the Chaldeans answered the king:

> There is not a man on earth who can meet the King's demand; for no great and powerful King has asked such a thing of any magician or enchanter or Chaldean. The thing that the King asks is difficult, and none can show it to the King except the gods, whose dwelling is not with flesh. (Daniel 2:10–12)

Daniel is then granted this gift from God in a vision and he is able to tell the king what his dream was[34] (2:31).

When, in our fourteenth century Arabic poem, Joseph interprets the dream, he elaborates on the seven years of plenty symbolized by the seven fat cows. The Egyptian setting is authentic and appropriate:

> The Nile shall be in full flood from bank to bank and the eyes of the clouds shall pour forth an abundance of rain. The tillers of the land shall be assured of water in their plough-land: there shall be no part of it which the blessed Nile does not cover and inundate. They shall strive to sow it all and they shall not leave a span of earth fallow. They shall build a spacious building for storage in every region with sturdy walls.[35]

There are echoes of two Ancient Near Eastern themes in this late medieval reworking of Joseph's story: the dependable fecundity of the Nile and the divinely inspired nature of dream-interpretation. These themes draw on the two distinct but linked civilizations that provide the background of the Biblical Joseph story, Egypt and Mesopotamia. The predictable inundation of the Nile was a basis of early Egyptian civilization, and the powers of dreams was long recognized in the Mesopotamian cultures. Much of this century's academic study of Genesis ties Joseph to its Egyptian setting. But it should not be overlooked that Joseph's origins were in Mesopotamia, the Biblical Aram Naharaim; he was the last of Jacob's children to be born in

Laban's household in Haran. Genesis 30:25 makes this association explicit; it ties together the birth of Rachel's first son with
the flight from Haran:

> When Rachel had given birth to Joseph, Jacob said to
> Laban, "Let me go, for I wish to return to my own home
> and country."

Joseph thus bridges the Mesopotamian and Egyptian experiences
of the Patriarchs, and, by extension, of the children of Israel. He is
born in Aram Naharaim, his youth is spent in Canaan, but he
grows to manhood and responsibility in Egypt. Long after his
death, when the children of Israel return to Canaan, they return
his bones to Canaan, land of his fathers. Symbolically, Joseph's
remains link Mesopotamia, Canaan, and Egypt.

Throughout our discussions of the Joseph story in its elaborated form we will see that this sequence of cultural settings—
Mesopotamia, Canaan, and Egypt, and the return to Canaan—
was used to great effect by post-Biblical commentators, folklore
anthologists, and, in the modern period, by novelists.

The Joseph Story in Polemical Literature

Even at this early point in our survey of the literature we
can see that the Joseph narratives were the locus of elaboration
and the subject of extensive commentary. A further indication of
the story's centrality and popularity is the frequency with which
it is cited in religious polemics. These include both Jewish-
Islamic polemics and Islamic sectarian polemics.

A. In the Jewish-Islamic Polemic

As Joseph/Yūsuf is a central figure in the two traditions, the
two distinct portrayals of him are not only of interest to the
modern student of narrative, they were understood by advo-
cates of each tradition to be of theological import as well. The
nature of the Jewish-Islamic polemic is markedly different from
that of the Jewish-Christian polemic. The difference is determined by Judaism's two "daughter religions'" relationship to the
text of the Hebrew Bible:

> For the Christian churches...the validity, sanctity,
> and authenticity of the Hebrew scriptures were beyond

challenge. The Christian churches recognized the divine origin of these scriptures in their entirety and considered them an integral part of the Bible...Radically different is the attitude of Islam toward the Hebrew scriptures: these do not form an integral part of Islam's holy writings. Islam ascribes holiness and authority solely to the Qur'ān."[36]

While Jews and Christians could debate the meaning of specific words and phrases in the Hebrew Bible, such an exercise would be meaningless in the Jewish-Islamic debate, for Muslims do not consider the text of the Torah sacred. When the *tawrat* (Torah) is cited in the disputations between Muḥammad and the Jews of his time, its antiquity is recognized—but Muḥammad accuses the Jews of having distorted it. These accusations are formulated in Islam as the doctrine of *Taḥrif*, a doctrine articulated four times in the Qur'ān.

The Muslims found occasion to deal with this concept in connection with those passages in the Qur'ān where Muḥammad accused the Jews of falsifying the books of revelation given them

There is a distinct charge of having falsified the text in Sūra 2:73. "Woe to them who write the scripture with their hands and say: this comes from Allah" and again in 2:91 "You make the scripture of Moses into leaves which you read out and suppress much of it;" which can only mean that in (Muḥammad's) opinion they removed the passages attesting to the truth of his mission from the copies which they used at their disputations.[37]

That the Jews will be punished for their rejection of Muḥammad is, according to Ṭabari, implied in Sūra 2:90—"And they were laden with anger"—(this refers to) the Jews, for their alteration of the Torah before the advent of the Prophet.[38] In the absence of a common textual ground for disputation (for the Jews did not accept the Qur'ān, nor the Muslims accept the Torah), stories common to both the Qur'ān and the Bible became the subject of polemic, and none assumed greater importance than that of Joseph. As the most extensively treated tale in the Qur'ān, and as one with a Biblical antecedent, the story of Joseph was a locus of debate. The debate had two aspects: 1) The question of what constitutes the complete story of Joseph and the related question of its significance in sacred history. 2) The fine details of the story, many of which are absent from either the Biblical or Qur'ānic text. Both aspects are illustrated in these comments of al-Bayḍāwī, the thirteenth century giant of Qur'ānic exegesis, in his *Tafsīr*.

Commenting on the opening of the sūra, "These are the signs of the manifest book" (12:1) al-Bayḍāwī offers an alternative reading to the simple meaning of the text:

> This is the sūrah which makes plain to the Jews that which they asked...it is recorded that their learned men said to the chiefs of the polytheists, "Ask Muḥam-mad why Jacob's family moved from Syria to Egypt, and about the story of Joseph," whereupon this sūrah was revealed.[39]

This reading, which recognizes the pivotal position of the story in Hebrew history (for in order for the Hebrews to be enslaved and liberated, Joseph must descend into Egypt and draw Jacob's family to him), echoes the Rabbinic homily, cited at the beginning of this chapter, which sees a new epic inaugurated with Joseph's story. al-Bayḍāwī's comment indicates that to the emerging Muslim community, the Muḥammad's superior knowl-edge of Biblical history was a sign of divine inspiration; Muslim expectation was that this knowledge would win the Jews over to the Muslim cause. For, in Muḥammad's attempt to win the allegiance of the *ahl al-kitab* (the Peoples of the Book), he was operating at a distinct disadvantage. As M. G. S. Hodgson put it:

> Muḥammad...had always expected that monotheists, whether Christians or Jews, ought to welcome his mes-sage and give him support in his work among the pagans. But...Muḥammad's versions of Biblical, Talmudic, and apocryphal Christian stories were too patently incoherent, and sometimes garbled, to win the respect of those who already possessed the older sacred books. There was little to encourage them to hail Muḥammad as a prophet even to their pagan neighbors.[40]

Against this background, in which Christians and Jews questioned the validity of Qur'ānic narrative, while the early community of Muslims affirmed it, it became all the more important
for Muḥammad to display knowledge of the "secret," unstated
details of the Biblical tales. This factor informs Baiḍawi's comments on Joseph's dream in which the sun, the moon, and
eleven stars bow down to him:

> Jabir tells a story to the effect that a Jew came to the
> Prophet and said, "Tell me Muḥammad, about the stars
> which Joseph saw," The Prophet was silent, then Gabriel
> descended and gave him this information, so he said,
> "These are the names of all of the eleven stars. Joseph
> saw these and the sun and moon descending from
> heaven and bowing down to him." And the Jew said, "Yes
> indeed, these are their names."[41]

In an another version of the story, (related by al-Thaʻlabī in
his Qiṣas al-anbiya), the encounter between the Jew and
Muḥammad had a more dramatic denouement. The angel
Gabriel tells Muḥammad the names of the stars, and Muḥammad then sends for the Jew and asks him if he will convert to
Islam if he reveals the stars' names to him. The Jew agrees and
Muḥammad then reveals the secret names that Gabriel had
revealed to him.[42] In this version, Muḥammad's knowledge of the
secret details so impresses the Jew that he converts to Islam.
Also of significance in al-Thaʻlabī's retelling is Joseph's seeming
bewilderment at his own dream. He turns to his father, who
assures him that this is a prophetic dream, "I see something
scattered but God will gather it up." Here we are not in the
company of the arrogant, preening Joseph of the Biblical story
(and of some Midrashim), but in the presence of a youth
bewildered by the divine call to greatness. He is not a victim of
his own youthful arrogance, but, rather, a young man destined
to be a Nabi (a prophet). Indications of his future greatness (e.g.,
his dreams) are not to be taken as indications of human striving
and weakness; rather they are "signs," presentments of the
fulfillment of God's plan.[43]

The "superior" narrative qualities of Sūrat Yūsuf, in com-
parison with the parallel Joseph narratives in Genesis, are
advanced by Muslim polemicists as an argument for the superi-

ority of Islamic revelation. Commenting on the Qur'ānic phrase, "the best of all stories," Al-Thaʻlabī quotes a tradition in which some of the companions of Muḥammad asked the sage Salmān al-Fārisi about the *tawrat*, the Torah of the Jews. "What," they asked, "is the best thing in it?" This incident was followed by the revelation to Muḥammad of Sūrat Yūsuf, and that revelation, this tradition asserts, proves that the Qur'ān is superior to the *tawrat*.[44]

Al-Thaʻlabī also offers another *isnād*, or "chain of transmission" for this tradition, one which links this saying directly to the Prophet. As a companion of the Prophet, Salmān's authority was considerable, and the attribution of this statement to him lent authoritative weight to this reading of Sura 12. This tradition amplifies the classical Qur'ānic commentators on the verse, some of whom assert that "best of all stories" refers to both the form and content of the Surah. In Muslim historiography, Salmān al-Fārisi, the first Persian convert to Islam, assumed legendary status. "The figure of Salmān has had an extraordinary development...the alleged site of his tomb very early became a center of worship...and the veneration accorded to Salman among the Sunnis is naturally exceeded among the Shīʻis."[45]

Two figures associated with the transmission of "Israelite" legends to Islam (and by extension, with the Jewish-Islamic polemic) are Kaʻb al-aḥbār (seventh Christian century) and Wahb ibn Munabbih (eighth century). Kaʻb al-aḥbār ("of the ḥaverim," the Rabbinical scholars) was a Yemenite Jewish convert to Islam. Said to have been a close associate of the Caliph Umar, he accompanied the Caliph on his march into Jerusalem. Kaʻb (his Arabic name may be a form of Akiba or Yakov) is often cited as a source for Jewish materials in Islamic legends, and he is quoted widely in the commentaries on Sūrat Yūsuf. Also of Yemenite Jewish origin was Wahb ibn Munabbih, who lived a generation after Kaʻb. He too is credited as the source of many Jewish (and Christian) stories which appeared in the *Isrāʼīlīyāt* compendia, and like Kaʻb, his authority is questioned at times because of his association with the "peoples of the book."[46]

B. In the Inter-Islamic Polemic

Sūrat Yūsuf, and parallel Jewish stories, served as proof texts in the Jewish-Islamic polemic. In disputations within the

Islamic community the debate centered on the text of the Qur'ān. Ibn Ḥazm, the eleventh century Andalusian polemicist and chronicler of Muslim sectarianism, described the beliefs and practices of the Kharijites, "that third party in Islam which anathematized both the majority Sunnis and the Shī'ī partisans of Ali."

There were, however, people who usurped the name of Islam, though all the sects of Islam agree that they are not Muslims. Thus there were sections among the Kharijites who went to the extreme, maintaining that the Salat (prayer) was not more than one bow in the morning and one in the evening. Others permitted marriage with granddaughters and daughters of nephews. They also maintained that Sūrat Yūsuf did not belong to the Qur'ān.[47]

Al-Shahrastāni, the twelfth century scholar who was considered the principal Muslim historian of religion, is more specific. He identifies the "extreme" sect as the Maimuniyya of the Kharijites, and says that the reason they rejected Sūrat Yūsuf as part of the Qur'ān was that they did not think that a love-story should be included in the Qur'ān. The reference here is to the Potiphar's Wife theme, which, though it highlights Joseph's virtue, seems to have been too erotically charged for the Maimuniyya's sensibilities. Their rejection of Sūrat Yūsuf is in keeping with extreme Kharijite ideology which "demands purity of conscience as an indispensable complement to bodily purity for the validity of acts of worship."[48]

Such an extreme position—rejection of an entire Sura from the corpus of the Qur'ān—is rare. We do find instances of a "lost" verse, one not found in our texts of the Qur'ān, being ascribed to Sūrat Yūsuf. Abū Wāq'id al-Laythī reports, "When inspiration came upon the Prophet, we would go to him and he would instruct us in what had been revealed. I went to him once and he said, 'God says, we sent wealth for the upkeep of prayer and alms-giving. Were ibn Adam ("a human being") to possess a wadi, he would desire another like it, which, if he had, he would desire yet another. Nothing will fill the maw of ibn Adam but dust, but God relents to him who repents.'" The verse was in Sūrat Yūsuf.[49]

Perhaps the choice of Sūrat Yūsuf for the placement of this "lost" verse is related to the centrality of the Potiphar's Wife motif in that Sura. The futility of desire, and the impossibility of fulfilling one's desires, are conveyed in the maxim that "Nothing will fill the maw of ibn Adam but dust." Yūsuf, by resisting temptation and conquering desire, exemplifies this theme, and therefore receives the rewards reserved for "him who repents."

Despite the different interpretations of Joseph conveyed in legends and polemics there is one area of agreement in the folklore of the confessional communities; they all attribute magical powers to both the living Joseph and to his earthly remains.

Joseph as Holy Man, Prophet, Magician

In Jewish tradition Joseph is not counted among the Avot, the Patriarchs. As one of the twelve sons of Jacob he is of the children of Israel, and among them he serves as the link between the Patriarchal Age and the Israelite sojourn in Egypt:

> On the literary level the Bible depicts Joseph as the heir and successor to the Patriarchs. He follows closely upon his fathers in carrying forth the ancestral heritage and in receiving, as did his fathers, the divine promise. (cf. Genesis 50:24).[50]

When, during Israel's bondage in Egypt, they "were groaning under their bondage and cried out," God who "remembered His covenant with Abraham, Isaac and Jacob, took notice of them" (Exodus 2:24). The narrative of their bondage begins with the new king who "arose over Egypt, who did not know Joseph." Joseph is the historical link to the covenant; but he is not one to whom the covenantal promises are directly made.

An early Midrash places Joseph in a quartet of men of great wisdom, men whose wisdom is exceeded only by Solomon. It comments on I Kings 5:11 "He [Solomon] was the wisest of all men: wiser than Etan the Ezrahite, and Heman, Calcol, and Darda the sons of Mahol." These are names unknown elsewhere in the Biblical narrative and therefore the impact of comparing Solomon to these men is somewhat muted. In order to solve that problem this Midrash identifies these names with well-known Biblical figures. "Calcol," the provider, "is identified with

Joseph."[51] Though excluded from the Patriarchal triad of Abraham, Isaac, and Jacob, Joseph is included in the list of the great wise men of Biblical history. He supplies both the Egyptians and the Israelites with grain and facilitates the settlement of Jacob's family in Egypt.

In Islam, Yūsuf also has an exalted position, one in which he is both the protagonist of the most colorful and elaborate of all suras, and a *nabi*—a prophet. In this latter role he is portrayed in the tradition as a precursor of Muḥammad. Joseph's success in Egypt serves as a model for Muḥammad endeavors in Medina; inspiring him to bring his monotheistic message to the pagan Arabs as Joseph did to the idolatrous Egyptians.[52]

Exalted as Joseph's position is in both the Jewish and Muslim traditions, it should be emphasized that in both traditions he is seen as secondary to Moses. According to S. D. Goitein:

> Moses (Mūsā) is the predominant figure in the Qur'ān. I would not like to lay too much stress on the quantitative aspect, although it is impressive enough; compared to Jesus, who is mentioned only four times in the Qur'ān during the Meccan, that is, formative period of Muḥammad's career, Moses' name occurs there over a hundred times. Much more important is the fact that the stories about Moses are not confined to certain chapters, but pervade the whole Qur'ān and the idea of Moses, the Prophet with a Book, possessed Muḥammad to such an extent that he immediately proceeded to produce a divine book of his own.[53]

In the Jewish tradition Moses' exalted status as prophet and lawgiver strengthened the tendency in both Bible and legend to de-mythologize him. In order to prevent his grave from becoming a shrine, its site remains unknown. Later in Biblical history the bronze serpent with which Moses stopped the plague (Numbers 21:9) is destroyed by Hezekiah so as to prevent it from becoming an object of further veneration. "He also broke into pieces the bronze serpent which Moses had made, for until that time the Israelites has been offering sacrifices to it; it was called Nehushtan." (2 Kings: 18:4). In the development of Moses as a literary figure, the functions of lawgiver and leader overshadow, and eventually exclude, the earlier roles of seer and magician.

Joseph, in contrast, is a figure ripe for mythologizing—he is neither patriarch nor national leader, and there is no danger in enriching his portrait with magical detail. With so much attention focused on Joseph by both scripture and its aggadaic elaboration, it was inevitable that he would become a popular figure in folk religion and that magical powers would be attributed to him. For Jews, Christians, and Muslims, the Ancient Egyptians were the magicians, par excellence, and therefore the Egyptian background of the narratives made the magical aspect even more appropriate to Joseph.

While I have been making the case that Moses is a more exalted and central figure than Joseph in both Judaism and Islam, one set of Muslim tales indicates that there may have been "competition" between the two prophets, and that this competition led to conflation of Joseph and Moses in the imagination of some storytellers. Al-Kisāʾī, the thirteenth century Muslim anthologist whose identity is something of a mystery, says on the authority of Kaʿb al Aḥbār and Wahb ibn Munabbīh, that Joseph's son Manasseh was "blessed with a child whom he called Moses, and this was *before* the time of Moses son of Amram." Like the later Biblical Moses, this Moses was also a spokesman for God and he was enjoined to remind his people of their covenant with God. Al-Kisāʾī's version closes with the affirmation that "Moses son of Manasseh recited all of that to the children of Israel, and they responded to him. He remained among them a long time before he died."[54] In some Islamic sources this Moses is identified with the mystical figure mentioned in the Qurʾān (Sura 18). Yet a third Moses, "Moses the Samaritan" appears in the chronologies of Muslim historians.

In Ibn Isḥāq's narrative, when the "primary" Moses, the leader of the Banū Isrāʾīl (the Children of Israel), was told that his time to die had come, he pleaded for his life. For he "hated death and found it distressing." The way in which he was convinced to embrace death was this:

> On the day that he was to die he saw a troop of angels digging a grave "more beautiful, green, splendid, and opulent than he had ever seen." When he asked the angels whose grave it was they replied "that it was for a servant of God who would have an eternal dwelling in heaven." The angels said to him, "Oh friend of God, do you wish to have this?" He said, "I would." They said,

"Enter, lie down in it, and face your Lord. Then breathe easier than you have ever breathed." So he went down and lay down in it and faced his Lord and expired. God took his spirit, and the angels raised their voices over him."[55]

The classical association of magic and death is also manifest in the Joseph tales. In these stories, in contrast to Moses' story, the hero's remains, tomb, and possessions, became objects of veneration. In weaving the story of his life, Jewish legends portray Joseph as a living, practicing magician, functioning and excelling in the "land of magic." In death, his power is transferred to his remains and effects. The Talmud states: Ten portions of magic descended to earth, nine were taken by the Egyptians.[56] This is a reflex of the Bible's focus on and condemnation of magic, particularly the magic of Egypt (Exodus 7:11, 7:22, 8:14). Moses and Aaron challenge the Egyptians' magical power, and best the Egyptians in a sphere in which that nation is known to excel. For post-Biblical Jewish writers, magic and Egypt would remain forever intertwined. In keeping with the spirit of this association, Genesis Rabbah has Joseph encounter these "nine portions of magic" as soon as he is brought down into Egypt:

"And his master saw that the Lord was with him" (Genesis 39:3), Rabbi Huna interpreted in Rabbi Aha's name: Joseph whispered God's name whenever he came in and whenever he went out...If his master bid him "Mix me a drink, and make it hot," lo, it was hot; Mix it lukewarm, it was lukewarm. What means this, Joseph!, exclaimed he; would you bring straw to Afrayim, or pitchers to Kefar Hananiah, or fleeces to Damascus, or witchcraft to Egypt—witchcraft to a place of witchcraft?

Joseph's Egyptian master suspects him of *ḥarshin* (black magic):

...How long did he suspect him of witchcraft?... Until he saw the Shekhinah standing over him. Hence it says: "And his master saw that the Lord was with him... and Joseph found favor in his sight."[57]

The use of the term *ḥarshin* (magic), is significant. It specifically refers to magical *praxis*, and in that sense it frequently appears in the magic bowl inscriptions, where *praxis* with evil intent is *ḥarshin bishin* (black magic). The Egyptians in this legend are masters of every *praxis*, both "black" and "white." Potiphar, in this legend, is able to distinguish between "good" and "bad" magic only because he can intuit the Shekhinah, the divine presence, hovering over the young Hebrew slave. As Jacob Neusner has noted, this Midrash "provides yet another opportunity for observing the same insistence that on the basis of extrinsic traits we cannot differentiate the Israelite from the gentile magician, either as to knowledge or as to deed."[58]

Numerous legends with magical or sexual themes weave themselves around Joseph's sojourn in Potiphar's house. A legend parallel to the magical one is that Potiphar was sexually attracted to Joseph, but his designs were thwarted through divine intervention. In some versions, this intervention takes the form of the castration of Potiphar and it is used to account for the description in some Biblical translations of Potiphar as eunuch. This variation appears in Jewish, Christian, and Muslim sources, and this illustrates that the cross-cultural diffusion of legends increases when sexual behavior or magic is the subject at hand.

And another "magical" legend: When Joseph is proclaimed "second to the King," he is paraded through the streets and the people proclaim before him: *'abrek* (Genesis 41:43). Though this is now understood by many scholars as an Egyptianism,[59] the *Book of Jubilees* (c. 200 c.e.) takes it to be a magical incantation, a contraction of *abir el* (the Great One of God)." Citing New Testament parallels, R. H. Charles comments that this, "may be a technical term for a great magician."[60] The *Book of Jubilees* continues in this magical vein in its retelling of the Joseph tale. When Joseph assumed his new position, the evil forces were propitiated: "Pharaoh's Kingdom was well ordered and there was no Satan and no evil person therein."

The Islamic legends about Joseph as a magician may echo these stories in Midrash and Jubilees, though as we have seen, the precise method by which these stories were transmitted is no longer clear. We find that in both traditions Joseph's powers inhere in his personal effects, especially his clothing and his diviner's cup. Early in the Genesis account Joseph is associated with the "coat of many colors" that Jacob gave Joseph; later we read of the cup with which Joseph practiced divination. Al-

Thaʻlabī tells us of another powerful object, an amulet that contained a blouse made of silk from the Garden of Eden. This blouse protected Joseph's ancestors, Abraham and Isaac, in times of danger. It was handed down to Jacob who placed it inside an amulet and hung it around Joseph's neck. In the pit, the angel Gabriel came to Joseph, took out the blouse, and placed it on the young man.[61] Much later in the tale, when the roles are reversed and Joseph controls the fate of his brothers, he uses their belief in the power of Egyptian magic as a ruse to bring them back to his court and provoke them into a confrontation with him. Al-Thaʻlabī lavishes description on Joseph's cup, which he used to measure grain. It was made of gold and set with gems. Previously, it had been the Pharaoh's cup.[62]

In this version, when Joseph's messenger overtakes the brothers they emphasize the cup's magic power, not its ornamental value. The messenger identifies it as the Pharaoh's cup of divination. Here we have an obvious echo of the Genesis account, for in Genesis 44:5 Joseph's brothers are told that they have stolen the cup with which Joseph practices divination. In the Qurʼān (12:75) no mention is made of the cup as a magical object. Here a Biblical narrative detail may have worked its way into an Islamic legend. In this Islamic retelling, when Joseph's brothers are brought back into his presence, they are taunted by him. Holding the cup he pretends that it has informed him that the brothers had a younger brother whom they sold into slavery. Benjamin asserts that if Joseph would inquire of the cup he would learn the real circumstances of the cup's disappearance. Joseph, overcome with emotion, has to leave his brother's presence, but when he returns he continues the deception and asserts that the cup will not vindicate Benjamin.[63] This demonstration so angers the brothers that they fly into a rage, leave Benjamin with Joseph, and return to Jacob in Canaan.

HIdden or "magical" meanings may reveal themselves in other ways. Some Jewish and Islamic commentators see a "number symbolism" operating in the sacred texts. For these readers the numbers used in straightforward narrative accounts, e.g., genealogies, life spans, census reckonings, have a hidden meaning and constitute an "internal-midrash." This is part of a larger view that Hebrew and Arabic words, of all parts of speech, can be understood in terms of their numerical equivalents. This view is expressed in the Jewish exegetical tool of *gematria*[64] and its Islamic equivalent *abjad.*[65] As Gershom Scholem noted, the system "consists of explaining a word or group of words according to the numerical value of the letters...the use of *gematria* was widespread in the literature of the magi and among interpreters of dreams in the Hellenistic world. Its use was apparently introduced in Israel during the time of the Second Temple." As for the interpretation of *numbers that appear in the text*, it is quite true, as Stanley Gevirtz says, that:

> ...no explanation of such numbers—whether ancient, medieval, or modern—can be conclusive. At best, only a reasonable solution to the problem of the origin of a given number can be hoped for: what magical, cultic, or theological significance that figure may have conveyed must always remain problematic.[66]

The number in the Joseph story that has attracted the attention of the Biblical commentaries is that of his life span: 110 years. "Joseph died at the age of 110 years. He was embalmed and laid to rest in a coffin in Egypt." (Genesis 50:26) The age of 110 was considered by the Egyptians to be the ideal life span.[67] This notion parallels the Hebrew ideal of a life span of 120 years, an ideal based on Genesis 6:3 ("My spirit shall not abide in man forever, for that he is also flesh, therefore, shall his days be a hundred and twenty years.") and on Moses' age and unfailing vigor at the time of his death (Deuteronomy 34:7). But, as S. Gevirtz states, "While Egypt may provide the cultural origins of the figure, (of 110 years) its mathematical derivation remains obscure."[68] Building on the work of earlier critics, recent writers on the topic, Gevirtz among them, discern a mathematical pattern at work in the age spans of the Patriarchs and Joseph. The pattern culminates in a "summation" life span for Joseph. There is a pattern of consecutive numbers at work here:

Patriarch	Life span
Abraham	$175 = 7 \times 5^2$
Isaac	$180 = 5 \times 6^2$
Jacob	$147 = 3 \times 7^2$
Joseph	$110 = 1 \times (5^2 + 6^2 + 7^2)$

Joseph is thus the successor in the pattern (7 - 5 - 3 - 1) and the sum of his predecessors $(5^2 + 6^2 + 7^2)$.[69]

J. G. Williams points out that:

> The number system in the Joseph story reinforces a great deal of textual evidence that the *Joseph figure is one that combines and embodies many of the features of the portrayals of the preceding patriarchs and matriarchs. In combining and embodying these features he transcends his predecessors.* He is like them and he is more than they.[70]

The legendary material surrounding Joseph, in both the Jewish and Islamic traditions, supports that contention. This is directly stated in the Midrash quoted above, "The following events transpired only on Joseph's merit."

Daniel Grossberg notes that Moses' life span, 120 years, which has come to be considered the ideal Hebrew life span, is the sum of a particular progression of square numbers: $2^2 + 4^2 + 6^2 + 8^2 = 120$.[71] Grossberg sees this as the symbolic expression of the Midrash's understanding of all aspects of the Exodus story—it is about the Hebrews rising above their oppressors. For the Egyptian ideal life span was 110 years. "We thus see that the numbers in those life spans provide an important additional dimension to the Biblical literary medium by complementing and underscoring the narrative."[72]

This number symbolism amplifies the impression created by the Biblical, Aggadic, and Qur'ānic sources that Joseph occupies a unique position in Jewish and Islamic folklore. He is successor to the patriarchs and matriarchs, bridge to the descent into Egypt, and, through the fulfillment of his brothers' promise to take his bones to the land of his fathers, link to the conquest and settlement of Canaan.

His uniqueness and centrality are underscored by the narrative art of the story's construction; by the story's frequent citation in religious polemics, and by the portrayal of Joseph as a wise man, magician, and the embodiment of personal and religious fulfillment.

The length and complexity of the Joseph narratives in Jewish and Muslim scripture and legend has its parallel in modern literary treatments of the Joseph stories. As one critic notes "few Biblical figures here inspired more extensive and more universal literary treatment than Joseph." Tolstoy, enchanted by the twists and turns of the Biblical tale, and obsessed with the narration of the pitfalls of sexual temptation, was inspired to study Hebrew when he was in his early seventies. He took a tutor, a Rabbi Minor, but found learning a new script and language at his advanced age too daunting. This new project also contributed to Tolstoy's domestic problems. In a letter to a friend, Tolstoy's wife Sonya wrote, "Leo is learning the Hebrew language to my intense regret...he is wasting his energy on foolishness."[73] But this did not diminish his enthusiasm for the manner in which Joseph's adventures were told. Thomas Mann, who read widely and deeply in many versions of Joseph's story, was to pay Joseph the greatest modern tribute when he embarked on the construction of his masterwork, *Joseph and His Brothers*, published as a series of novels between 1933 and 1944. Mann began writing the series in 1928 and toured Egypt and Palestine in 1930. At the time of that journey he was already deeply immersed in the Joseph story and noted that "it could hardly be called a trip for the purpose of study; it rather served for verifying on the spot the things of this sphere with which I had been concerned at a distance."[74]

For Mann, as for Tolstoy, the center and essence of the Joseph story was the Potiphar's Wife episode. Mann considered his retelling of the "mournful story of her passionate love of the Canaanite major domo of her pro forma husband" as the artistic zenith of his life's work.

In their enthusiasm for the story of Joseph these two twentieth century literary giants echo the assessments of Jewish and Muslim readers and writers in earlier centuries. Let us proceed then to the story of the favored young man and his master's wife and examine the earliest expressions of this celebrated motif. The tale of the encounter between Joseph, the "well-favored," and his master's wife, a woman of great beauty and determination, has its parallels in Ancient Egyptian and classical literature. An examination of the narrative variations on their encounter will enable us to come to some tentative conclusions about the antiquity of this motif and the degree to which these respective Near Eastern cultures—Ancient Egyptian, Jewish, and Islamic—influenced each other's storytelling traditions. The storytelling traditions of the Greek world and their expression in the Homeric epics are also relevant to our discussion. Some scholars posit a direct connection between

Homeric epic and Ancient Near Eastern myth, and the shared motifs of the Potiphar's Wife story may serve to add supporting evidence to this theory. For those who reject this "Mediterranean model" of the transmission of the Potiphar's Wife motif, early attempts to forge a connection between Greece and the Near East—the Roman historians and the Church fathers engaged in such speculation—are of themselves of great interest.[75]

Joseph and Potiphar's Wife

The Spurned Woman: Potiphar's Wife in Scripture and Folklore

"Lie with me!"—the laconic terseness of the original text cannot be surpassed.

It goes without saying that there can be no chastity where there is no capacity—honorary captains and mutilated sun-chamberlains, for instance, are not chaste. We set out with the premise that Joseph was a whole and virile man.
—Thomas Mann, *Joseph in Egypt* (1934)

Though I have alluded to the Potiphar's Wife motif throughout the introduction and first chapter, I have not yet considered fully the earliest known expressions of this motif. I will begin with the ancient Mediterranean traditions, those of Egypt, Greece, and Israel, and then proceed to the treatment of the motif in later Jewish texts and Islamic sources.

I. The Ancient Near Eastern Background and the Biblical Tale of Potiphar's Wife

"A woman makes vain overtures to a man and then accuses him of attempting to force her." The folklorist Stith Thompson thus succinctly describes a motif whose earliest known expression appears in the literature of the second pre-Christian millennium.[1] The motif remains a popular one in many literatures and folklores. The appeal of the tale seems to be universal, and it appears in cultures that have no demonstrable links to the scriptural monotheisms. In the cultures influenced by the Bible and the Qur'ān, the motif was very widely diffused. The Islamic story of the "Prophet" Yusuf and his master's wife, Zuleikha, spread throughout the Middle East and Asia. The linguist Maurice Bloomfield noted in the 1920s that "to this day the tale of Yusuf and Zuleikha is recited by minstrels in Kashmir in the Kashmiri language."[2] In our own time the success of Michael Crichton's novel, *Disclosure*, in which a powerful female executive assumes the Potiphar's Wife role, attests to the staying power of the Joseph and Zuleikha story.

This motif, embedded in the Joseph story in Genesis, has affinities with similar stories popular in Egypt of the Amarna age (the fourteenth century B.C.) and Greece of the age of Homer (the ninth century B.C.). One could describe the earliest known forms of this story as Mediterranean in origin. The relationship of the Biblical tale to the *Tale of Two Brothers* has long been debated;[3] classical scholars have noted parallels to our motif in Greek and Roman literature: the earliest expression of the motif in the classical world appears in the Iliad as the tale of Bellerophon.[4]

The Joseph narratives enjoy a central position in both the Jewish and Islamic traditions. Of the various motifs operating in the Joseph stories "Potiphar's Wife," with its elements of intrigue, romance, revenge, and vindication, must have appealed strongly to the popular imagination and contributed to the Joseph story's popularity. These narrative elements, and the lessons to be drawn from them, may explain the Qur'ān's reference to Yūsuf's tale as "the best of all stories." And these same elements helped to make the *Tale of Two Brothers* a popular Egyptian tale, and to ensure the Bellerophon story a place in the Homeric cycle.

As the setting of the Bellerophon story lies outside of the Middle Eastern cultural sphere with which we have been concerned until now, let me situate this episode in the story of the Iliad. The tale of Bellerophon is told by his grandson Glaukos, an ally of the Trojans. Glaukos is about to engage the Greek warrior Diomedes in combat. But combat is pre-empted by conversation and the two fighters exchange stories of their heroic ancestors. They discover that their grandfathers were once friends and therefore Glaukos and Diomedes decide not to fight one another. As a legacy, they leave us the story of Bellerophon.

In this chapter, I will first compare and contrast three early versions of the motif: the Egyptian, the Homeric, and the Biblical. Each version will be studied in the context of the culture from which it emerged; similarities and discrepancies between the versions will be analyzed using the comparative method. I will then move to the post-Biblical Jewish retellings of Joseph's adventure with his master's wife, and from there, proceed to the way the story is treated in the Qur'ān and later Islamic sources. Like Joseph himself, the story of his encounter with his master's wife is attractive and enticing. While these religious and cultural traditions "made the story live" and transmitted it across generations, they also saw fit to exercise control over the story. Each culture produced a variant that was uniquely its own. It could not be too frivolous or entertaining; in some retellings it was encumbered with didactic moralizing, and we have seen that some Muslim sectarians called for the exclusion of the Potiphar's Wife motif from their scriptural canon.

As a recent study of the Ancient Egyptian version of our story notes, the *Tale of Two Brothers* tells "the nearly universal story of a handsome and chaste young shepherd who rejects seduction by a powerful older woman and, after many adventures, becomes king." In all of our "Joseph" stories, the young hero is described in mythological fashion; he is endowed with divine characteristics. In the Egyptian tale, the two brothers, Anubis and Bata, are granted the names of Egyptian divinities, and their story has affinities with the Osiris myth. In the Iliad, Bellerophon, a child of the god Poseidon, resists the beautiful Antéia, and travels in the "blameless convoy of the gods." He is able to overcome mythical beasts and fearless warriors and, in some sources, is associated with the winged horse Pegasus. In the end, it is the gods themselves who destroy him. In the Bible, Joseph, like the two brothers Anubis and Bata, and like the semi-divine Bellerophon, is later given a theophoric name (a name associated with the divinity), Jehosaph (Psalm 81:6). His ability to interpret dreams, and his status as provider of food for a starving Egypt, places him in the company of other semi-divine hero-kings of Ancient Near Eastern myth.[5]

As befits a figure of mythic stature, the hero figure of all of these tales is endowed with great beauty and strength. Of Bata we are told that "there was no one like him in the entire land," that Joseph was "well built and handsome," and that "to Bellerophon the gods granted beauty and desirable manhood."[6] The hero proves irresistibly attractive to the female protagonists of the tales: the wives of Anubis, Proitos, and Potiphar, respectively. Each of these proposed liaisons have an incestuous aspect. The hero is a member of the household, not a stranger, and in each situation a relationship between the "adopted son" and the woman of the family would constitute a betrayal of both human trust and divine law. Anteia, we are told, "could not beguile valiant Bellerophon, whose will was virtuous." In the Bible Joseph responds to his master's wife's entreaties saying "How then could I do this most wicked thing, and sin before God?" And in the *Tale of Two Brothers* Bata states, "see here— you are like a mother to me, and your husband is like a father to me! Because—being older than I—he was the one who brought me up. What is this great crime which you have said to me? Don't say it again!"

In each case the seduction attempt is direct and the request is bluntly stated; the woman's passion overwhelms her. Of Bellerophon we read, "Beautiful Anteia was stricken with passion to lie in love with him." Anubis' wife tells Bata, "Come, let's spend an hour sleeping together." And Potiphar's wife is most succinct, "lie with me." Later retellings were less comfortable with such direct speech. That such directness was offensive to the sensibilities of some Rabbinic exegetes is demonstrated by the Midrash that contrasts the crassness of Potiphar's wife's attempt at seduction with the subtlety of Ruth's approach to Boaz (Ruth 3:9),[7] an approach that is ultimately successful.

When her advances are rebuffed, the woman accuses the hero of attacking her. The accused is banished; he is either forced to flee (Bata), sent to exile in a distant land (Bellerophon), or placed in prison, a place of internal exile (Joseph). Banishment does not provide refuge for the hero; even in exile or prison he is not safe. The husband threatens revenge and only supernatural intervention can save the hero. In each of the stories the type of intervention presented in the narrative is determined by the cultural norms of the story's provenance. In Bata's case the intervention is sudden and supernatural. The god Re causes a lake full of crocodiles to appear, separating the brothers and allowing Bata to escape to the Valley of the Cedar. As befits a Greek hero, Bellerophon is able to kill the Chimaira and defeat the Amazons. Only later will the gods take their revenge on him. Joseph, sojourner in a land ruled by magic and necromancy, frees himself through his ability to interpret dreams. He becomes second to the king and rises above the station of his former master.

The protagonist is vindicated by this intervention and subsequently rewarded. He is raised in station and becomes king or
the vice-Regent. Bata becomes a god; Bellerophon is granted "half
of all kingly privilege"; Joseph is told, "only in the throne will I be
greater than thou." In addition to rank and temporal power, each
hero is given a beautiful and aristocratic wife by the god or king.
Khnum himself fashions a companion for Bata. She was, "more
beautiful in body than any woman in the whole land, for the fluid
of every god was in her." Bellerophon is granted the daughter of
the King of Lykia. The Pharaoh gives Asenath, daughter of
Potiphera, the priest of On, to Joseph. A compensatory mechanism is at work here: each hero is given a beautiful woman as
compensation for resisting an earlier forbidden sexual temptation.

Each of these women give birth to children who become
heroes in their own right. Bata's family line is continued through
a cycle of magical transformations and reincarnations and he
lives eternally among the gods. Though these animal-human
transformations might seem bizarre to modern sensibilities, and
the details might seem excessive when contrasted with the
conciseness of the Biblical version, they are very much in keeping with the Ancient Egyptian view of the goings on among the
gods.[8] In the Iliad, Bellerophon's descendant Glaukos, a warrior
at the walls of Troy, relates Bellerophon's tale. Glaukos too is a
great hero, and he reminds us that his own father sent him to
Troy, "and urged upon me repeated injunctions to be always
among the bravest, and hold my head above others, not shaming
the generation of my fathers." In the Bible, the tribes descended
from Joseph and Asenath's children, Ephraim and Manasseh,
are victorious warriors; they are described by Moses as, "the
horns of the wild-ox, with them he shall push the peoples, all of
them, even to the ends of the earth. And they are the ten thousands of Ephraim and they are the thousands of Manasseh."
(Deuteronomy 33:17)

Affinity between the lives of the protagonists of our three
tales extends beyond the confines of the Potiphar's Wife motif.
Though there are similarities in the final outcome of each story,
not all of our heroes come to the same end. Bata, through a
series of magical transformations, becomes a god-king and
rules Egypt for thirty years. Bellerophon is denied these plea-
sures. Because he is "blameless" he incurs the wrath of the
gods, and he spends his remaining days, "skulking aside from

the trodden track of humanity." Joseph, elevated to the rank of second to the king, dies at the advanced age of 110 and lives to see children of the third generation.

We are thus witness to the parallel development of our motif, each embedded in a larger story, and each story firmly anchored in its own culture. *The Tale of Two Brothers* strikes us as characteristically Ancient Egyptian. The setting is pastoral. Humans converse with animals, women are impregnated by splinters of wood, the gods freely meddle in the affairs of men. Here, too, there is a didactic intent, and with its echoes of the Osiris myth the story demonstrates the eventual victory of good over evil.[9]

Bellerophon's tale is Greek in its tragic aspect. It is the fate of the beautiful and blameless hero to be punished by the gods. Though he has proven himself guiltless by slaying mythical beasts and performing other heroic deeds, he is "hated by the immortals," and condemned to "wander about the plain Aleios, eating his heart out." In one variation on the Bellerophon story, the lost play *Stheneboia* by Euripides, the spurned older woman plots revenge against the blameless hero. To defend himself he uses his wiles to entrap and destroy her. Offering to flee with her he persuades her to mount the winged horse Pegasus. "When they are out over the sea he throws her down to her death."[10]

The Joseph stories are a Hebrew creation set in Egypt, and as such, they may have many authentic Egyptian touches but their primary purpose is to be a narrative of sacred history—to explain Israel's sojourn in Egypt. The Bible's approach to the Potiphar's Wife motif is didactic; it provides a moral lesson to the reader and demonstrates the rewards of virtue. Joseph, though unfairly condemned to imprisonment, has God with him. Soon, he will rise to greatness. Many scholars have asserted that the *Tale of Two Brothers*, which has been dated to the thirteenth century B.C., influenced the construction and elaboration of the Joseph story. The validity of this assertion has been debated since the publication of the Tale in 1860.[11] A minority opinion has also postulated Egyptian influence on the development of the tale of Bellerophon.

The post-Biblical legends and the parallel tales in the Muslim tradition have a more distinct lineage and a more demonstrable relationship. They both emerge from the "Biblicist" milieu of the Near East in the first Christian centuries. The Bible, which had been translated into Greek in the third pre-Christian century, had diffused into the various cultures of the Hellenistic and early Roman Near East. Biblical heroes were familiar figures in Near Eastern folklore. The post-Biblical legends that grew up around the Joseph tale preserved both the narrative and didactic intent of the Bible; they provide the reader with details that enhance the narrative, and serve to explain, entertain, and edify. Some legends, as we have seen, attempt to control the material by making it less sexually provocative and more pietistic. Other legends, soon to follow, heighten the erotic content of the stories and make Joseph's resistance to Potiphar's wife that much more heroic.

II. Midrash

The post-Biblical Jewish sources treat the Potiphar's Wife episode as a cautionary tale. The reader is encouraged to resist sexual temptation, as did Joseph. As recompense, he or she (for it should not be imagined that this exhortation is directed only at men) is promised glory in this world and reward in the hereafter. In rabbinic literature, Joseph's self-control becomes paradigmatic for all who are tempted by the flesh, and Potiphar's wife becomes the archetype of the "strange woman" of Proverbs. As Susan Niditch has noted, "One of the dominant themes in Proverbs is to keep one's distance from the loose woman, the adulteress. Joseph exemplifies the wise man: hardworking, sober, God-fearing, and able to resist forbidden fruit." Midrash Rabbah applies the verses of Proverbs chapter 7 to different episodes in the Joseph story.[12]

In order to make Joseph's resistance that much more dramatic, and his title of ha-tzadik (the righteous one) well-deserved, the seduction attempt is presented in elaborate detail. Both Joseph and Potiphar's wife are portrayed as very handsome people; their natural beauty is enhanced by artifice: cosmetics, perfumes, and sumptuous clothing. The wife's seduction attempt (in some aggadot there are several such attempts), is carefully orchestrated, and it is almost successful. It is only through strength of character, or divine intervention (or, in some versions, a combination of both) that Joseph is able to overcome temptation.

Some Rabbinic elaborations of the Potiphar's Wife motif seems to hold Joseph responsible for the drama that ensues. He is not innocent of his appeal to women. It is Joseph's vanity about his looks that brings upon him the test of Potiphar's wife:

> "His master's wife cast her eyes upon Joseph." What verse precedes this passage?
> "And Joseph was well built and handsome." [Genesis 39:6] It may be illustrated by a man who sat in the street, pencilling his eyes, curling his hair and lifting his heel, while he exclaimed:
> "I am indeed a man." "If you are a man," the by-standers retorted, "here is a bear; up and attack it!"[13]

The "bear," of course, is his master's wife. This Midrash echoes other Aggadic descriptions of Joseph in which his eyes, hair, and shoes are featured. Just as Joseph is not blameless, Potiphar's wife is not villainous. Her plight is rendered human by the strength of her feelings, and the reader feels some sympathy for her. One Midrash explains her persistent attempts to seduce Joseph as the result of misunderstood divine guidance. The court astrologers told her that she would be the mother of Joseph's descendants. This confirmed her feelings for the Hebrew slave. Only later would she realize that this prediction was about her daughter, Asenath, who would marry Joseph and bear him two sons. In her desperation, Potiphar's wife, who is named Zuleikha in most of the Aggadic narratives, and named Ra'il in others,[14] appeals to Joseph's vanity and gives him beautiful clothes. But this is to no avail: "he remained equally steadfast when she lavished gifts upon him, for she provided him with garments of one kind for the morning, another for noon, and a third kind for the evening."[15]

When gifts do not have their desired effect Zuleikha resorts to flattery, praising Joseph's physical beauty and talents. A Talmudic Midrash has Joseph ready with a pious retort for each of Zuleikha's seductive praises. She pursued him day after day with her amorous talk and her flattery, saying:

> "How fair is thy appearance, how comely thy form! Never have I seen so well-favored a slave as thou art." Joseph would reply, "God, who formed me in my mother's womb, hath created all men."
> Zuleikha: "How beautiful are thine eyes, with which thou hast charmed all Egyptians, both men and women!"

Joseph: "Beautiful as they may be while I am alive, so ghastly they will be to look upon in the grave."

Zuleikha: "How lovely and pleasant are thy words! I pray thee, take thy harp, play and also sing, that I may hear thy words."

Joseph: "Lovely and pleasant are my words when I proclaim the praise of my God."

Zuleikha: "How beautiful is thy hair! Take my golden comb, and comb it."

Joseph: "How long wilt thou continue to speak thus to me? Leave off! It were better for thee to care for thy household."

Zuleikha: "There is nothing in my house that I care for, save thee alone."

But Joseph's virtue was unshaken. While she spoke thus, he did not so much as raise his eyes to look at his mistress.[16]

In their attempt to provide every detail of the encounter between Joseph and Zuleikha, later *aggadot* pose a reasonable question: What language did the "Hebrew slave" (for it is as such that she refers to him in Genesis 39:17) and the Egyptian woman use to communicate?

At first, Joseph pretended not to understand the Egyptian language, in order that he might be spared the passionate words of the infatuated woman. After a while he could no longer feign ignorance of the language. When she saw that her words were of no avail, she attempted to use force.[17]

Al-Kisā'ī describes the first encounter of the Hebrew slave and his master's wife. Zuleikha tells Joseph, "How beautiful is your language, but I do not understand it." "It is the language of my grandfather Abraham," said Joseph. "Were it not forbidden to polytheists, I would teach it to you."[18]

Joseph's mastery of Ancient Egyptian and other languages is attested to in a number of Jewish legends. In one tale, Joseph is about to be released from prison in order to interpret Pharaoh's dreams. The angel Gabriel comes to him and teaches him "the seventy languages of man" in one night. Pharaoh is amazed at Joseph's linguistic skill and cites it when appointing him "second to the king." That a knowledge of many languages was seen as a sign of holiness and power is attested to by the Talmudic statement that after teaching him all the languages of humankind Gabriel added the letter *heh* to Joseph's name, thus forming the name "Jehosaph," the name by which he is known in Psalm 81:6.[19] While the addition of this divine element to his name may have been taken in an earlier period as a mark of a great hero touched with a spark of the divine, in the Talmudic era it was seen as a sign of accomplishment and erudition.

The idea that mastery of language is the key to power was a common one in the Ancient Near East. In Egypt, mastery of the scribal arts provided access to the corridors of power and ambitious young men were encouraged to enter the scribal profession. Jewish and Muslim legends concerning "the wisest of all men," King Solomon, emphasize his mastery of all human languages, as well as his ability to communicate with the animal kingdom and the Jinn.[20]

One Midrashic portrayal of the seduction attempt gives us both the time and the setting of the encounter. The time is the "Nile Festival" which celebrated the inundation of the river. Potiphar and his retinue have gone to celebrate the festival on the banks of the river, while Zuleikha remains home, feigning illness. Joseph has been assigned to work in the fields. The setting is the receiving room of Potiphar's estate. Zuleikha dresses and perfumes herself and sits in the vestibule through which Joseph will have to pass. When Joseph comes in from the field, "Zuleikha stands before him in all her beauty of person and magnificence of raiment and repeats the desire of her heart."[21] Here we find echoes of the seduction attempt in the *Tale of Two Brothers*. In that tale, Anubis, the elder brother, is away when Bata comes in from his work in the fields. Bata finds his brother's wife fixing her hair and it is then that she tries to seduce him.

In the Biblical account we are told, "One such day, he came into the house to do his work." Rabbinic opinion was divided as to what that "work" was. And this divided opinion speaks to the question of Joseph's intentions. According to Rashi, the Rabbis differed in their interpretation of the Biblical verse.

> Rav and Samuel disputed regarding the interpretation of this phrase—one said it literally implies his work and the other said it implies to yield to her.[22]

A later Midrash compilation, the Yalkut Shimoni, further extends the range of opinion about Joseph's intentions by adding this pietistic variant: "The day on which Joseph came into the house to do his work was the Sabbath day, and the work consisted in repeating the Torah, which he had learned from his father."

This divided opinion also extended to the interpretation of Joseph's resistance to Zuleikha's advances. One group of Aggadists sees Joseph's refusal as a manifestation of self-control and a reluctance to betray the trust that Potiphar placed in him. This interpretation seems closer to the simple meaning of the Biblical text, and it echoes the parallel moment in the stories of Bata and Bellerophon. In Thomas Mann's twentieth century elaborate narration of Joseph's encounter with his master's wife, the young man's youth and virility are contrasted with the disinterest and passivity of Potiphar, the high-ranking court eunuch. Here too Joseph's resistance is a triumph of self-control and the realization that restraint is in his self-interest. For "it goes without saying that there can be no chastity where there is no capacity—honorary captains and mutilated sun-chamberlains, for instance, are not chaste. We set out with the premise that Joseph was a whole and virile man."[23] Earlier storytellers portray Joseph as about to succumb to Zuleikha but being prevented from doing so *by divine intervention.* The intervention takes the form of a vision. In one source it is an image of his mother that appears to him, in another it is one of his father.[24] In the Midrash Hagadol, the thirteenth-century anthology in which there is a tendency to conflate details from variants of a tale, we read that both of Joseph's parents appear to him in a vision.

In a remarkable variant in an earlier Midrash, divine intervention takes a physiological form: "The bow was drawn but not relaxed....That is Joseph actually went into sin but found himself impotent....Rabbi Isaac said: His seed was scattered and issued through his fingernails."[25] In this variant, as one modern scholar noted, "Joseph's intended offense is deterred either by the censoring vision of his parents or by the impairment of his sexual capacity.[26]

Though Joseph has rebuffed her, Zuleikha does not relent. She tries again on numerous occasions. The Aggadists see support for this in the Biblical phrase "much as she coaxed Joseph day after day." (Genesis 39:10)[27] Even after he is imprisoned, Zuleikha visits Joseph, promising him his freedom if he will give himself to her.

But he would say "better it is to remain here than to be with thee and commit a trespass against God." These visits to Joseph in prison Zukheila continued for a long time, but when finally, she saw that all her hopes were in vain, she let him alone.[28]

III. In Qur'ān and Islamic Legends

Some of these Midrashic elements may have been transmitted to Muslim compilers of legend. This may have occurred through *cultural diffusion*—legends of Biblical heroes were circulating in the Jewish and Christian communities of pre-Islamic Arabia and later throughout the Islamic empire, or through *direct transmission*—Jewish converts to Islam often brought with them tales and fragments of tales that would later enrich Islamic elaborations of "Biblical" themes. One of these converts, Ka'bal-Aḥbar, will figure prominently in our discussion of Islamic elaborations of the Joseph tales.

In my analysis of the Egyptian, Greek, and Hebrew treatments of the Potiphar's Wife motif, I demonstrated that each variation on the motif is firmly anchored in the culture from which it emerged, that each retelling is distinctive and appropriate to its own cultural norms. In a similar fashion, Midrashic embellishments are the product of the pietistic world-view of the Rabbinic exegetes. In the Qur'ān, and in later Islamic versions of the tale, we move even further away from the world of the Heroic Age of ancient Israel and more to the realm of the pietistic. In Sūrat Yūsuf, elements of our motif are crafted into an artfully constructed moral tale; its world view is that of early Islam. The motif thus remains within the Mediterranean tradition from which it emerged, yet develops its own distinctive Islamic voice.

As noted earlier, Sūrat Yūsuf is the only chapter of the Qur'ān that is devoted solely to one personage. Its narrative form is of a more continuous and cohesive nature than other chapters. Within that narrative the Potiphar's Wife story is the central episode of the Sura and is recounted in considerable detail.

If we look back to the Ancient Near Eastern and Biblical versions we can see a set of affinities that the stories of Bata, Bellerophon, and Joseph share. Schematizing our analysis will enable us to see how the Qur'ān's treatment of the motif differs from the earlier versions. We noted five areas of similarity between the various retellings.

1) The hero has achieved semi-divine status.
2) His is strong and handsome.
3) His master's wife attempts to seduce him, and the attempt is sudden and direct.
4) He rejects her advances and is punished.
5) He is eventually vindicated and rewarded.

In Sūrat Yūsuf and in the Islamic genre of Qiṣaṣ al-anbīyā', each of these elements is woven into the story in a distinctively Islamic manner. The intent is didactic; Yūsuf's actions are a "sign," and the reader is to strive to emulate the prophet. Let us examine the way Muslim tradition responded to these elements of the Joseph story.

Semi-divine Status

In Islam, Joseph is not a semi-divine hero, he is a holy man, and a *nabi*, a God possessed messenger, a prophet. In Sura 40:34, we are told that Yūsuf was sent as a prophet but his people rejected him. After his death it was thought that Allāh would not send another prophet. Yūsuf is thus seen as a precursor of Muhammad. Al-Tha'labī related that Muhammad was dazzled by Yūsuf's beauty when he saw him in heaven.[29] This theme also appears in the *mi'raj* literature (the descriptions of Muhammad's "Night Journey"), where we are told that Muhammad meets Yūsuf in a position of honor in the third heaven. This meeting is also depicted in some of the illustrated manuscripts of the mi'raj.[30]

Beauty

The women of the city in Sura 12 are dazzled by Yūsuf's beauty. They cry, "This is no mortal; he is no other but a noble angel." This exclamation implies that his physical beauty is inseparable from his divine attributes; he is both human and angelic, and thus underscores Yūsuf's direct relationship to the earlier prototypes of the legend. The beautiful man-god figure appears in legend as early as the Mesopotamian stories of the

Gilgamesh cycle. Gilgamesh's beauty was described as a mixture of the human and the divine. Like Joseph he was both a dreamer and interpreter of dreams and had been granted the power of prophecy. In Islamic tradition Yūsuf's beauty and prophecy are evoked in one description of Muhammad's father ʿAbd Allāh, the son of ʿAbd al-Muttalib of the clan of the Quraysh: "ʿAbd Allāh was, for beauty, the Joseph of his times. Even the oldest men and women of Quraysh could not remember having seen his equal. He was now in his twenty-fifth year, in the full flower of his youth...could it be that ʿAbd Allāh was the expected Prophet? Or was he to be the father of the Prophet?"[31]

The Seduction Attempt

Beautiful Yūsuf is the object of sexual desire. In a commentary on 12:21 "Or we may take him for our own son" al-Ṭabari states that Qiṭfīr, the name given in Arabic sources for the Egyptian master of the house, was sexually attracted to Yūsuf and therefore wished to take him into his household. This echoes Rabbinic tradition where we find that the Egyptian's designs on Joseph were thwarted when God made him a eunuch.[32] His wife's plans, on the other hand, almost come to fruition. As in the earlier stories the woman's statement is direct, "Come, take me," and Joseph is at the point of responding with full ardor—but "he sees his master's proof." In this explanation for the curbing of Joseph's passion, the Qurʾān is anticipated by the Midrash quoted earlier, which tells us that the image of his father Jacob appeared before him. What is unique in Sūrat Yūsuf is that although the hero is proven innocent (his shirt being torn in the back) and his master is aware of his innocence, he nevertheless must be imprisoned, for that is the next step on his predestined path.

The Qurʾān implies that only God could save Joseph from temptation. The Qurʾān has Yūsuf stopped by the *burhan rabbihi*, the "image or proof of his lord," variously interpreted by the commentators as that of his father, or of Potiphar, or by some other apparition. The Qurʾān's approach is in consonance with the doctrine of *qadr* (predestination).[33] Yūsuf's actions are not the consequence of his own will but are predetermined. He is not a hero for resisting, he resists because he is divinely ordained to do so. But not all of the accounts in the Tales of the Prophets literature depict Joseph as a helpless victim of Zuleikha's lust. In al-Kisāī's retelling, it took more than a vision of the divine, or of his father, to dampen Joseph's ardor.

> She threw herself upon him and untied seven of the knots in his trousers, one after the other. For she desired him; and he would have taken her (Qur'ān 12:24), had not just then Gabriel descended in the form of his father Jacob, biting his own fingertips.[34]

Despite this piquant detail, the emphasis here is on predestination, and on Yūsuf's tale as a "sign," a didactic allegory for the community of believers, and this differentiates it from the three earlier versions, the Ancient Egyptian, the Greek, and the Biblical. These were products of an Heroic Age, one in which the heroes did as they wished and acted as their impulses guided them. If they did resist temptation, that too was an act of heroism. But in Rabbinic and Islamic sources the Potiphar's wife episode becomes a tale of instruction, extolling the moral values institutionalized by a religious community.

Vindication and Reward

In the ancient treatments of this motif, when our hero is vindicated he is not only rewarded by elevation to a high social station, he is also granted a beautiful wife, just compensation for resisting a woman forbidden to him. But this theme is not operative in Sūrat Yūsuf. As it was divine intervention that prevented him from succumbing to Potiphar's wife, Joseph is not granted a wife in reward, for in his case we cannot say that he resisted temptation.

Because Yūsuf is portrayed as guided by fate, and not by the normal human impulses, his motives are never brought into question. There is no implication in the Qur'ānic tale that Yūsuf may have been vain or arrogant, and that he therefore "earned" his fate; or that, as the Midrash put it, he deserved to be confronted by "a bear." This view of Yūsuf applies to his whole career; in his relationship with his brothers *he* is viewed as the wronged-one, the victim, and they are wrongdoers. In the Genesis narrative the portrayal of Joseph is not quite so sympathetic. His arrogance and vanity manifest themselves of an early age. We read of his grandiose dreams (Genesis 37:5–12) and are told he brought the evil report of his brothers back to his father (Genesis 37:2). Some Rabbinic exegetes were quite harsh in their judgment of Joseph. We have seen Joseph's vanity condemned. But, as we have noted, other Jewish exegetes saw the inexorable hand of fate operating in the tale and this is the attitude that may have influenced the Islamic retellings of our story.

In its portrayal of Joseph the Qur'ān has moved away from the richly descriptive modes of an Heroic Age, modes in which the vagaries of personality and passion hold sway. This move from the heroic to the holy was apparent earlier in the Rabbinic period. With this transition from the heroic type of description to the didactic type, Joseph becomes less of a hero and more of a holy man.

But some of the Qur'ānic commentators and Muslim historians emphasize Yūsuf's enthusiastic participation in this erotic encounter. Commenting on the verse, "For she desired him; and he would have taken her, but that he saw the proof of his Lord," al-Ṭabari relates the following tradition: "Ibn 'Abbas was asked how far Yusuf went in following his desires. He said, 'He loosened his waistband and sat with her as one who possesses (a woman) would sit.'" Another tradition, also in the name of Ibn 'Abbas, follows. "How far did Yusuf go in following his desires?" He said, "She lay on her back for him and he sat between her legs removing his clothes."[35]

But this is a legend, not a scriptural detail. From a literary standpoint, Joseph emerges *in the Qur'ān* as something of a "flat" character, one without much depth. This mode of portrayal changes in some of the Islamic elaborations on the tale, both in the *tafsīr* and in the *qiṣaṣ* literature. The portrayals of Ra'il/Zuleikha, on the other hand, are even more fully developed; her human drives are fully acknowledged. Zuleikha is seen as motivated by passion and animated by *kayd* (deceit or malice). Her behavior, therefore, is portrayed in a less deterministic manner and is more in the heroic tradition.

The Qur'ān attests to the strength of her passion and quotes her companions, who said of Yūsuf , "He smote her heart with love." Al-Ṭabarī quotes a tradition that gives this metaphor a physical sense. "For her love for Yusuf had reached the pericardium of her heart, entered beneath it, and overpowered her heart. The pericardium is the cover and veil of the heart."

IV. The Wiles of Women/The Wiles of Men

In the Qur'ān, Potiphar's wife is accused by her husband of acting out of guile or deceit; it is not only her individual guile that is condemned, rather it is the guile of all women, "This is of your women's guile; surely your guile is great." Al-Bayḍāwī, in his commentary on the Qur'ān, notes that in the Arabic phrase *min kaydikunna*, "The plural pronoun is addressed to her and to those like her, or to women as a whole."[36] Though the actions of one woman are condemned in this story, the concept of *kayd* is generalized and applied to all women.

That women are capable of guile, and that men are susceptible to their wiles, was an idea that derived from a set of assumptions about gender relations, assumptions that functioned to maintain a social order in which men dominated in both the private and public spheres. In this world view relations between the sexes must be controlled; a disruption of these controls can destabilize the wider society. In Islamic societies, as Paula Sanders has noted, "Although men and women presumably bore equal responsibility for illicit relations, that responsibility was construed in terms of certain assumptions about the natures of men and women. Men were considered susceptible to seduction and the actors, whereas women were considered to be both seductresses (that is, tempting men to act in certain destructive ways) and the recipients of the men's acts." Thus "women's guile" is viewed as an inherent female characteristic against which men must be warned, and if possible, protected. As Gordon Newby put it, "In this androcentric view female sexuality, unless controlled, leads to evil and destruction."[37]

In the Sirah, the early biography of Muḥammad, the danger of women's *kayd* is illustrated in an episode said to have taken place toward the end of the Prophet's life. The episode illustrates that even within the Prophet's household, among his trusted wives, he was both suspicious of, and susceptible to their wiles. When he knew that his end was near Muḥammad wanted to emphasize his choice of Abu Bakr as successor by having him lead the community in prayer. But Muḥammad's wives, Aishah and Hafsah, conspired to prevent this. When Hafsah was about to speak, "the Prophet silenced her with the words: "Ye are even as the women that were with Joseph. Tell Abu Bakr to lead the prayer.""[38]

An analysis of the use of the term *kayd* in the Qur'ān indicates that "guile" or "deceit" is a misleading translation of the Arabic original, and that *kayd* is a quality attributed to men and women. "Artifice" or "strategem," terms that do not have pejorative connotations, would be more appropriate translations of *kayd*. Elsewhere in the Qur'ān *kayd* is not a stratagem of men and women only, it is also utilized by God against unbelievers. There are at least thirty-four uses of the Arabic root K.Y.D. in the Qur'ān, and a number of them refer to God's actions. In Sūrat Yūsuf itself (12.76) God's kayd is celebrated.[39]

In Sura 7:182 we also find *Kayd* as an attribute of Allāh:

And those who cry "lies" to our signs
we will draw them on little by little
whence they know not
And I respite them
Assuredly, my guile (kayd) is sure[40]

The ability to be guileful is not then in itself a negative characteristic; it can be used for good or for evil. Admiration of this quality is typical of the literature of a culture's Heroic Age. As we have seen, the Potiphar's wife figure of the Bible and its Ancient Near Eastern parallels, is still closely tied to that age, while Joseph of the legends, whose character has been transformed into that of a holy man, is more a figure of a pietistic age. For Zuleikha, more than for Joseph the nabi (prophet), *kayd* is an appropriate characteristic.

One can adopt the *kayd* interpretation of behavior and retroject it to the Biblical Patriarchal Narratives. The actions of the women in these narratives, including Rebecca, Rachel, Tamar, and Serah, may be viewed through the prism of *kayd*. Whether women are the primary tricksters of the narrative and whether the Biblical text implies that there is an *essentially* guileful quality in women, is a question that I will examine in chapter V, "The Women of the Joseph Story."

In Genesis 27, Rebecca plots to fool her husband Isaac and secure his blessing for Jacob. When she is successful, she is wise enough to send Jacob to her brother's house in Haran. Isaac realizes that he has been duped and tells Esau: "Your brother came here by a ruse (*mirmah*) and he carried off your blessing" (Genesis 27:35). Mirmah is here used in the same sense as *kayd*. It is Jacob that is accused of *mirmah* (trickery); Isaac, presumably, does not know of his wife's role in the matter.

Rachel uses deceit and trickery when she steals the *teraphim*, the household "idols," from Laban's house (Genesis 31). In doing so she deceives both her father and her husband, who have no knowledge of her plan (31:32). When her effects are searched she resorts to further trickery by asking that she be left alone because she is menstruating. The incident of the *teraphim*, and the subsequent encounter with Laban, sparks Jacob's impassioned speech in which he justifies his decision to leave for Canaan.[41]

Tamar uses considerable guile to entice her father-in-law Judah. When she succeeds in her plan and is pregnant with Judah's children he acknowledges that she is justified (Genesis 38:26). Tamar's *kayd* ensures the continuation of Judah's lineage. Her children are the ancestors of the Davidic line, and by extension, of the Messianic line. (Ruth 4:18–22)

Dinah, in Genesis 34, is the catalyst in a drama in which trickery plays a pivotal role. Outraged at Shechem's rape of their sister, Jacob's sons trick the men of Shechem into believing that they will be accepted by Jacob's family if they are circumcised. As in the story of Jacob and Esau, the text uses the term *mirmah* to describe the hidden agenda behind their offer of acceptance.

> Jacob's sons replied to Shechem and his father Hamor with mirmah (guile). (Gen. 34:13).

Weak from the pain of circumcision, the Shechemites are easy prey for Simon and Levi, who destroy the city. They kill all the males, take the women and children captive, and plunder the livestock (34:26–29). Jacob condemns them for their impetuousness, fearing the wrath of his Canaanite neighbors (34:30). Though it is the men who are deceitful here, Dinah is not a completely passive figure in the drama. Some commentators see her as an active participant in the early stage of the drama, for she "went out to see the daughters of the land."

We have seen that the stories of Rebecca, Rachel, Tamar, and Dinah (Genesis 27; 31; 34; 38) all utilize the *mirmah/kayd* motif.[42] This sequence of stories foreshadows, and anticipates the full development of the motif in the Potiphar's Wife story in Genesis 39. In all of these instances it is the establishment of a proper genealogy, and the preservation of the family group through which the divine promise is to be fulfilled, that is of overriding concern to the Biblical narrator. Rebecca saves the birthright for Jacob; Rachel ensures that Jacob obtains the *teraphim*, the symbols of authority. After the rape of Dinah, Simon and Levi prevent the union with the Canaanites of Shechem, and the story of Tamar provides a link to the historical future when Judah's descendants will rule the nation. We have here a series of stories in which the use of *mirmah/kayd* is justified, and one might say, valorized. Uppermost is the need to ensure the continuity and purity of the family line. In the culminating story, Joseph resists Potiphar's wife, marries Asenath, and the family line is preserved through their progeny.

A thirteenth century compendium of Islamic folklore, *The Subtle Ruse*,[43] presents all of Sūrat Yūsuf (and not only the Potiphar's Wife episode) as a series of stories of *kayd*. The anonymous author of this work retells each of the episodes of the story, indicating in each how the characters are constantly deceiving others or being deceived themselves. A number of examples, all based on the Qur'ān or on Islamic legends, will indicate his approach:

1) Joseph is the victim of a ruse when his brothers entice him to the well to drink and then throw him in to die.
2) Jacob is the victim of his sons' ruse when they bring Joseph's bloody clothes to him.
3) When given the opportunity, Joseph plays a number of tricks on his brothers in Egypt. He thus keeps them in a continual state of suspense and anxiety.
4) When Jacob sends his sons to Egypt for a second time he uses a ruse in his attempt to outwit the "evil eye." He tells his sons not to enter the same gate together when they reach Egypt; this would subject them to the power of the evil eye. Rather, they should enter by different gates.

A view of *kayd* as a dominant factor in human behavior permeates the greatest collection of Islamic folklore, the *'alf layla wa-layla, The Thousand and One Nights*.[44] One full section of the work, the *Sindibadnama*, is dubbed by some translators as *The Malice of Women*, though on closer examination it is not only the *kayd* of women that is celebrated here, but the *kayd* of all beings: men, women, and the jinn, those spirit beings, "created from unsmoking fire,...who exercise direct and formative influence upon the affairs of humanity."[45] In this section of the *Nights*, much is made of "women's kayd," and the spirit in which these tales are told encourages the translation of *kayd* as "malice." For the protagonists delight in the results of their trickery. After hearing tales that tell of women's guile, the women of the story then have their opportunity to counter-attack. They respond by relating corresponding tales of the "wiles of men." Despite the obvious advantages granted to their male antagonists (they get to tell their stories first, and have more of them to tell), the women acquit themselves honorably.

This cycle of stories, the *Sindibadnama*, was based on a Persian saga of the ninth century c.e. Later translated into Arabic, it became one of the core elements in the formation of the loosely-defined corpus of tales that made up the *Thousand and One Nights*. But before its inclusion in that corpus it was translated into Syriac and Hebrew. These translations preserved both the framework and engaging contents of the saga, whose Persian original no longer survives.

The narrative device used to structure or "frame" the 1001 nights is in itself a tale of "the wiles of women and the wiles of men." Both King Shahriyar and his brother Shahzaman discover that their wives deceived them in their absence. Discouraged and disillusioned, they leave their respective kingdoms and set off for the wilderness. There they have an adventure that proves to them that even the jinn are helpless before the wiles of women. And here, in the opening chapter of the *Nights*, the Potiphar's Wife motif is cited by the woman who tricked the jinn and then forced the king and his brother to have sex with her.

> Take warning, then, *by Joseph's history*, and how a woman sought to do him bane...For great the wonder were if any man alive from women and their wiles escape unharmed away.
>
> When the two Kings heard this they marvelled and said "Allah, Allah, there is no power and no virtue save in God the most High, the Supreme! We seek aid of God against the wiles of women, for indeed their craft is great."[46]

This encounter fuels Shahriyar's resolve to never trust a woman again and, "...he took an oath that every night he would go unto a maid and in the morning put her to death."[47] Shahrazad, his vizier's daughter, saves the women of the kingdom with her masterful storytelling abilities. She entertains and intrigues Shahriyar and at the end of the "1001 nights" of her storytelling (during this period she bore the King three sons) the King rescinds his order and a great celebration is held.

Many of the stories in the *Nights* are tales of trickery and cunning.[48] This is especially true of the so-called "Malice of Women" section, whose structure is modeled on that of the complete *Nights*. Its "frame device" is a direct reference to the Potiphar's Wife motif:

> Without issue in his old age, a King prays to the Prophet and begets a son. When the prince attains young manhood, his tutor perceives by the stars...that if he speaks one word during the following seven days he will die. He commits him to his father's favorite damsel to be entertained by the music girls, in numerous flower-scented apartments, until the danger passes. The damsel, falling in love with him, offers to poison his father and set him on the throne. When she is repulsed she goes with torn clothes and a tale of attempted rape to the King who immediately condemns his son to death. The chief vizier, however, changes the King's mind with two tales.[49]

The champions of the prince and the damsel are called upon to present stories that support their respective cases. There ensues a debate in the form of storytelling in which tales of "the malice of women" are matched by tales of "the malice of men." In a fashion that is unique in the *Nights* (where the storyteller generally shies away from a didactic tone) each tale ends with a moralistic conclusion. The point of each episode is made very explicit, *e.g.*, "beware of women's speech," "beware of the malice of men," "one can be suspicious without due cause," etc. This emphasis on the didactic intent of each story further ties this section to the Islamic view of the Joseph story and lends credence to the supposition that "the malice of women and the malice of men" was an earlier independent work which was later incorporated into the larger *Nights*.[50]

The *kayd* section of the *Nights* ends with a peaceful resolu-
tion in which the two sides are reconciled. Convinced that the
malice of *both* men and women have been amply demonstrated,
"The prince declares that the damsel should be forgiven and
sent away. The King proudly confers his throne on his marvellous son."[51]

In one manuscript tradition of the *Nights*, direct linguistic
reference to *Sūrat Yūsuf* appears in a related tale. One of the
viziers tells the story of *The Husband and the Parrot*, and uses it
to "prove" the deceitfulness of women. He addresses the king,
saying "Oh King, I have informed you of this only so that you
may know that the wiles of women (*kaydahunna*) are mighty."
This is a rephrasing of Potiphar's words to Zuleikha.[52] An
instructive parallel may be found in the "wiles of women" sections of the great Japanese novel, Lady Murasaki's *Tale of Genji*.
The gentle (and not so gentle) mockery of women that the young
men of the court display in their stories is later countered and
subverted by the mirror-images of these tales, told by women,
in which men are mocked for their fickleness and cupidity.[53]

Despite the passage of centuries the Potiphar's Wife motif
remained vital in Islamic folklore. It permeated both the structure and the content of the *Thousand and One Nights*, which,
while anthologized in the thirteenth and fourteenth centuries,
draws upon stories that had been circulating in the Middle
East, North Africa, and Southern Asia for a millennium. Its
earliest written sections date to the ninth century.[54] The roots of
some of the tales reach into the second pre-Christian Millennium and they echo motifs present in the tales of the Ancient
Near East and stories of the Bible. Scholars have noted Persian
and Greek influence on the *Nights*, specifically in the areas of
structure and plot respectively. But let us not de-emphasize the
Islamic genius of the *Nights*. Von Grunebaum called for "greater
emphasis on the genuinely Arabic" when we analyze any given
episode in the *Nights*. And in a poetic and insightful image he
noted that "the structure of Islamic civilization repeats the
structure of the *Nights*. Islamic civilization is thoroughly
syncretistic, and it proves its vitality by coating each and every
borrowing with its own inimitable patina."[55] That Joseph lives as
a symbol of beauty in the *Nights*, and that the themes that
dominated the scriptural Joseph material are also present in
this great folklore anthology, is a further example of the remark-

able cultural continuity of Middle Eastern and Mediterranean civilization. Hodgson observed that some Qur'ānic tales are "reminders of episodes which are often presumed to be known to the audience." In the early Islamic centuries other Near Eastern episodes and themes were disseminated throughout the Islamic world, eventually making their way into the *Thousand and One Nights* and other forms of literature. "Biblical" figures, greater and lesser were also known to Islamic audiences, but none achieved the popularity of Yūsuf.

The preservation and transmission of *Nights* tales and manuscripts was an endeavor in which Muslims, Jews, and Christians participated. Goitein noted that the first recorded use of the title *A Thousand and One Nights* is found in the Cairo Genizah book lists of a twelfth century Jewish physician of Cairo.[56]

Jewish storytellers of thirteenth century Provence produced the *Mishle Sendebar*, a Hebrew version of the *Sindibadnama*. This version contains a delightful story which both affirms the world view of the "Wiles of Women" literature while at the same time subverting the notion that women's cunning can be anticipated. "The story tells of a man who thought he had written down all the wiles of women. At the last stopping-place on his journey, he boasts to the governor's wife of his accomplishment. She immediately makes overtures to him and as he is about to succumb, she shouts for her husband. The stranger faints of fright. When the governor arrives, his wife says merely that the visitor was so sick he almost choked when she fed him. When the governor departs, she asks the stranger whether he had ever beheld this variety of cunning before. He destroys his notebooks and admits that his research has been in vain."[57]

In tracing the development of the Potiphar's Wife motif, we have traveled through the Biblical Land of Israel and the cities of Islam. Egypt, the original setting of our motif, may have slipped into the background. Let us restore the Egyptian setting to its place of significance and see how that milieu—real or imagined—affected the telling of the tale.

Joseph Led into Prison

3

The Egyptian Background of the Joseph Story

With Genesis 37 we come to the saga of Joseph, which is one of the most appealing narratives in world literature; for in it are blended the spirits of Israel and Egypt.
—C. H. Gordon (1965)

Egyptology and the Study of the Narratives

In the Joseph Story, the episode most evocative of Ancient Egyptian culture and societal norms is "Potiphar's Wife," a tale also embedded in the mid-thirteenth century B.C. text, *The Tale of Two Brothers*. Was this Egyptian story an inspiration for the Biblical author or redactor? Shall we take the inclusion of this motif in the Biblical Joseph narratives as an indication of the Biblical author's familiarity with Egyptian culture, a familiarity that would then authenticate the historicity of this Biblical novella and lend it an air of antiquity and authority? Some material that may help us answer these questions has already been provided. Other clues may lie in the general Egyptian background of the latter part of Genesis.

Is Genesis' portrayal of Ancient Egypt accurate? Are the people, places, and events named in the Joseph narratives representations of an historical reality? Or are they merely shadows of an imagined Egypt, one conjured up by a late Biblical writer or editor? The secondary literature on this question is voluminous and there are several book-length treatments of the topic. According to Donald Redford, the author of a monograph on the Biblical Joseph, "Over the past century and a half, many Egyptologists have been attracted to the Joseph story. The list comprises something of a "Who's Who of Egyptology."[1] Many of these early studies focused on the dating of the Joseph story, with an assigned date ranging from the nineteenth to the fourteenth centuries B.C.E. But as there is no Egyptian corroboration of the specific events and personages of the Joseph story (or of other Biblical stories set in Egypt), such attempts at dating are notoriously difficult. As the study of ancient Egypt became independent of the study of the Bible, the question of the date of the narratives was no longer asked by scholars outside of Biblical studies.

More recently, interest in the narratives' Egyptian background has shifted from an attempt to "validate" the Biblical text through Egyptological proofs to a more literary approach, one which discerns in the Genesis account a successful attempt to provide the reader with authentic details of daily life in Ancient Egypt, much as a novelist might provide the reader with an accurate evocation of the historical past. As early as the 1950s, Janssen noted that:

> As the chronological problem, and especially the problem of synchronism, is rather complicated, it seems to be preferable to avoid it and to focus our attention on questions where chronology is not of prime importance...Egyptian sources can be helpful in elucidating the Bible text and to see better the background and circumstances of several topics dealt with by the narrator.[2]

Considerable scholarly effort has been devoted to these investigations, and it has been asserted by one authority that "At every turn the Biblical author shows knowledge of Egyptian conditions...The whole Joseph story is to be understood against the Egyptian background."[3]

Not all scholars agree. The end of the nineteenth century and the first decades of the twentieth century witnessed the tendency to view Ancient Egypt (and all of the Ancient Near East) through a Biblical prism. This has changed radically since mid-century. There is now a tendency among Egyptologists (and their colleagues in parallel disciplines in the study of Ancient Mesopotamia) to distance themselves from Biblical connections. For both the Biblicists and non-Biblicists among scholars of the ancient Near East, the focus of the argument often revolves around Genesis, and when Egypt's relation to the Bible is under scrutiny, around the Joseph narratives, and the descriptions of what befell the Hebrews when there arose a "King who knew not Joseph." (Exodus 1:8)

From its inception, European and American scientific archaeology was subject to the push and pull of the public's interest in the history of events they knew from the Bible. The impetus to much of early archaeological excavation lay in the expectation of excavators (and their financial backers) that the new science would "affirm the Biblical truths." The actual recovery of ancients texts, and their decipherment and interpretation, were influenced by theological and social concerns. With the shift in interest to a literary reading of the narratives, and the achievement of a "consensus that the Joseph story is a novella, a genre category that facilitates the original conceptions of an artist rather than the patterns of a traditional folk story,"[4] scholarship has shifted away from an "affirming" mode and has focused on elucidating the rich novelistic detail that girds the story.

One aspect of the Joseph narrative that cries out for elucidation is the constant reference in Genesis to the social barriers erected by the Egyptians in order to maintain their separation from and superiority over foreigners—in our case the Hebrews. Both ancient and modern historians note that the Egyptians considered themselves distinct from, and superior to, all other peoples. It is a persistent theme in Herodotus' *History*, and it has echoes in the remarks of modern historians:

> For the Egyptian there could be no doubt that his country was quite distinct; it was a universe on its own, unrelated to other lands abroad. To be away from Egypt was to be divorced from reality; being an Egyptian meant living in Egypt, worshipping Egyptian gods (who had nothing to do with the world outside), dying and, above all, being buried in Egypt. The special features of Egyptian life reflected this egocentric view, which treated all things Egyptian as being of their kind unique.[5]

In order to keep this sense of separateness alive, social distinctions were enforced both *within Egypt*, when Egyptians were confronted with foreigners living among them, and *abroad*, when Egyptians lived among the "uncivilized" Asiatics. In the latter case, the resident Egyptian felt uncomfortable even when living the "good life." This is vividly illustrated in the *Romance of Sinuhe*, the tale of the adventures of an Egyptian official in a foreign land who is left in exile when his pharaoh falls. "He had everything an Asiatic could want. But to an Egyptian, even an Asiatic paradise was bitter exile. All Sinuhe's prosperity was in vain because of his longing to return to his native land." Some of the parallels between Sinuhe's story and Joseph's are so striking (especially in the sequencing of events), that one scholar has suggested that Sinuhe was the prototype of the Joseph story.[6]

In the following section, I will examine those social barriers alluded to in the Biblical text. This provides us with a case study of the way our knowledge of ancient Egyptian life can be used to enhance our understanding of the Bible's Egyptian "background." When we move to the post-Biblical period, Jewish and Muslim legends, and their treatments of the Egyptians aspects of the Joseph story, provide a case study in the use of imagined "Egyptian" elements in folkloric retellings. For the civilization of Ancient Egypt was by then only a series of ruins. But in the popular imagination these ruins came to life through imaginative retellings of sacred history. By the same token, the study of these legends illustrates the reciprocal and complex relationship between the folkloric traditions of Jews and Muslims.

Egyptians and Hebrews:
Social Contacts and Social Barriers

Within the Biblical Joseph story we find four references to social barriers between Egyptians and Hebrews. These are in the areas of 1) dress and general appearance, 2) language, 3) eating habits, 4) means of earning a livelihood. The first two barriers are implied in the Biblical text:

1) Thereupon Pharaoh sent for Joseph, and he was rushed from the dungeon. He had his hair cut and changed his clothes, and he appeared before Pharaoh.
(Genesis 41:14)[7]

2) They did not know that Joseph understood for there was an interpreter between him and them.
(Genesis 42:23)

The latter two cases are reports of Egyptian measures taken to prevent social interaction between Egyptians and foreigners, and are directly stated:

> 3) They served him by himself, and them by themselves, and the Egyptians who ate with him by themselves; for the Egyptians could not dine with the Hebrews, since that would be abhorrent to the Egyptians.
>
> (Genesis 43:32)

> 4) So when Pharaoh summons you and asks, "What is your occupation?" you shall answer, "Your servants have been breeders of livestock from the start until now, both we and our fathers"—so that you may stay in the region of Goshen. For all shepherds are abhorrent to Egyptians.
>
> (Genesis 46:33-4)

Both of the latter verses use the Hebrew *to'evah* (abomination, abhorrence), to express the Egyptians attitude toward social interaction with foreigners.

These social barriers are alluded to in Ancient Egyptian literature and in Jewish and Muslim retellings of the Joseph story, but the degree to which these barriers are emphasized or glossed-over differs greatly from one culture to another. Let us proceed chronologically, moving from what the Egyptian texts reveal about the construction of social identity in Ancient Egypt to the imaginative recreations of that identity in later Jewish and Muslim texts.

Contacts and Barriers: The Egyptian Background

1) Dress and General Appearance

A. S. Yahuda points out that:

> In the eyes of Semitic people the beard was a mark of dignity, long hair an ornament on warriors and heroes, and only prisoners and slaves were shaved as sign of humiliation and dishonor. The Egyptians had an exactly opposite view, and the first thing every Egyptian of better

upbringing was anxious to do, as soon as he came of age, was to deliver his head and face to the razor of the barber. He only grew beard and hair when mourning for a near relative. Thus Joseph wanted to appear before Pharaoh not as a barbarian and in foreign garb, but as a dressed and well-shaven perfect Egyptian gentleman.[8]

In Egyptian art the Egyptians are always neatly dressed and shaven while the Asiatics are hairy and somewhat slovenly:

> We encounter these Semitic "barbarians" everywhere on the Egyptian monuments, and we are never left in doubt as to how completely foreign and outlandish in dress and appearance they were regarded by the Egyptians…The inhabitants of the Nile Valley were accustomed to shave their hair and wear wigs, but the foreigners permitted their hair and beards to grow long. In fact, their hair fell in thick masses around the back of their heads as low as the neck and was usually confined by a sort of fillet above the forehead; and their yellowish brown faces were framed by heavy dark beards which ended in a point beneath the chin.[9]

The Egyptian disdain for the hairy Asiatic is expressed orthographically in the hieroglyphic determinative of the word *nwn*, meaning to be disheveled, which is a standing figure with two flying locks.[10] In contrast the Semitic ideal was that long locks were a sign of the great warrior. Thus, Judges 5:2, has been translated, as supported by some of the Septuagint manuscripts, "When long locks of hair were worn loose by warriors in Israel."[11] This ideal of the longhaired warrior both antecedes Biblical Israel and extends beyond its borders. "Long hair was associated with heroic strength…It is interesting to note that precisely during the epic age of Israel, long hair was a feature of the heroic male."[12] Parallels may be found in Mesopotamian, Greek, Cretan, and Egyptian representations of warriors.

Some find vestiges or echoes of this practice in reports of life among the Bedouin in the past century. In his *Travels in Arabia Deserta*, Doughty remarks that:

> Seldom or never have the nomad women very long hair, and it is not thick. Side locks are worn by men at

their natural length: so it is said in praise of a young man's fortunate beauty "he has great and long horns"... The Bedouins say, commending a prince "It is a fair young man, he has goodly horns," Elder men at length renounce this ornament of their regretted youth..."[13]

The importance, for the Egyptians, of socially appropriate hair and dress is highlighted in the story of Sinuhe. When Sinuhe returns from his Asiatic exile, we are told that:

The King received him well and summoned the Queen and the royal children. When they came into the court and saw Sinuhe, about whom they had heard so much, they screamed on seeing him clad like an Asiatic. They could not believe that the person before them was Sinuhe, but the King assured them that it was he. Then Sinuhe was clad in fine linen, perfumed, shaved and given an estate and royal support.[14]

The romance of Sinuhe provides us with a context in which we can understand the ceremony in which Joseph is designated "second to the King."

Pharaoh further said to Joseph, "See, I put you in charge of all the land of Egypt." And removing his signet ring from his hand, Pharaoh put it on Joseph's hand; and he had him dressed in robes of fine linen, and put a gold chain about his neck.

(Genesis 41:41–42)

This is similar to "Sinuhe's elevation in rank together with royal gifts of robes and other honors."[15]

2) Language

In Genesis 42:23 Joseph has a translator act as an intermediary between himself and his brothers. Though this was a ruse on his part, for he understood the language of his brothers, it does indicate that the Egyptians needed the services of a translator in order to communicate with foreigners. The term for translator, melitz, is a rare Biblical word. It occurs only once in the Pentateuch. In the three other times that it occurs in the Bible (Isaiah 43:27, Job 33:23, II Chronicles 32:31) it has the sense of intermediaries, or emissaries.[16] That the word means "translator" in Genesis 42:23 is indicated by internal evidence. If we translate this verse "And they did not know that Joseph heard (*sham'a*) and the interpreter was between them," and position it in its Egyptian setting, *sham'a* can only mean "*understand*," "*comprehend*," and not merely "*hear*." As A. S. Yahuda noted:

> At the beginning of his conversation with Joseph, Pharaoh says: "I have dreamed and there is none that can interpret it; but I have heard say of thee that thou understandest a dream to interpret it." For "understand" the Hebrew has "to hear": "thou hearest a dream". This corresponds entirely to the Egyptian use of *sdm* "to hear" = "to understand," a meaning which is most clearly shown by its use in the phrase, *Sinuhe* 31f.: sdm.k rˁ n km.t: "thou hearest the mouth of Egypt" *i.e.*, "thou understandeth the language of Egypt, or in Wen-Amon," 77: iw.f *sdm* md.t km.t: "he hears the speech of Egypt," *i.e.*, he understands the language. Likewise in Genesis 42.23 "hear" stands for understanding the language, exactly as in Egyptian.[17]

Such linguistic isolationism was to be expected, as the Egyptians' ethnocentricity and sense of superiority also extended to their attitude towards language:

> ...the hieroglyphic script, was a medium of communication developed specifically for the use of the tongue spoken in Egypt, and it was incapable of adaption to the requirements of other languages...the methods developed in the earliest times remained, in general terms, satisfactory for the needs of the Egyptian people and over the centuries required only the modifications resulting from natural development within a fairly closed culture. This self-sufficiency, which amounted almost to a sort of cultural stagnation, is well demonstrated in the matter of writing...[18]

There were periodic exceptions to this linguistic isolationism. One exception that would dovetail nicely with the details of the Joseph story is the period known to modern scholars as the

Amarna Age the era of cultural, religious and political ferment of the fourteenth century B.C.E. In the Amarna Age we do find the Egyptians using Akkadian, the Mesopotamian language that was the lingua franca of the period. To this period belong much of what we in the West find most attractive in Ancient Egyptian culture: the artifacts in the tomb of Tutankhamen, the exotic beauty and mystery of his wife Nefertiti, and the strikingly modern artistic and religious sensibilities of the reign of his kinsman Akhenaten. The Amarna Age's appeal to Americans is summed up in James Henry Breasted's description of the "heretic pharaoh" Akhenaten as "the first individual in history."

In contrast to the Amarna Age, during other periods the Egyptians would insist on communicating with outsiders in the language of Egypt. The new attitude towards other languages was part of the "Amarna revolution" in which Egypt emerged from its cultural isolationism.

> The changed was thoroughgoing. Art was revolutionized as well as religion, with the breaking down of old canons, and the introduction of new trends. Modernistic realism and distortion suddenly appear in the art of what had been the world's most conservative country.[19]

3) Dietary Restrictions

The two social barriers that the Bible describes as Egyptian *prohibitions* against contact with outsiders were the Egyptians' distaste for eating with foreigners, and their aversion to associating with shepherds. In both cases, the Bible uses the word *to'evah* indicating abomination or abhorrence. There are direct Biblical references to these aversions. "For Egyptians could not dine with the Hebrews, since that would be abhorrent to the Egyptians." (Genesis 43:32) And "For all shepherds are abhorrent to Egyptians." (Genesis 46:33)

If we examine the use of *to'evah* in the Old Testament, we find that it has both a *ritual* sense: *e.g.*, idolatry, child sacrifice, witchcraft; and an *ethical* sense: it is used to denote the sacrifices of a wicked person, or to condemn unchastity.[20] The Hebrews are enjoined from participating in any activity of the *to'evah* category.

The injunction to avoid acts of the *to'evah* category is seen as separating Israel from the nations (e.g., Deuteronomy 13:14–15: "that abhorrent thing was perpetrated in your midst").[21]

Unique to the two aforementioned citations in Genesis is that they display a remarkable degree of cultural relativism, and they stand in contrast to the Bible's usual condemnation of Egyptian practices. For in Genesis *to'evah* is used to describe the *Egyptian aversion to things Hebrew* and not the Hebrew aversion to Egyptian, or any other nation's objectionable practices. Both the aversion to eating with the Hebrews and to associating with shepherds may be compared with Herodotus' report of the Egyptians, which affirms that:

> The pig is regarded among them as an unclean animal...hence, too, the swineherds, notwithstanding that they are of pure Egyptian blood, are forbidden to enter into any of the temples, which are open to all other Egyptians, and further, no one will give his daughter in marriage to a swineherd, or take a wife from among them, so that the swineherds are forced to intermarry among themselves.[22]

4) Means of Earning a Livelihood: The Aversion to Shepherds

Genesis 46:33–34 indicates that Jacob's sons counted on a negative response to their announcement that the family supported itself by herding sheep. On Jacob's counsel they used that anticipated response to ensure that the Pharaoh would grant them Goshen, a land rich in grazing areas. In explaining why "all shepherds are abhorent to Egyptians," Rashi states that this was because sheep were considered divine by the Egyptians. This understanding of the aversion to the Hebrews as shepherds is paralleled in the Greek understanding of the Egyptian aversion to keepers of cattle. Describing the cult of the Egyptian temples, Herodotus notes that:

> The male kine, therefore, if clean, and the male calves, are used for sacrifice by the Egyptians universally; but the females they are not allowed to sacrifice, since they are sacred to Isis. The statue of this goddess has the form of a woman but with horns like a cow, resembling thus the Greek representation of Io; and the Egyptians, one and all, venerate cows much more highly than any other animal. This is the reason why no native of Egypt, whether man or woman, will give a Greek a

kiss, or use the knife of a Greek, or his spit, or his cauldron or taste the flesh of an ox, known to be pure, if it has been cut with a Greek knife.[23]

In both reports we see that among the Egyptians the veneration of, or aversion to, a specific animal extends to anyone who may have touched or consumed this animal. Against this background, the two taboos, eating with the Hebrews and associating with shepherds, can be seen as related: the aversion to sheep, "a reflection of the age-old fear and hatred the Egyptians entertained for the beduoin of the desert,"[24] is extended to any contact with shepherds, including the act of sitting down to eat with them.

The connection between the two prohibitions, between eating with foreigners and associating with shepherds, is implied by the description of both as *to'evah.* In the Biblical text's choice of the term, A. S. Yahuda sees a deliberate use of an Egyptianism:

> The conception of something being an "abomination" *bw.t* which is expressed in Hebrew by *toevah,* especially in connection with Egypt, e.g., Genesis 43:32, "for it was an abomination to the Egyptians" (to eat with Hebrews): or 46:34, said of the shepherds as "an abomination to Egypt," or Exodus 8:26, of the cattle sacrifices, *is typically Egyptian. It occurs profusely in both sacred and profane literature of all epochs and is an expression of loathing and strong abhorrence against everything disgusting, repugnant or execrable.*[25]

It is of note that three out of four social barriers (the matter of dressing and shaving for the Pharaoh is a mark of Joseph's transition from Hebrew slave to Egyptian noble) are mentioned after Joseph's brothers descend into Egypt. For the reader of the Biblical story, this highlights the ease with which Joseph had become an Egyptian, and the ease of his transition to a new identity is sharply contrasted with the difficulty that his less polished brothers encountered.

For some critics the mention of these social barriers at a point late in the story serves a structural function, it is not an indication that the Egyptians actually were bound by these taboos:

The Biblical author enters into some detail in presenting the Egyptian setting of the story in an attempt to provide verisimilitude for his work...In a few instances however, with regard to the author's notice about Egyptian distaste for shepherds and their unwillingness to dine with Hebrews, he moves beyond the verifiable and even the plausible in the service of a good story. These notices serve a narrative function, allowing the brothers to be alone with Joseph at a critical moment and permitting their settlement in Goshen, and, they contribute to a sense of wonder at the strange land of Egypt.[26]

One verse that we have cited as evidence of a social barrier, that the Egyptians could not dine with the Hebrews (Genesis 43:32), also serves as a reminder of another widespread, but often unrecognized, social institution of Biblical Israel, fratriarchy, the exercise of authority by one sibling over others. For the following verse tells us, "And as the men took their seats at his direction, the oldest in the order of his seniority and the youngest in the order of his youth, they gazed at one another in astonishment." (Genesis 43:33). Cyrus Gordon notes that "...fratriarchal organization was widespread throughout the East, including Israel,"[27] and he cites our verse as a reference to, "fratriarchal etiquette whereby brothers at a banquet are seated in order of seniority."[28] This verse's somewhat oblique reference to fratriarchy, is one illustration of the observation that "The Biblical narratives give us casual glimpses of fratriarchal authority."[29]

Joseph's troubled relationship with his brothers was only one aspect of the complex family dynamic operating among Jacob's children. At different points in the Patriarchal narratives, Reuben, Jacob's first born, and Judah the fourth son, assume leadership positions. With the descent of the family into Egypt, Joseph, one of the two youngest sons, assumes the leadership of the family. And in one sense, he becomes the "eldest" son, assuming authority in all the brothers' affairs. "Joseph provided the family with property and provisions upon their arrival in Egypt, and functioned as their fratriarch until his death."[30]

If we use the fratriarchal model to understand Joseph's actions at the banquet with his brothers, we gain further insight into the structure of the Joseph narratives as a whole. For the power struggle between the brothers, a struggle that was interrupted, but not concluded, with Joseph's descent into Egypt, again comes to the fore when the brothers are reunited:

> No one who reads the Joseph story can help but be struck by the symmetry of the plot. Settings and roles appearing in the development are duplicated with subtle contrasts in the resolution [the scene in Chapter 45 is at once the duplicate and the contrast to the scene at Dothan in Chapter 37]...The last time Joseph was alone with his brothers he was a weak powerless lad, and they tore his clothes off and threw him into a pit to die. Now, the first time they meet with him alone since that day long ago at Dothan, the situation is completely reversed. They are the destitute, he the powerful.[31]

By seating his brothers, "the oldest in the order of his seniority and the youngest in the order of his youth" Joseph is legitimizing the proper fratriarchal order. He is reversing his implied threat to usurp power in the family, and thus this verse becomes the symmetrical response to the fear that the brothers expressed in their youth, "Do you propose, the brothers asked him, to rule over us? Are you to be our master?" (Genesis 37:8)

Contacts and Barriers: In Jewish Legend

There are two opposing tendencies at work in the interpretations that the Rabbinic exegetes and Aggadists give to the four social barriers. One is the tendency to elaborate upon the behavior of the Egyptians, to embellish the terse Biblical reports with details that make the tales even more Egyptian and thus more "authentic." The other tendency is to "de-Egyptianize" the material and depict the behavior of Joseph and his brothers in a manner more acceptable to the norms of Rabbinic Judaism. Both of these tendencies are at work in the legends concerning the most striking cultural interaction of the story, Joseph's marriage to Asenath, daughter of the Priest of On. We will discuss Asenath in chapter V, but let us note now that some of the Rabbis deny Asenath's Egyptian parentage. They imagine her as the abducted daughter of Dinah, daughter of Jacob and Leah.

Joseph is thus freed from the obliquity of having an Egyptian wife, a situation unacceptable to the Rabbis. But in describing Asenath's alleged abduction and upbringing in the house of Potiphera, the Aggadists filled the legends with details that they considered "Egyptian": Asenath is carried to Egypt by a hawk, a bird associated with Egypt, she is placed by that bird on the altar of On at which Potiphera officiates, and she adopts Egyptian manners and speech.[32]

As Louis Ginzberg noted in his seminal essay on "The Significance of the Halakhah for Jewish History," "the Aggadah is the handmaiden of the Halakhah." In this traditional view the stories found in Rabbinic literature are far less important than the legal material in which these stories are often embedded. And throughout his voluminous work on Jewish legends Ginzberg emphasized that "it was not possible to understand Jewish history and culture without a thorough knowledge of *halakhah*."[33] In constructing elaborations of Biblical narrative the factor that determined for the Rabbis when any one interpretive approach was to dominate was the *legal* implication of the legend at hand. To uphold the prohibition against marrying non-Jewish women the Egyptian ancestry of Asenath has to be denied. In our discussion of Asenath we will see that this "exegetical management" (to borrow Reuven Firestone's phrase) demanded considerable work on the part of the Rabbis. But this did not obviate the literary impulse to make Asenath's story even more "authentically" Egyptian, especially when such embellishment did not clash with rabbinic norms of behavior.

As we look at representative commentaries and legends about the four social "barriers" we will see that these opposing tendencies, the legalistic and the literary, rather than detracting from the richness of the *aggadot*, make them even more complex and appealing. The tension between the need to emphasize Jewish separateness and the impulse to authenticate an exotic tale added to the complexity and texture of the composite Joseph legends.

1) Dress and General Appearance

We read in Genesis Rabbah, "They brought him hastily out of the dungeon, but first Joseph, out of respect to the King, shaved himself, and put on fresh rainment, which an angel brought him from paradise, and then he came in to Pharaoh."[34]

The haste alluded to by the Aggadist is no doubt a conclusion drawn from the terse style of 41:14. "Thereupon Pharaoh sent for Joseph, and he was rushed from the dungeon. He had his hair cut and changed his clothes, and he appeared before Pharoah." As Donald Redford noted:

> When the physical action itself is speeded up the writer can suit his syntax to the requirements of the new speed...In the succession of six converted imperfects in 41:14 the reader easily senses the haste and excitement which attends the summoning of Joseph by Pharaoh. When the verse begins Joseph is in prison, ignorant of what has been transpiring at court. Then follows verse 14, and after fourteen words he has run the gamut from the most miserable surroundings to the most sumptuous court in the land.[35]

The Talmud further dramatizes Joseph's appearance on his release from prison. It was, no doubt, festive, for all of the events that are compressed into this verse took place on Rosh Hashanah. Other sources add that, "It was on this same day that Joseph's grandfather Isaac died. Joseph's joy was therefore mixed with sadness."[36]

2) Language:

We have seen that the linguistic isolation of Egypt is the background against which we can best understand the text's contention that, "there was a translator among them." One Midrash is more specific, it tells us who the translator was. It was Joseph's son Manasseh.[37]

As Manasseh was the elder son and had grown up in Egypt (and at the same time it was assumed that he learnt Hebrew from his father) he was an apt choice for the role of intermediary. From the Biblical text, the reader knows that Joseph can understand his brothers' deliberations. We know he understands Hebrew, though his brothers do not realize this. Later elaborations describe Joseph as master of all languages. Here too we have an expansion of a reference in the Bible to folkloric proportions; a popular Midrash relates that "Joseph knew all the languages of mankind," some sources say that he knew all seventy languages of the earth.

3) Dietary Restrictions

Commenting on Genesis 43:32, (They served him by himself, and them by themselves, and the Egyptians who ate with him by themselves) Midrash Tanhuma relates:

> The table was set in three divisions: for Joseph, for his brethren, and for the Egyptians. The sons of Jacob had not ventured to eat of the dishes set before them; they were afraid that they might not have been prepared according to the ritual prescriptions.

In this Midrash, the Hebrew aversion to eating with the Egyptians was a matter of following the laws of Kashrut. Onkelos, the second century C.E. translator of the Bible into Aramaic, comments:

> The Egyptians, again could not sit at the same table with the sons of Jacob, because the latter ate the flesh of cattle to which the former paid divine worship.[38]

With these elaborations Onkelos has changed the episode from one in which the Egyptians are protecting their cultural isolation into a tale of *mutual aversion*; each group is prohibited from dining with the other. The Hebrews must follow their dietary laws, the Egyptians had to follow their own.

Rashi highlights the *Egyptian* aversion and mentions that "Onkelos has given an explanation for the phrase: "since that is loathsome": it is despicable to the Egyptians to eat with the Hebrews."[39] The Rabbinic insight that the Egyptians' behavior might be explained by the cultic sanctity of certain animals also extends to their explanation of the aversion to shepherds. We have noted Rashi's comment on Genesis 46:34: "For sheep were a divinity to the Egyptians." Ibn Ezra, the twelfth century exegete famous for his naturalistic explanations, has this to say on Genesis 46:34:

> "For every shepherd is abhorrent to the Egyptians": This indicates that in those days the Egyptians did not eat meat. And they did not associate with anyone who sacrificed sheep, as is the case today with the people of India. And he who is a shepherd is abhorrent for he

drinks the milk. To this day, the people of India neither eat nor drink anything that derives from a sentient being.[40]

In this remarkable excursus on comparative religion, Ibn Ezra ties together both of our "taboos," implying that the aversions to eating with the Hebrews and the prohibition against associating with shepherds are both functions of the Egyptian refusal to eat the flesh of animals. And he notes that this aversion should not surprise the reader, for the people of India have similar rules.

In these representative selections of Rabbinic interpretation of the social barriers separating Egyptians and Hebrews, we can see both the recognition of another nation's taboos, and the Rabbi's understanding of Jewish dietary prohibitions as constructed to enforce the separateness of the Jews. For these legends are a reflex of the Rabbinic legal codes and are therefore "handmaidens of the law." In our discussion of related Islamic legends we shall find both parallels and divergences from this pattern of what we might call *legalistically determined folklore*, folklore that uses "exegetical management" to bring a scriptural story into line with the norms of law.

Contact and Barriers: Ancient Egypt in the Qur'ān and Islamic Legend

Unlike Genesis 37–50, the Qur'ān does not concern itself with the Egyptian background of the Joseph story. More important to the Qur'ānic retelling is the didactic force of the tale. This didactic intent distinguishes Qur'ānic tales as a genre. Commenting upon Sūrat Yūsuf, a contemporary Muslim author states that:

> ...and the whole of this Surah might be described as a series of variations on the theme "judgement as to what happens rests with none but God," explicitly enunciated only in verse 67 of Sūrat Yūsuf, but running like an unspoken leītmotif throughout the story of Joseph.[41]

Egypt (*Misr*) is mentioned only twice in Sura 12. In verse 21, "And the man from Egypt who brought him," and in verse 99, when Joseph greets his family thus: "Enter Egypt! If God so wills, you shall be secure."

In the report of the King's dreams, he is called only "the king" and not the "Pharaoh"—although elsewhere in the Qur'ān we find the term *fir'awn*, used for the Pharaoh of the oppression.[42]

Consistent with this lack of Egyptian background is the absence of any reference to the social barriers discussed above. Where we do find mention of them is in the commentaries on the Qur'ān and in the collections of Islamic legends.

1) Dress

Al-Tha'labī relates that on the day that Yūsuf was released from prison he bathed, put on new clothes and went to see the Pharoah. Before he walked out of the jail he wrote the following inscription on the wall: "This is the tomb of the living and the abode of sorrows. This place is a test of the faith of the friends of God, and my experience here will make my enemies rejoice."[43] In accord with the Biblical account, al-Tha'labī has Joseph prepare to meet the king. Such preparation is to be expected of a commoner who is about to enter the presence of royalty. No mention is made of Joseph cutting his hair, a detail that has import only in the Ancient Egyptian context, and one that may have found an echo in the Genesis account.

Al-Tha'labī's account of Joseph's release from jail, which includes a transcription of Joseph's writing on the prison wall, had its counterpart in medieval Egyptian Islamic folkways. The impulse to identify the sacred places of scripture manifested itself in an attempt to identify the site of Yūsuf's prison. The Egyptian historian al-Maqrīzī (d. 1442) notes that "The knowledgeable are unanimous in their opinion that Yūsuf's prison was in the area of Giza. As the prophet Yūsuf received revelation there it is a place where prayers are answered." al-Maqrīzī, to validate his claim that Giza is the authentic site of the prison, quotes a fascinating account by the eleventh century historian al-Musabbīḥī. This account tells of a yearly pilgrimage to Yūsuf's jail (*sijn yūsuf*). This took place in the early summer, and in the year that al-Musabbīḥī writes of, 1024, the Caliph a-Zahir participated in the festivities of this pilgrimage, which extended over a two week period. These included storytelling, a procession, and a performance of shadow-plays. The procession was so large that "for all practical purposes it shut down the regular business of Cairo, for the populace would flock to the markets to see the procession and watch the performers." Despite the raucous nature of the festivities, the more pietistic aspects of pilgrimage were not forgotten. Al-Maqrīzī, in recounting the history of the site and its associated festivities and rituals, quotes a contemporary sage who said that "if a man journeyed from Iraq to Egypt only in order to see Yūsuf's prison and pray in it, I would have scolded him."[44]

2) Language

Prepared to meet the king, Joseph enters the royal presence. As al-Thaʿlabī tells it Yūsuf addressed the Egyptian ruler in Arabic. "Which language is that?" said the king. "It is the language of Ishmael my uncle." Yūsuf then spoke in Hebrew, and in answer to the king's query said, "this is the language of my father Jacob." Wahb ibn Munabbīh said that the king knew seventy languages. Each time Yūsuf spoke in a language the king responded in kind. Acknowledging Yūsuf's mastery of languages, the king admitted that even his own priests and magicians were not so knowledgeable.

Neither in this case, nor in his later encounter with his brothers, is any mention made of the presence of a translator, a figure who appears in Genesis. Both the king, in his capacity as ruler and diplomat, and Joseph, as a prophet predestined for this role, know "seventy" languages.[45]

In this Islamic retelling, when Joseph's brothers come down into Egypt, he communicates with them without a translator. They address him in Hebrew and he asks them to tell their story. "We are people of Syria," they say, "we are tired, and have come for food."[46]

3) Dietary Restrictions

We have seen that the Egyptian aversion to eating with the Hebrews was taken by some Rabbinic commentaries to have a cultic meaning related to Ancient Egyptian beliefs. Islamic legend preserves the reference to the aversion, but it sees it as an indicator of the need to maintain social distinctions, not religious barriers. When the Pharaoh recognizes Yūsuf's abilities he makes him a member of the court, but does not want the Hebrew to eat with him. Yūsuf counters this insult by celebrating his ancestry: "I am the descendant of Abraham, Isaac, and Jacob. In truth I should not lower myself to eat with you."[47]

Yūsuf here overcomes a social barrier by using his wit. In effect he is saying to the king: as a member of the aristocracy I should be prevented from eating with you, but I will overcome my aversion if you overcome yours.

Here we have a concept similar to that expressed in some of the above-mentioned Rabbinic legends about the eating prohibition. Both parties feel that they cannot sit down to eat with the other, and each for their own reasons. In al-Tha'labī's version, Yūsuf, on his rise to power, is able to present himself in such a way that he can sit down with the king. Yūsuf's invocation of his lineage hearkens back to the notion of an Ancient Near Eastern "ecumene," a social order in which all members of the higher strata of society, whatever their country of origin, were on an equal footing.[48]

In our case study of representative elements in the Joseph story we have seen how extensively the Ancient Egyptian background pervades the tale in both Jewish and Islamic legends. In both scripture and legend, daily life is described in exhaustive detail; the portrayal of the Egyptian tendency to stay aloof from foreigners lends an authentic tone to this tale of foreigners trying to make their way in an alien and hostile land. As a young Hebrew in Egypt, Joseph is forced to adjust quickly to his new situation. Potiphar's wife, sorely tempted by the presence of the young man, fails to comply with her society's norms. What was it about Joseph that proved so irresistible? The following chapter will attempt to answer that question.

Zuleikha Pursues Joseph

4

A Portrait of Joseph

"Extolled is the perfection of Him who has made thee a
temptation to all creatures."
(The Thousand and One Nights)
(c. 1400)

Joseph's Beauty: The Details

Genesis 39:6 tells us that Joseph was "well built and handsome."[1] That the text speaks of Joseph's physical beauty is
beyond doubt; his attractiveness to women is the pivot on which
the upcoming narrative turns.[2] This description of Joseph as
beautiful is artfully placed; it follows the announcement of his
appointment as manager of Potiphar's household and precedes
(and thus explains) the precipitous actions of Potiphar's wife.

Sura 12 vividly dramatizes Yūsuf's beauty. In the Qur'ān,
not only the Egyptian's wife, but her companions, the "women
of the city," are smitten with the young man. Invited by Potiphar's wife to attend a banquet at which she plans to have
Joseph appear, each woman is given a knife and some fruit.
When they see Joseph "they so admired him that they cut their
hands, saying 'This is no mortal; he is no other but a noble
angel.'" Legends in both the Jewish and the Islamic traditions
embellish the handsomeness of Joseph and seem to outdo each
other in extolling the uniqueness of his appearance and its
compelling appeal. Though other attributes of Joseph are emphasized in these legends (his intelligence, piety, chastity) it is
his handsomeness that is most often highlighted.[3] This is an
appropriate characteristic to emphasize in a narrative which
reflects the values of an heroic age, an age in which heroes,
both male and female, were often depicted as beautiful. In con-

trast, "In spiritual or pietistic literature, virtue, but not beauty is stressed. Thus Rabbis or Church Fathers are not singled out as beautiful."[4] Though there are some exceptions to this rule, one thinks of the few Rabbis singled out in the Talmud as "handsome" or "beautiful," it is generally true that in later religious literature good works are a greater spiritual asset than good looks.

In the Bible *yafeh/yafah* (beautiful), is a term used most often to describe women; occasionally, it is used to describe men.[5] The term is applied to eight women and only three men: Joseph, David, and Absalom.[6] In the Song of Songs, the female-male ratio is even greater; the term is used eight times to describe a woman and only once to define a man. The adjective *yafeh/yafah* may be used in a general sense, to describe the pleasing effect of a person's appearance, or it may be applied to a specific feature. The eyes are often singled out. Of David we find, "of beautiful eyes" (I Samuel 16:12); of the Shulamite we read, "Behold, thou art fair, my love; Behold thou art fair; Thine eyes are as doves" (Song of Songs 4:1).

In Israel's pre-monarchic Heroic period the Biblical historian makes note of a character's beauty. In later periods, with the notable exception of the Book of Esther, less attention is drawn to the purely physical. As the culmination and fulfillment of the patriarchal genealogy, Joseph is cast in the mold of the beautiful, semi-divine hero. The antecedents of the Joseph figure in the development of Potiphar's Wife motif, Bellerophon and Bata of Homeric and Ancient Egyptian myth, were both blessed with great beauty.[7] In this respect Joseph displays affinities with another figure of Near Eastern myth, Gilgamesh. Like Gilgamesh, Joseph rules as a king; it is only the official designation of kingship that is withheld from him (Genesis 41:40). And, like Gilgamesh, he is provider to his people, and dreamer of prophetic dreams. E. A. Speiser points out that the phrase used to describe Potiphar's wife's obsession with the Hebrew slave, "His master's wife cast her eyes upon Joseph" (Genesis 39:7) is similar to the phrase used to describe the goddess Ishtar's designs on Gilgamesh.[8] Gilgamesh is praised as two-thirds divine and one-third human, and this motif reverberates in a Midrash that portrays Joseph as possessing, "...two-thirds of the beauty of mankind."[9] Al-Tha'labī, quoting Wahb ibn Munabbih, the early Muslim storyteller who was a convert from

Judaism, tells us that Yūsuf had nine-tenths of the world's beauty.[10] It is as if there is competition within the folkloric material, and each author attempts to outdo the other in extolling Joseph's charms.

Such grand statements about a character's physical attractiveness are unsatisfying unless they are accompanied by descriptive detail. The reader might well ask, "in what way was Joseph 'well built and handsome' or 'handsome of figure and features?'" And where did these good looks come from? Did they appear suddenly in the family or were they inherited? The answers to these questions may be found in the Biblical text and its attendant Midrashim. The phrase used to describe Joseph is also used of his mother Rachel—she too is "beautiful of form" (Genesis 29:17)—the Aggadists concluded that Joseph inherited his mother's beauty; therefore he both resembled her and was her equal in beauty.[11] Muslim authorities, al-Tha'labī among them, also make this connection to Rachel. Other Midrashim trace Joseph's handsomeness to his father Jacob. One source relates that Joseph resembled his father both in the beauty of his appearance and in having been born circumcised.[12]

The Qur'ān, in contrast to the Bible, does not mention Joseph's beauty in connection with his master's wife. In Sura 12 the seduction attempt is preceded by a different narrative link and by a didactic exhortation.

And when he was fully grown, we gave him judgment and knowledge. Even so we recompense the good-doers. Now the woman in whose house he was solicited him...

But, after her failed attempt at seduction, when Ra'il (or "Zuleikha"), in desperation, invites her female friends to that "bloody banquet" her physical attraction to him is underscored by her friends' excitement and exclamations. Now that they too have seen Joseph's beauty she can exclaim "So now you see. This is he who you blamed me for." In elaborating upon this episode, the Qur'ānic commentators and the Muslim folklore anthologists do speak of Yūsuf's physical attractiveness, and in their descriptions we have a fusion of the spiritual and the physical. Razi notes that "when Yūsuf walked through the streets of Egypt, the reflections from his face shone on the walls like sunlight lighting up the sky."[13] The historian al-Ṭabarī (d. 923), is most extravagant in praise of Joseph's beauty. He opens his narration of Joseph's history with this phrase: "Jacob's son Joseph had, like his mother, more beauty than any other human being."

Al-Tha'labī elaborates upon this genealogy of good looks, tracing the family's beauty through Isaac/Isḥaq and his mother Sarah. Sarah inherited her beauty from her grandmother, Ḥawa, or Eve, and we can now think of this as the Ur-beauty, the God-bestowed splendor of the "mother of all flesh."[14] Sarah's beauty, alluded to a number of times in Genesis (in Genesis 12 and 20 her beauty attracts the attentions of the local King), is elaborated upon in one of the prototypes of early Midrash, *The Genesis Apocryphon* of the Dead Sea Scrolls.

Jewish sources emphasize the power and depth of Joseph's eyes, "Your eyes are so beautiful, you have enchanted with them all men and women of Egypt."[15] We have noted that in I Samuel David's eyes were singled out for their beauty. Elsewhere in the Bible eyes are seen as a source of sexual power, "Turn away thine eyes from me, For they have overcome me" (Song of Songs 6:5). Though Joseph's eyes were naturally beautiful he insisted on beautifying them further by applying makeup. And this wasn't the only artifice that he employed. An early Midrash tells us that Joseph's beauty did not go unadorned; it was the result of both artifice and natural endowment. In addition to wearing *kohl* around the eyes, he wore the ancient equivalent of high heels and elaborately dressed his hair.[16]

Islamic sources praise Yūsuf's face. It is often compared to the moon. As we noted in our discussion of the depiction of Joseph's beauty in the earlier Mediterranean "versions," descriptions to this effect are found in the accounts, both in prose and poetry, of Muḥammad's "night journey"—the *mi'raj*, his ascension to heaven. This followed the *isrā*, the journey "from the sacred mosque to the farthest mosque" that is described in sura 17 of the Qur'ān. On the *mi'raj*, Gabriel takes the Prophet through the seven heavens. In each heaven they meet one of the earlier messengers of God. In al-Tha'labī's account, Muḥammad is astounded by Yūsuf's beauty and asks Gabriel "Who is that?" "That is Yūsuf...and his appearance was like that of the full moon." In the Sirah, the early biography of Muḥammad, the Prophet meets Yūsuf in the third heaven: "And there was a man whose face was as the moon at full. This was my brother Joseph son of Jacob."[17] We have also seen that Muḥammad's father, 'Abd Allāh, was "for beauty, the Joseph of his times."

A later poetic account of Joseph echoes these descriptions. In an anonymous thirteenth century poem we read:

The Lord of the Throne had given Joseph an endowment of beauty sufficient to supply the new moon with radiance.[18]

In Islamic manuscripts and paintings that illustrate the *Tales of the Prophets* literature, Yūsuf, in contrast to other prophets, whose portraits tend to resemble each other, has a distinctive appearance. His portraits often incorporate elements of the divine. In a fifteenth century manuscript of the *Miraj Nameh* produced in Herat, there is a picture of Jacob and Joseph greeting Muḥammad and Gabriel, "Jacob and Muḥammad are portrayed with oval faces, beards and mustaches; Gabriel, Joseph and Buraq have round faces."[19] Joseph is in this way placed in the same category as the angel Gabriel and Buraq the supernatural steed of the Prophet, for they too have the round faces of the divinely illumined.

A composite portrait of Yūsuf is presented by al-Thaʿlabī in the name of Kaʿb al-aḥbar, the eighth century Yemenite Jewish convert to Islam.

Yūsuf was light skinned. He had a beautiful face, curly hair and large eyes. He was of medium build, his arms and legs were muscular, his stomach "hungry" or flat. He had a hooked nose, and a small navel. The black mole on his right cheek was an ornament to his face, and between his eyes there was a spot white as the full moon. His eyelashes were like the feathers of an eagle, and when he smiled the light flashed from his teeth. When Yusuf spoke rays of light beamed from between his lips. No one can (fully) describe Yūsuf.

His Effect on His Admirers

What effect does Joseph's beauty have on its beholders? Though each person in the Joseph narratives (and the subsequent elaborations) reacts to him differently, they are all deeply influenced or attracted. And this is not a passing infatuation;

his admirers' destinies are changed irrevocably through their encounter with him.

A Midrash tells us that Joseph's resemblance to Rachel had a powerful effect on his father Jacob and that this resemblance was, "reason enough for distinguishing him among his children."[20] Through his father's love for him the enmity of his brothers was aroused. Early on in his life it was Joseph's destiny to arouse strong emotions, but not necessarily emotions of love. Philo saw Jacob as employing psychology to offset the strength of these feelings, "Jacob sent his sons away for a time, retaining only Joseph with him...and when he thought that the ill feelings of his sons against Joseph had subsided he sent the latter to enquire after their welfare."[21]

When Joseph's beauty fails him, the result is dramatic. The Midianites paid a low price for such a distinguished youth, because his appearance was affected by the days he spent in the pit.[22] In an Islamic legend told by al-Kisāʾī, Joseph's beauty is revealed only when the caravan owner, Malik ibn Dhu'r, reaches Egypt with the Hebrew slave that he purchased in Canaan. Upon arrival, Malik said to Joseph, "Boy, get down here. Take off your shirt and wash in this river." When he had washed and performed ablutions with the water, the earth itself shone from his beauty, and the light of prophethood gleamed from his eyes and penetrated the very walls of Egypt, filling the entire country with light."[23]

In both Jewish and Muslim legends, Potiphar finds the restored and rehabilitated Joseph very attractive, and is willing to pay a very high price for the young man. As we noted in Chapter 3, in some legends he finds the young man sexually desirable. In Midrash and Biblical commentary, Potiphar's sexual preference is the subject of much speculation. The question is related to the meaning of Potiphar's Hebrew title, *saris* of Pharoah (Genesis 37:36 and 39:1). While some translators and commentators take *saris* to be a title of the nobility, others, including the Septuagint, translate *saris* as eunuch. Genesis Rabbah also understands the term this way. Potiphar as eunuch offered a challenge to the Aggadists and commentators and it is worth noting Albright's observation that "while a eunuch may have a whole harem, and is often blessed with his share of erotic proclivities (see Juvenal's sixth satire and the Arabian Nights) it is at least unusual to find a married *saris*."[24]

The legend that Potiphar was sexually attracted to Joseph is also found in the Talmud and is mentioned by Jerome in his Latin translation of Genesis.[25] It later surfaced in some Jewish and Islamic folklore. In some versions the Egyptian's designs on Joseph were thwarted when the angel Gabriel mutilated Potiphar and made him a eunuch. There is, of course, a logical and chronological problem here. Genesis terms Potiphar *saris* before he meets Joseph. How then can the punishment be meted out before the crime is committed? "Displaying little regard for the sequence of events, the Midrash takes the "eunuch-hood" of Potiphar as the punishment visited upon the Egyptian for having purchased Joseph allegedly for the purpose of sodomy."[26] Variations on this theme appear in al-Ṭabarī and al-Thaʿlabī. Al-Ṭabarī adds that Qiṭfīr (the Potiphar figure in Islamic legend), "was a man who did not have intercourse with women, though his wife Rāʿīl was beautiful and tender, and had property and possessions."[27] These circumstances of neglect, coupled with Joseph's irresistible attractiveness, led Potiphar's wife to seek Joseph's attentions.

Neither the Bible nor the Qurʾān give "Potiphar's wife"/"the Master's wife" a name. Feminist critics note the absence of women's names in other narratives in the Bible. A woman may be identified through her husband (Noah's wife in Genesis 7:7) or through identification with a place, as in the case of the wise woman of Abel-beth-maacah (II Samuel 20:14–22), but she is seldom presented in the narrative with her own name. In the case of Potiphar's wife, this strikes both the modern reader, as it struck the pre-modern exegete, as a serious omission. Various exotic names were suggested by the authors of legends. Potiphar's wife is named Rāʿīl in the accounts of al-Ṭabarī and al-Thaʿlabī. Gordon has suggested that Rāʿīl is a theophoric name that echoes ancient Egyptian and Semitic sources. The name may thus be read as a composite of *Re*, the Egyptian sun god and *El* the Semitic deity. Al-Bayḍāwī mentions the name Rāʿīl *and* the name Zuleikha. In the Jewish work *Sefer Hayashar* and in later Persian Islamic folklore, Potiphar's wife is consistently named Zuleikha.[28] Al-Kisāʿī also calls her Zuleikha and goes so far as to give us her father's name: "Then Potiphar brought Joseph to the palace of Zuleikha, the daughter of Akahira."[29]

When Zuleikha's attempts at seduction fail, and she is spurned by Joseph, she accuses him of assaulting her. A piquant detail of the circumstance of her report to her husband is provided by Genesis Rabbah: "And it came to pass when his master heard..." (39:19) R. Abbahu said: "This happened during cohabitation."[30] This detail is inconsistent with the above-mentioned assertion of conjugal neglect, and it contradicts of the traditions which portray Potiphar as a eunuch. This serves to remind us that these disparate and often contradictory fragments of folkloric elaboration were not conceived of as a discrete and consistent entity. It is only in the modern period that attempts were made to blend these tales together. When we read a modern reworking of Jewish legends, such as Ginzberg's *Legends of the Jews* or Bialik and Ravnitsky's *The Book of Legends*, we expect, and, for the most part, find, internal consistency. This tendency is also evident in Jan Knappert's *Islamic Legends: Histories of Heroes, Saints and Prophets of Islam*. But this consistency is the result of the modern anthologist's efforts. When we read the great medieval anthologies of legends, both Jewish and Islamic, we find that the creation of a coherent narrative consistent in its details is not the anthologist's primary aim. Rather, the editor wants to make available all authoritative elaborations of the scriptural text under discussion.

An even more surprising twist in the narrative is provided by al-Tha'labī and al-Bayḍāwī. They both say that Yūsuf and Ra'il became man and wife after Yūsuf's appointment to the office of vizier. According to al-Tha'labī, "At the time of his appointment Ra'il was still a virgin; she later was to bear Yūsuf two sons."[31] al-Bayḍāwī is even more specific, "These were born to him, from Ra'il, Ephraim and Manasseh, who was the ancestor of Joshua son of Nun and of Rahmah, wife of Job."[32]

These Islamic legends may reflect the Bible's assignment to Joseph of Asenath, "daughter of Potiphera priest of On." For most Jewish exegetes Potiphera is identified with Potiphar, and Joseph thus marries the daughter of the family which he served as a servant. This is, in J. Robin King's phrase, "an exquisitely ironic victory." In the Islamic tradition, where no Asenath figure is mentioned, legends tell of Joseph marrying Potiphar's wife after she had repented of her sins. In some Islamic pietistic texts, and especially in the great poetic epics of Rumi and Jami, Zuleikha's life becomes a paradigm for the power of repentance.

Perhaps the most dramatic response to Joseph's beauty is that of the "women of the city" in Sura 12; they swoon and cut their hands when he enters the room in which they are sitting with Zuleikha. To make their response even more dramatic Wahb ibn Munabbih related that there were forty women at this banquet and that seven of them died of longing for Joseph.[33]

In Thomas Mann's modern retelling of the episode, he highlights the power and inevitability of that moment.

This oft-described scene has by some been thought to be apocryphal and not belonging to the story as it happened. But they are wrong; for it is the truth, and all the probabilities speak for it. We must remember, on the other hand, that this was the most beautiful youth of his time and sphere; on the other, that these were the sharpest little knives that the world has ever seen and we shall understand that the thing could not happen otherwise—I mean with less shedding of blood—than as it actually did.[34]

Even the warden of the Egyptian prison is not impervious to Joseph's charm and good looks. The Targumim and Josephus interpret Genesis 39:21, "and disposed the chief jailer favorably toward him" to mean that the warden was taken with Joseph's beauty and wisdom.[35] This motif is echoed in Islamic sources where Joseph's fellow prisoners tell him, "We loved you as soon as we saw you."[36]

The people of Egypt are also taken with Joseph's beauty. Commenting on Genesis 41:43 "Thus he was installed over the land of Egypt," the Midrash Hagadol says that, "The women of the nobility looked out of the windows to gaze upon Joseph's beauty and they poured down chains upon him, and rings and jewels, that he might but direct his eyes toward them."[37] As we saw in the previous chapter, adorning the king's favorite with jewelry, especially with gold, is very much in the ancient Egyptian tradition of the mid-second millennium. Amarna Age art abounds with the pictorial image of a similar ceremony, and the custom is also reflected in the written texts of the period.[38] For those scholars who date the Joseph story to the Amarna period (fourteenth century B.C.), this Biblical parallel to actual Egyptian ceremony is a colorful piece of supporting evidence.

Elements of His Appeal

In Joseph's appeal to both men and women there is an element of the androgynous. We have already alluded to these feminine aspects and to the observation in both Midrash and *qiṣaṣ al-anbiyā* that Joseph inherited his mother's good looks. The smooth, clean-shaven face depicted in Islamic art, and the use of makeup and elaborate clothes attributed to him in various legends, also emphasize the feminine aspect. His masculine appeal is attested to in the story of the "woman of the city." But an undertone of androgyny informs another Midrash, which speaks of the birth of Jacob's children:

> "With every tribal ancestor a twin sister was born... Abba Halpa the son of Koriah said: An additional twin sister was born with Benjamin."[39]

This legend provides an answer to a question which vexed the Rabbis: who were Jacob's sons to marry when they reached adulthood? Weren't they surrounded by the Canaanites, whose daughters were forbidden to them? The ingenious answer: the sons, children of Jacob's two wives and two concubines, would marry their half sisters. According to one version of this Midrash, Benjamin had two twin sisters, while Joseph had none. The implication of these legends is that Joseph combined both male and female characteristics, and therefore there was no need for the legends to provide him with a twin sister.[40] His destiny was to be the one son who would grow up in an alien land, and when he rose to prominence in that land he married a daughter of the nobility.

As a character who has androgynous appeal to both sexes, Joseph became a standard of beauty, both male and female. In *The Thousand and One Nights*, where Joseph's beauty is often extolled, a woman is described as being, ":as beautiful as Yūsuf in form."[41] In another tale in the collection, a *man* is praised in a similar fashion. *The Thousand and One Nights* epitomizes this view of Joseph's beauty in the following phrase, which could serve as an epigram for all of the Joseph narratives, "Extolled is the perfection of Him who has made thee a temptation to all creatures."[42]

The "misfortune of love," is a persistent theme in both the Jewish and Islamic Joseph legends. Joseph is aware that adoration and infatuation have their price:

> Love has caused me a great suffering; my father's love brought upon me my brethren's hatred, which resulted in my being sold as a slave; the love of Potiphar's wife for me lodged me in prison."[43]

An Islamic evocation of this theme is quoted in Tabari's Qur'ānic commentary.

> Yūsuf has arrived in prison and his fellow prisoners shower him with affection. He turns to them and says "By God, don't love me, for every time someone has loved me it has caused me misfortune. My aunt loved me, and only misfortune followed. The same was true of my father, and of my master's wife. So please don't love me." But the prisoners refused his request, "for they wanted his companionship and his wisdom."[44]

The aunt who loved him, a situation that appears only in Islamic sources, was an unnamed aunt of Jacob's who cared for Yūsuf after his mother's death. She grew so attached to her young charge that when Jacob requested him back she refused to relinquish him.[45] In the next chapter we will see this episode folded into other tales of the young Yūsuf's entanglements.

In conclusion, we can see that the praise and depiction of Joseph's physical beauty and great charm play a pivotal role in the Joseph narrative. In the Ancient Egyptian, Biblical, and Qur'ānic accounts, and in the subsequent Jewish and Islamic embellishments, Joseph's portrait hovers on the border between the human and the angelic. Both men and women were attracted to him, and much of the plot revolves around the consequences of their actions and reactions. Despite the androgynous undertone in many of the descriptions, and despite the early Rabbinic legends about Potiphar's designs, it is Joseph's appeal to women that is most often highlighted. And despite the fact that a "wiles of men" trope balances the "wiles of women" theme of so many of the retellings, it is that latter cultural construct that is dominant throughout the history of the Joseph stories.

In the following chapter, on the women of the Joseph story, we will again encounter, as Joseph did, Potiphar's wife, her companions the "women of the city," and his Egyptian wife Asenath. But it is not only women in potential erotic relationship to Joseph (a relationship either real or imagined) who enliven our tales. We have seen that in one account his aunt, acting as his guardian, becomes unduly attached to him. Other women—his mother Rachel, his kinswomen Tamar, his aunt Serah bat Asher—are also pivotal figures in Joseph's tale. It is to the stories of all of these women that we now turn.

Zuleikha Complains of Joseph to Her Husband

The Women of the Joseph Story

The Egyptian women, daughters of Kings, desired to gaze
upon Joseph's face, yet he would not look at any of them.
                              Genesis Rabbah (c. 600 C.E.)

In the patriarchal narratives, both as described in scripture
and elaborated upon in legend, women play a major role.
Though the primary identification of each of the matriarchs,
Sarah, Rebecca, Rachel, and Leah, is as the *wife* of Abraham,
Isaac, and Jacob, each woman also has a greater or lesser
degree of agency in the unfolding saga of the people of Israel. Of
these women, Rebecca is the most assertive; it is her attentive-
ness and "guile" that enables her son Jacob to earn his father's
blessings. In a similar manner, her niece Rachel's theft of the
teraphim, symbols of household authority, foils the plans of her
father Laban and empowers her husband Jacob. While these
strategies may be seen as examples of the "wiles of women,"
they do not mark women as essentially more guileful or decep-
tive than men. Because of their powerlessness in some spheres
of life women may have to resort to guile. But dispossessed men
in quest of power also have to resort to guile. Jacob's very name
conjures up the idea of the trickster.

I emphasize this lack of distinction between the aims (and
strategies) of women and men to take issue with the view that
the sexes are treated in *fundamentally* different ways in the
Biblical narratives. While it is clear to the Biblical author that
men most often have power and privilege, it is made very clear
that they must often gain this power and privilege by their wits.
It is also understood that they may lose this power, often at the
hands of a woman. As the feminist critic T. Frymer-Kensky put
it "There is nothing distinctly 'female' about the way that women

are portrayed in the Bible....the 'Biblical' image of women is consistently the same as that of men. In their strengths and weaknesses, in their goals and strategies, the women of the Bible do not differ substantially from the men."[1]

Some scholars note that in contrast to the earlier parts of Genesis there is "a comparative absence of women in the Joseph tales."[2] The women of Joseph's world are portrayed as less assertive and determined than their immediate ancestors, the matriarchs of an earlier but not too distant period. Despite this scaling down of women's roles, we can point to a number of important women in "Joseph." Dramatic changes in Joseph's situation are inextricably linked to the actions of the female characters in the narrative. If these tales are judged to be "the best of all stories" no small measure of their popularity may be attributed to the lively role of the female characters. Though marginalized in other parts of the Biblical saga (one thinks of the narratives of the conquest and settlement of Canaan) women have significant roles in almost all episodes of Joseph's story, though their centrality is less apparent than it is in the earlier foundation stories of the nation.

In this chapter, I will describe and analyze the role of the women in the Joseph narratives, and demonstrate that we can sense a shift in attitudes as we move forward in the history of the retelling of our story. The women in the Biblical Joseph story, and in the patriarchal narratives that proceed them, are portrayed in the heroic tradition. Their stories are of a period when women's status, at least among the aristocracy, was depicted as an elevated one.[3] Some of the legends indicate that vestiges of this attitude towards women were retained at a later date. Stories told at a later time, when the status of women was diminished, may very well reflect women's elevated status in an earlier time—as well as the aspiration for future social change and the return to an earlier model of male-female relationships.

The legends of women in "Joseph" also lend themselves to analysis in terms of cross-cultural and inter-denominational borrowings (Jewish, Christian, and Muslim). As with the magical aspect of the tales, the "feminine aspect" is one that tends to encourage such borrowings.

The five women prominent in the larger Joseph narratives—Rachel, Tamar, Asenath, Serah, and Potiphar's wife—share a number of characteristics. They are all described (in scripture or legend) as beautiful; they are highly intelligent, and capable of great wisdom and cunning. They are all "worthy of saga" and enliven as well as propel the narrative. And, I contend, the portrayal of these women changes dramatically as we move from the more literary scriptural traditions to the folkloric traditions of legend and elaboration that flourished in the Jewish and Islamic cultural spheres.

Rachel

In Genesis, Joseph and his mother Rachel are described by exactly the same Hebrew phrase, though the impact of this identical phrasing is not conveyed in most English translations:

Rachel was shapely and beautiful. (Genesis 29:17)

Joseph was well built and handsome. (Genesis 39:6)

While the Hebrew uses the adjectives yafeh/yafah, in their masculine or feminine form, the English translators have taken liberties with the sense of the text and leave us with a culturally determined "gender-appropriate translation." Joseph was "well built and handsome," while Rachel was "shapely and beautiful."

Both of these verses are followed by the consequences of such beauty. In Rachel's case it is that, "Jacob loved Rachel" (29:18). In Joseph's it was that, "His master's wife fixed her eye on Joseph" (39:7). As we saw in the previous chapter, Jewish and Islamic sources concur in the observation that Joseph inherited his beauty from his mother. (Though some legends also credit his father Jacob as a source of Joseph's beauty.) The Zohar states that it was Joseph's resemblance to his mother that consoled Jacob in his grief over her death. Jacob, therefore, was rendered disconsolate when Joseph himself was presumed dead.[4] The Muslim commentaries on the Qur'ān vied with each other in praising Raḥil's great beauty, just as they did in extolling Joseph's charms.[5] For commentators of both traditions this is one of many ways in which the lives of Rachel and Joseph parallel one another. In the case of Joseph, who more than any other child of Jacob is tied to and identified with his mother, we may rephrase the Rabbinic dictum that "The deeds of the fathers are signs of the deeds of the sons."[6] To read "The deeds of the mothers are signs of the deeds of the sons."

Both Rachel and Joseph are the younger, more beautiful, and more favored siblings of their respective families. Jacob, as husband and father, favors both of them (Genesis 37:3), and the text relates that "Israel loved Joseph best of all his sons, for he was the child of his old age." Later, Joseph's own charm and beauty win Jacob over.

In Genesis 46 the Bible ties together the fate of Rachel and Joseph when it lists the "names of the Israelites, Jacob and his descendants, who came to Egypt." Though the three other mothers of Jacob's children (Leah, Bilhah, and Zilpah) are mentioned in the list, only Rachel, mother of Joseph and Benjamin, is designated "Jacob's wife." Some Midrashim tell us that the personalities and behavior of mother and son were similar. Rachel's successful attempt to steal the *teraphim*, and thereby acquire the symbols of family authority and cultic leadership, is paralleled in the legends that report Joseph as stealing idols and other symbols of authority. This motif surfaces in Jewish legends and these in turn may have influenced the Qur'ān and its Qur'ānic commentators. Al-Bayḍāwī, commenting on Qur'ān 12:77: "If he is a thief, a brother of his was a thief before" states:

> ...they mean Joseph. For it is said that his aunt inherited from her father Abraham's girdle; and she used to nurse Joseph and love him, and when he grew up to be a youth, Jacob wished to withdraw him from her influence, so she tied the girdle round his waist and then proclaimed that it had been lost; so a search was made for it, and it was found tied around Joseph, and thereby she became the most entitled to him according to their law. *Another story is that Joseph's mother's father had an idol which Joseph stole, broke and threw among the carrion.*[7]

In al-Bayḍāwī's account it is Joseph who completes the mother figure's appropriation of—and desecration of—her father's idols. A similar tradition about the brothers is recorded in early Jewish legends. But there, the theft is imputed to Joseph's younger brother Benjamin. In Genesis Rabbah, the brothers accuse Benjamin of being a "thief and a son of a female thief," referring to his mother's theft. This Jewish legend may have been transposed in its Islamic counterpart from Benjamin to Joseph in order to strengthen the Joseph-Rachel parallels.

These mother-son parallels extend beyond our protagonists' lives and into the depictions of their deaths and burials. In some legends both Rachel and Joseph are perceived as having died prematurely. Rachel dies in childbirth with Benjamin. "It was Jacob's unintentional curse against her on that occasion [stealing the *teraphim*] that caused Rachel's premature death. The curse would have taken effect at once were it not that she was destined to bear Jacob his youngest son."[8] Joseph, too, dies "prematurely," for there are legends that characterize Joseph's death at age 110 as early, for it falls short of the ideal Biblical age of 120.

In Genesis, both Rachel and Joseph are buried elsewhere than the family tomb at Hebron. Rachel is buried near Bethlehem, and Joseph at Shechem. In Rachel's case the text itself provides an explanation for the choice of her burial site. As she died in childbirth on the road to Ephrat, her tomb was erected at that very spot and Jacob consecrated it (Genesis 35:20). No explanation is given in the text for the site of Joseph's burial, though the commentaries attempt to explain the choice of Shechem in ingenious ways. Rashi (on Genesis 50:25) quotes a legend that says: as his brothers sold him near Shechem, in Dothan, it was to that place that they were obligated to return him.[9]

Significantly, the Jewish and Islamic traditions provide complementary tales regarding the *intended* burial places of Rachel and Joseph. A poignant Midrash informs us that Jacob wanted Rachel buried next to him in the tomb of Hebron, but God refused his request.[10] There is a parallel Islamic tradition that Joseph, according to his own wish, *actually was buried* in the *Haram* at Hebron. This may reflect the influence of an early Jewish legend that Hebron is where Joseph *wished* to be interred.[11] We shall return to these traditions in our final chapter, "Joseph's Bones: Linking Canaan and Egypt."

Much later in history the tombs of both mother and son became important religious centers and places of supplication. In the case of Rachel's tomb, the Biblical text alludes to the tomb's importance in a later generation:

Thus saith the Lord: a voice is heard in Ramah, lamentation and bitter weeping, Rachel weeping for her children. (Jeremiah 31:15)

The Rabbis understood this Biblical verse to be a reference to the efficacy of supplication at Rachel's tomb.

> This is the source of the Midrash that when the Israelites were driven into captivity by Nebuzaradan, and the supplications of the patriarchs and of Moses proved to no avail, Rachel arose from her grave and implored God's clemency, basing her plea upon her own self-abnegation with regard to her sister. God thereupon promised her the restoration of Israel. (Lamentations Rabbah)[12]

Medieval Jewish chroniclers noted the celebration of what we would call popular religious practices at the site of Joseph's tomb in Shechem. At Rachel's tomb we find similar practices in medieval and modern times:

> The tomb is especially visited on the new moons, during the whole month of Elul, and on the 14th of Heshvan, the traditional anniversary of the death of "our mother Rachel." Jews donated oil, sacred curtains and charity for the tomb structure. They were also accustomed to inscribing their names on the tombstone and measuring it with red woolen threads, which were tied onto children and the sick as a remedy for good health and healing.[13]

The magical elements in these practices are obvious: the visits during the new moon, the dedication of sacred objects to the shrine, and the invocation of sympathetic magic in order to protect children and the sick. In the Aggadic imagination Rachel and Joseph were linked in death as well as in life.

Tamar

Most readers of Genesis do not consider Tamar a character in the Joseph tales. For many critics and readers, the tale of Judah and Tamar as told in Genesis 38 is an intrusion into the narrative flow that begins with Chapter 37 and ends with the closing of Genesis in Chapter 50. One of the ingenious solutions to this problem, based on the Documentary Hypothesis, is that the inclusion of Chapter 38 at this point in Joseph's unfolding story is the result of a redactor's compromise between Northern (Israelite) and Southern (Judean) claims to authority and leadership. In an attempt to satisfy both claims to legitimacy, the redactor wove the story of Tamar, a southern or Judean tale which affirms Judean legitimacy, into the Northern story of the origins of the Joseph tribes. This type of explanation was anticipated by the fifteenth century Jewish savant Don Isaac Abrabanel. He recognized that competing claims to kingship were at issue in the latter part of Genesis and explained the "intrusion" of Chapter 38 into the Joseph narrative as a reminder that the "House of Joseph" because of its descent from "Asenath the Egyptian" did not remain the tribe of royalty. The kings of the tribe of Judah, descended from Tamar (who the Rabbis described as "daughter of Shem") and Judah, were the rulers destined to be "God's holy Kings for all time." Today, many scholars have accepted the view that Chapter 38 derives from the same source as the surrounding narrative (the J or Jehovist source) but claim that, "The narrative is a completely independent unit. It has no connection with the drama of Joseph, which it interrupts at the conclusion of Act I."[14] A more organic view of Chapter 38 and its placement was advanced by C. H. Gordon, who views the break in the Joseph story as a literary device:

"Where an entirely different tale is interposed, may it not be that the Biblical author or editor purposely inserted this long chapter for suspense. For, while Joseph is left behind as a slave in Potiphar's house, we must go through all of Chapter 38 before we get back to the fate of the hero."[15]

That there is a thematic link between Chapter 38 and the surrounding chapters was recognized by the classical Jewish commentaries, foremost among them, Rashi (d. 1105). In making this link Rashi and other commentaries were building on Midrashim which tied together the Joseph story and the tale of Judah and Tamar. Rashi's comments on Genesis 38:15:

Why was this section adjoined here? It interrupted the section of Joseph. To teach us that his [Judah's] brothers removed him from his rank. When they saw the grief of his father, they said "you said to sell him. Had you said to return him we would have listened to you."[16]

Judah's misadventure is thus linked to the plot of the Joseph story. Judah's complicity in Joseph's disappearance is not forgotten; because he neglected his brother he will now be punished. He will be humiliated by Tamar. The narrative digression thus serves a didactic purpose. In other attempts to link the two stories, the sexual abandon of Judah and his sons is contrasted with Joseph's chastity.

One striking Rabbinic commentary on the question of the two stories' proximity affirms the innocence of both Tamar and Potiphar's wife. Genesis Rabbah quotes Rabbi Samuel ben Nahman to the effect that the stories of Tamar and Potiphar's wife are linked to teach us that "as the former was actuated by pure motive, so was the latter." For Tamar foresaw that she would give birth to the ancestors of the kings of the Davidic dynasty, and Potiphar's wife saw that she would be the "mother" of Joseph's descendants.[17]

This comment maps on nicely to the higher criticism view that Chapter 38 displays concerns about authority and leadership in Ancient Israel, a concern demonstrated in the integration of Israelite and Judean origin tales. The Rabbinic tradition, aware of the contending northern and southern claims to kingship and authority, validates them both and fuses their claims through the stories of Tamar and Potiphar's wife. Tamar on the Judean or Southern side, and Potiphar's wife on the Israelite or northern side, acted honorably and with the future interests of all Israel uppermost in their minds.

For scholars who emphasize the "trickster" motif in Genesis, Tamar's justified entrapment of Judah is both the tale of the disenfranchised woman as trickster and an instance in which male wrongdoing is punished, though in a roundabout manner. Some scholars have suggested that Judah's entrapment and embarrassment balances the brother's misdeed to Joseph. "As Joseph was taken in ambush, so Judah is taken by deception and forced to do his duty to Tamar."[18] Robert Alter's analysis of Chapter 38 also places Judah and Tamar within the wider context of the Joseph narrative:

There is thematic justification for the connection (between the two stories) since the tale of Judah and his offspring, like the whole Joseph story, and indeed like the entire Book of Genesis, is about the reversal of the iron law of primogeniture, about the election through some devious twist of destiny of a younger son to carry on the line. There is, one might add, genealogical irony in the insertion of this material at this point of the story, for while Joseph, next to the youngest of the sons, will eventually rule over his brothers in his own lifetime as splendidly as he has dreamed, it is Judah, the fourth-born, who will be the progenitor of the kings of Israel, as the end of Genesis 38 will remind us.[19]

There is a voluminous secondary literature on the function and placement of Genesis 38.[20] Alter's observation that, "Tamar wants to become the channel of the seed of Judah" echoes the Midrash about Potiphar's wife that I cited earlier. She was told by the court astrologers that she would bear Joseph's children. Therefore she tried to seduce him. What she did not realize was that the prediction meant that her daughter Asenath would bear Joseph's children, Ephraim and Mannaseh.[21]

Tamar and Asenath are also linked by a set of legends about their genealogy. The Rabbis were obviously troubled by the non-Israelite origins of both women; as described in the Bible Tamar was a Canaanite and Asenath an Egyptian. To legitimize their roles as ancestors of the Kings of Judah and Israel, legends ascribe to each of them "appropriate" ancestors. Tamar is described as a direct descendant of Shem, which places her among a righteous and genealogically acceptable family; of Asenath it is said that she was the daughter of Jacob's daughter Dinah.[22]

Though Tamar never *directly* enters into the Joseph tale, her tale is very much of a piece with both the spirit and circumstances of the Joseph narratives. A midrash establishes this link through a familiar hermeneutical device. It cites two parallel episodes in otherwise unconnected narratives and uses the newly-found connection as the basis for a homily. "The Holy one Praised be He said to Judah, you deceived your father with a kid of the goats. By your life, Tamar will deceive you with a kid of the goats."[23] The goat in whose blood the brothers dip

Joseph's coat, and the goat that Tamar demands as payment for her services to Judah, is the symbolic link between Judah's complicity in Joseph's disappearance and his punishment—in the form of humiliation—at the hands of Tamar.

The Women of the City

The women discussed thus far are characters that are mentioned, however briefly, in the *Biblical* text. Potiphar's wife, of course, occupies a central role in the Genesis narrative. The nineteenth century Orientalist E. Meyer claimed that this motif represented the oldest layer of the Joseph material, and that it may have been directly influenced by the Egyptian *Tale of Two Brothers*.[24] In this section we shall discuss a group of women not mentioned in the *Tale of Two Brothers* or the Bible: the "women of the city," those companions of Potiphar's wife who gossiped about her designs on Joseph and whose actions later serve to prove her point about Joseph's irresistible charms. They appear in the Qur'ān, where it is related that Potiphar's wife, after her attempts to seduce Joseph fail, invited her companions to a banquet and presented them with fruit and knives. She then called Joseph into the room. Overcome by his beauty they cut their hands and exclaim: "This is no mortal: he is no other but a noble angel."

Is this episode an Islamic contribution to the larger narrative? Or can it be traced to an earlier Jewish prototype? A Jewish form of this episode is found in the Midrash Tanhuma, "...where it is introduced with the formula 'our masters say' which indicates that an old source was made use of."[25] In the Jewish version the women are cutting *etrogim* (the citrus fruit associated with the holiday of *sukkot* or Tabernacles) when Joseph appears among them. The story also appears in Midrash Yashar, but according to L. Ginzberg, "Whether Yashar made use of Qur'ān 12:30–33 is doubtful; the Jewish origin of the legend as given in Tanhuma is beyond dispute."[26] An examination of the sources cited reveals that Ginzberg's conclusions are not as self-evident as he makes them out to be, and it is not clear that this is an episode first told in a Jewish source. For these Midrashim are very difficult to date and it may be that the episode originated in the Qur'ān and was later transmitted to Jewish anthologists. S. D. Goitein noted that:

This scene [that of the ladies of the party], which has often been depicted by Muslim painters, is found in Hebrew literature *later* than the Qur'ān. It may have been told to Muhammad by a Jew, *although it does not occur in the ancient Midrash*, but it is more likely that the very un-Arab theme had come to the Arabs from some Persian romance and was introduced by Muhammad himself into the story of Joseph. *Later on, it also found its way into popular Jewish literature.*[27]

If Goitein's reading of the evidence is correct, this vivid episode, the cutting of the hands, serves as an example of cultural borrowing and repayment. Later Jewish folklore, influenced by legends circulating in an Islamic milieu, adopted this Qur'ānic episode and added a detail—the citrons—which "authenticates" it as a Jewish story. But this specific Muslim-Jewish exchange of narrative detail does not end with the development of a Jewish variant of a Qur'ānic tale. In al-Tha'labī's eleventh century retelling of Sūrat Yūsuf, the women of the city are given a variety of fruits to eat, including pomegranates, bananas, and *atraj*. This is the Arabic equivalent of the Hebrew *etrog*, the citrus fruit associated with the holiday of Sukkot that is mentioned in Jewish versions of the story. In the process of cultural cross-fertilization this Islamic anthology of tales absorbed folklore material from a Jewish source, and make the ceremonial citrus of Jewish ritual the fruit served to the women. These women, of course, were characters first delineated in Islamic scripture.

The *etrog*, the *citrus media* whose botanical origins lie in India or Iran, might strike the reader as a strange choice of fruit to offer at a banquet. Its rind is thick and its taste quite bitter. But it is not its taste, but its associative value that must have generated this detail. For the *etrog*, known in medieval sources as the "lust apple," is said in one Jewish legend to have been the "fruit of the Tree of Knowledge" that Eve offered to Adam. In the banquet episode it evokes both sexual knowledge and the underlying trope of the "wiles of women." A popular Egyptian folktale has it that tangerines were the fruit that Zuleikha served to her friends. In Egyptian colloquial Arabic the tangerine is called "yusef effendi" ("mister Joseph"); named, according to some authorities, after the events of that fateful banquet.[28]

Though the question of the original provenance of the "cutting the hands" episode proves difficult to answer conclusively, there is another question which may be more fruitfully posed. Why were the "women of the city" added to the narrative in both Jewish and Islamic legend? Wasn't the Potiphar's Wife story "sufficient unto itself?" Hadn't it satisfied readers for a millennium? Four answers suggest themselves:

1) Their presence in the story heightens the drama, it adds an element of court intrigue to what was an intimate, personal story. Potiphar's wife's method of involving her female companions is a manifestation of *kayd*, or guile, an attribute valorized in many other tales of women *and* men in pursuit of their aims.

2) The women's reaction to Joseph emphasizes his great beauty and irresistible sexual charms. Overcome by passion, they cut their hands instead of their fruit.

3) This is an example of a familiar literary device, "build up and climax."[29] Joseph not only has to resist the charms of Potiphar's wife, he has to contend with a full bevy of beauties, each of whom would like to seduce him. In some Midrashim each of the "women of the city" attempt to seduce Joseph on a number of occasions.

4) In the earlier accounts the encounter between Zuleikha and Joseph is personal and intimate. With the involvement of her companions, "the passion itself becomes social."[30] Al-Tha'labī quotes Wahb ibn Munabbih who tells us that seven of the forty women "died from longing." Baiḍawi says that there were forty women at the banquet, and that five of them were the gossips who instigated the campaign against Potiphar's wife. "These women were the wives of the chamberlain, butler, baker, prison-keeper, and head groom."[31] In her description of her encounter with Yūsuf, Zuleikha does not spare her companions any of the graphic details of their meeting, or her plans for their future together. As al-Ṭabarī tells it she pointed to Yūsuf and said, "This is the one on whose account you blamed me. I asked of him an evil act, but he proved continent. And after he had loosened his trousers, he remained continent. I do not know what appeared to him. But if he does not do what I order—

that is, have intercourse—verily he will be imprisoned and brought low."[32]

The intensity of these women's response to Joseph is highlighted in al-Bayḍāwī's comment on the phrase "And when they saw him they so admired him." He first quotes the traditional interpretation of the verse, "And when they saw him they thought him marvellous and were awed at his superlative beauty." Then he states:

> Another interpretation is that 'akbarna has the sense here of "menstruated," since one says of a woman 'akbarat (she has grown up) meaning "she menstruated" because a woman enters on adulthood with menstruation. In this case the -hu attached to the verb is a pronoun representing a verbal noun (a cognate accusative, maful mutlaq) or, it refers to Joseph with omission of the preposition "for" i.e., they menstruated because of him out of the violence of lust.[33]

As the contemporary critic Abdelwahab Bouhdiba noted, the symbolism of the cut hands, in juxtaposition with the onset of menstruation, is both obvious and effective:

> The emotion felt of the sight of Joseph was so great that the charming assembly was seized by a collective physiological pain...the menstrual blood has its corollary and counterpart in the blood shed on their own hands. Their admiration for Joseph was such that they could no longer distinguish between either the fruit and their hands, or the blades and handles of their knives! The symbolism could not be more transparent: the oranges and knives are substitutes for an act of love so desired by the women, but refused by Joseph, the mere sight of whom brings on a collective orgasm on their part. The eroticism here derives from the divine, angelic character of Joseph. Love and prophecy are identified; the beautiful reveals the sacred.[34]

Al-Bayḍāwī's note on the intensity of the women's responses to Joseph serves to emphasize the theme of inexorable fate that operates throughout our tale. Zuleikha is helpless in the face of her passionate attachment to Joseph, and she proves it by having him elicit the same passionate response from her companions. Joseph's subsequent imprisonment and elevation to nobility are also seen as predestined, as is his union with Asenath, daughter of the priest of On, city of the Sun God.

Asenath

"And he gave him as wife Asenath, daughter of Potiphar, Priest of On." (Genesis 41:45) An Egyptian reading of Asenath's name has been advanced by modern scholars. It is the Egyptian *iw.s-n-nt,* "She who is given by the goddess Neith."[35]

As I mentioned above, Joseph's marriage to the daughter of an Egyptian priest troubled the Rabbinic exegetes. For how could the favored son of Israel marry one of "the daughters of the land." One attempt at "exegetical management" of the Biblical text was to make Asenath a more acceptable wife for Joseph (and, by extension, a more acceptable mother for his children) by claiming that though brought up in the Egyptian nobleman's house, she actually was the daughter of Dinah and Shechem. An early form of this legend is found in *Pirke De R. Eliezer* (Chapter 38):

> Dinah went forth to see those girls who were making merry; and Shechem seized her, and he slept with her, and she conceived and bare Asenath. The sons of Israel said that she (the child) should be killed, for they said that now people would say in all the land that there was an immoral daughter in the tents of Jacob. What did (Jacob) do? He wrote the Holy name upon a golden plate, and suspended it about her neck and sent her away. She went her way...Michael the angel descended and took her, and brought her down to Egypt to the house of Potiphera; because Asenath was destined to become the wife of Joseph.[36]

This Midrash, which serves as a recapitulation and elaboration of Genesis 34:1, notes that Dinah "went forth to seek those girls who were making merry." In doing so it elaborates on the spare narrative of the Bible and supports the contention that

Dinah was not merely a passive participant in the ensuing drama. An earlier Midrash, Genesis Rabbah, commenting on the verse "and Dinah the daughter of Leah went out" (Genesis 34:1) portrays Dinah as a "loose woman." A more complimentary view of Dinah's behavior places her "going out" in a Mediterranean cultural context.

As C. H. Gordon pointed out in *Homer and the Bible*:

> Maidens might go strolling in search of a husband. Nausicaa is portrayed thus in Odyssey 6:1 ff., amongst her maids. It is possible that Genesis 34:1-2 reflects similar usages and should be translated: "And *Dinah*, daughter of Leah, whom the latter bore to Jacob, went out to be seen among the daughters of the land, and Shechem saw her..." (after taking her violently) Shechem became enamoured of Dinah and sought her hand in marriage.[37]

This legend places Dinah in a heroic context. Her daughter Asenath would be an appropriate spouse for Joseph, who is second only to the King and also a member of the aristocracy. Elaborations of this legend were soon to follow. In a later Midrash (Ruth Rabbah) we read:

> When Jacob and his sons, Simeon and Levi had found out that Dinah was with child by Shechem, they threatened her with death if the seed of Shechem would be borne. Therefore when the day approached on which Dinah was to give birth she went out into the wilderness. There she gave birth to a girl. She laid the child down and stationed herself weeping behind a thornbush. An eagle, whose nest was in Egypt, where it received its sustenance from the sacrifices of On, the deity of the Egyptians, carried off the child and brought it to the altar of On. On the following morning, when Potiphar, the priest of On, ascended the altar for the purpose of burning incense, he noticed the girl. He rushed back to his house in great haste and related the miracle to his wife. Both of them hastened forthwith to the temple of On, where they found the child protected by the outspread wings of the eagle. Potiphar's wife

adopted the child, secured a nurse for it, and both rejoiced exceedingly, for they were childless.[38]

This legend implicitly recognizes and emphasizes the Egyptian setting of the tale. By providing us with details that are commonly identified as Egyptian—the eagle and its outspread wings, the sacrifices, the altar, and the office of priesthood—the Midrash strives to make its embellishments authentically Egyptian, while at the same time validating the Jewish origins of the child by distancing the reader from the acceptability of marriage with non-Jews. Supporting this view of Asenath's parentage is the Midrash that explains her name as a Hebrew acronym, and not that of an Egyptian goddess:

> The Alef in Asenath stands for *On*, where Potiphar was priest; the Samek for *Setirah*, Hidden, for she was kept concealed on account of her extraordinary beauty; the Nun for *Nokemet*, for she wept and entreated that she might be delivered from the house of the heathen Potiphar; and the Taw for *Tammah*, the perfect one, an account of her pious, perfect deeds.[39]

Not all of the Rabbis granted Asenath an Israelite genealogy. Rabbi Joshua ben Levi (third century C.E.) is quoted in Genesis Rabbah as saying, "The wife of Potiphar had seen in her horoscope that she was destined to have descendants through Joseph, but she did not know that her daughter was meant."[40] The intent of the legend is to explain the ardor and persistence of Potiphar's wife, but it also indicates that Rabbi Joshua felt that Asenath actually was Potiphar's daughter and thus of Egyptian parentage. She was not a hidden daughter of Israel. That Asenath was born into the Egyptian aristocracy is the basic premise of the Hellenistic Greek text *The Prayer of Asenath*, which "presents Asenath as a model of a Jewish proselyte."

Islamic sources mention the Asenath legend only in order to deny its veracity. In his extended polemic against Jewish traditions and rituals, the eleventh century Muslim theologian and man of letters Ibn Ḥazm cites a number of aggadot about Asenath. He then proceeds to attack their veracity.

> Then they say, furthermore, in several of their books, that after Shechem, the son of Hamor, had violated

Dinah and has acted unchastely toward her, Dinah became pregnant and gave birth to a daughter, and that an eagle carried off the bastard child and brought her to Egypt, where she was placed in the chamber of Joseph, who brought her up and subsequently took her as his wife. The story resembles the lying gossip which the women utter as they sit spinning in the night.[41]

It seems that it was the more elaborate and "Egyptianized" version of the Joseph legends that Ibn Ḥazm had heard and then rejected. This legend was also rejected by the Samaritans. In the view of some scholars the Samaritan-Islamic "agreement" on this point—that it would have been out-of-the-question for Joseph to marry his sister Dinah's daughter—was the result of their commonly shared prohibition against uncle-niece marriages.[42]

Later Midrash anthologies implicitly reject the Asenath-as-daughter of Dinah legend. In the following legend, Joseph presents Jacob with a *ketubah*, a marriage contract, to prove that his marriage to Asenath is sanctioned by Jewish law.

> Jacob saw that when he wanted to bless them (Joseph's sons) the Shekhinah left him. When Jacob saw this he thought that they might be unfit for a blessing. He said to Joseph, "Who are they?"..."They are my sons." This teaches us that he brought [as evidence] his *ketubah* from Asenath.[43]

Here Jacob expresses doubts as to the legitimacy of Jacob's marriage to Asenath and questions whether his grandchildren were to be accepted into the lineage. If Joseph's wife was an Israelite he would have no such doubts; the *ketubah* is produced to demonstrate that Asenath has become a halakhically acceptable wife.

The anthologies that quote this legend were composed after the twelfth century. Therefore, "it is possible that in this rejection of our narration (the Asenath-Dinah legend) the influence of Ibn Ḥazm's attacks is manifest."[44] It may be that Jewish sources, influenced by Muslim attacks on some Aggadic traditions, shied away from presenting Asenath as Dinah's daughter. If this is so, it provides another example of the "feedback" mechanism that existed between Jewish and Islamic lore. In this instance we are witnesses to one Jewish source's rejection of a legend as a response to polemical attack from non-Jewish sources.

Perhaps the most intriguing legend about Asenath is one that ties her directly to the Potiphar's Wife episode. As we saw in chapter 2, Joseph, accused by his master's wife, was vindicated in a number of ways. Jewish legends provide us with the names of witnesses who come forth to testify to Joseph's innocence. In some stories these witnesses are unnamed children. According to one Midrash:

> Asenath had saved Joseph's life while she was still an infant in arms. When Joseph was accused of immoral conduct by Potiphar's wife and the other women, and his master was on the point of having him hanged, Asenath approached her foster-father, and she assured him under oath that the charge against Joseph was false.[45]

In the Qur'ān we read that it was an unnamed person, "a witness of her folk" who bore witness to Joseph's innocence. It was she who suggested that the condition of Joseph's shirt— whether it was torn from behind or in front—should determine who is telling the truth. The Qur'ānic commentators cite many opinions on who this witness was. Some say that it was a female cousin of Zuleikha, while others say that it was a child in its cradle. But as the Qur'ān does not speak of Joseph's marriage to his master's daughter (a union mentioned only in Jewish sources), there was no narrative impulse to link this child witness to the woman who would become Joseph's wife.[46]

In reward for her defense of Joseph, God promises Asenath that she will be the mother of Joseph's children. That Joseph is rewarded for his chastity when, later in life, he is given a beautiful wife, is an idea underscored by this legend, which makes Joseph's future wife, Asenath, the witness who vindicates him when he is accused by Potiphar's wife. A further delightful twist is provided by the author of *The Prayer of Asenath*, the second century C.E. Greek work. He relates that "the son of Pharaoh was so transported with Asenath's beauty, that he made the plan of murdering Joseph in order to secure possession of his wife." The plot is foiled by Joseph's brothers, Simon and Levi, those same brothers who destroyed the city of Shechem to avenge their sister's honor.[47]

In one legend Joseph pays a great and final tribute to his wife Asenath, while at the same time linking her fate with that of his mother Rachel. As part of his request to his brothers that they bury him in the land of his fathers he asks them to bury Asenath in Rachel's tomb beside the road to Ephrath.[48]

Seraḥ

In Jewish tradition, as reflected in both the Biblical text and the aggadaic elaborations, a number of people are granted immortality. Prominent among them are two men, Enoch (Genesis 5:25) and Elijah (II Kings 2:1). According to the Rabbinic tradition, the only woman to appear in this select company is Seraḥ, daughter of Asher. In a Midrash, we learn that she was rewarded for her kindness to Jacob. When his sons returned from the second encounter with Joseph in Egypt, they did not know how to break the good news to their father:

> "On coming close to their habitation, they caught sight of Seraḥ, daughter of Asher, a very beautiful maiden, and very wise, who was skilled in playing upon the harp. They summoned her unto them and gave her a harp, and bade her play before Jacob and sing that which they should tell her. She sat down before Jacob, and, with an agreeable melody she sang the following words, accompanying herself upon the harp: 'Joseph, my uncle, liveth, he ruleth over the whole of Egypt, he is not dead.' She repeated these words several times, and Jacob grew more and more pleasurably excited. His joy awakened the holy spirit in him and he knew that she spoke the truth...Jacob rewarded her with the words, 'My daughter, may death never have power over thee, for thou didst revive my spirit.' And so it was, Seraḥ did not die, she entered Paradise alive."[49]

Seraḥ's *kayd*, in contrast to that of the other women of our story, is of a gentler kind. She uses a deceptively sweet medium —words set to music—to deliver a shocking, though joyful, message: that Joseph still lives. That Seraḥ was immortal seems to have been suggested to the aggadist by the inconsistencies between the Biblical verses in which she is mentioned:

"She is counted among the seventy members of the patriarch's family who emigrated from Canaan to Egypt (Genesis 46:17), and her name occurs in connection with the census taken by Moses in the wilderness (Numbers 26:46)...The fact of her being the only one of her sex to be mentioned in the genealogical lists seemed to the Rabbis to indicate that there was something extraordinary in connection with her history."[50]

For the Aggadists, the fact that she was counted both among the people going down into Egypt, and among those leaving it during the Exodus, had to be resolved. In the aggadaic imagination the only possible solution to this problem was the assumption that Seraḥ was immortal. Therefore, she was able to span the four hundred and thirty year gap between the descent into Egypt and the Exodus from it.

Despite this exegetical basis for her saga, Seraḥ's tale is a Rabbinic story, not a Biblical one. In the numerous legends that arose about her, Seraḥ is portrayed as both a beauty and a member of the aristocracy, qualities she shares with the other women of the Joseph tales. In the following Midrash, Seraḥ's origins are "worthy of saga,":

Asher's first wife was Adon, the daughter of Ephlal, a grandson of Ishmael. She died childless, and he married a second wife, Hadorah, a daughter of Abimael, the grandson of Shem. She had been married before, her first husband having been Malchiel, also a grandson of Shem, and the issue of his first marriage was a daughter, Seraḥ by name. When Asher brought his wife to Canaan, the three year old orphan Seraḥ came with them. She was raised in the house of Jacob, and she walked in the way of pious children, and God gave her beauty, wisdom, and sagacity."[51]

Of note in this Midrash are parallels to the descriptions of the other women in both the scriptural and post-scriptural Joseph tales.

1) Like Tamar, Seraḥ is portrayed as descended from Shem, son of Noah. (In fact she is granted double "Semitic"

lineage in that her mother's first husband was also a descendant of Shem's.)

2) Like Asenath (as she is portrayed in those legends that claim her as the daughter of Dinah), Seraḥ is an adopted child.

3) Seraḥ is granted, "beauty, wisdom, and sagacity," qualities that are attributed to the other women in these tales and, in fact, to Joseph himself.

From the many legends about Seraḥ, we can construct a short biography. She grows up in Jacob's house, "whose affection she won by her remarkable piety and virtue."[52] She must also have won his trust, for Jacob comes to believe her when she gently, but repeatedly, tells him that Joseph is alive.[53] Her role in announcing Joseph's place among the living is replicated in the legends about Joseph's bones. Just as she was able to bear witness that Joseph was among the living, she was later able to expedite his return and burial to the land of his fathers by identifying his place among the dead. Legends gives her the credit for recovering Joseph's remains and thereby enabling the Hebrews to fulfill their vow to Joseph and leave Egypt. The magical powers attributed to Seraḥ are related to her beauty and immortality, and she uses these powers to help Moses recover Joseph's bones as the Israelites leave Egypt. In our concluding chapter "Joseph's Bones: Linking Canaan and Egypt," we will assess the wider implications of this tale of recovery, burial, and enshrinement.

In the Islamic versions of her story Seraḥ is not given a name but is called "the old woman of the children of Israel." In al-Ṭabarī's *History* a spare, concise version is extant. In al-Thaʿlabī's legends, as in Midrash, the woman is blessed with eternal youth. But this "youth" is granted as a reward for her help in finding Joseph's bones; it is only after the recovery of the coffin that her youthful beauty is restored.

Al-Ṭabarī's version tells of the Israelites' confusion after they had crossed the sea. They could not proceed on their journey and Moses enquired of the elders as to the cause of the problem. They told him of the promise to take Joseph's bones and concluded that with that promise unfulfilled they could not make their way out of the desert. None of the men could help Moses with his search. An "old woman of the Children of Israel," who heard them talking, offered to help if Moses would grant her a place in paradise. He agreed to her request, carried her to the banks of the Nile, and together they retrieved the coffin. Al-Tha'labī cites a similar version and follows it with a more fanciful coda. In it the old woman asks for a place in paradise and the restoration of her youth and beauty. Moses is reluctant to grant her both of these requests, but God tells him to give her what she wishes.

In this story from al-Tha'labī's *Tales of the Prophets*, we see the "old woman" transformed as the result of her cooperating with Moses. This is in marked distinction to the Jewish legends in which she is graced with beauty from birth (a beauty which is "eternal") and helps Moses on her own volition. As the frame of reference in the Jewish tales is Biblical, the storyteller assumes that Seraḥ, who was among the first Hebrews in Egypt, would know of the brothers' promise to redeem Joseph's bones, and that she had already been rewarded for her part in telling Jacob that Joseph still lived. She does not have to be convinced of the importance of her mission. In the Islamic traditions, the woman who finds Joseph's remains is not identified as a member of Jacob's family. She is not the woman who brought the good tidings to Jacob. She has to be convinced of the importance of the task and rewarded for her assistance. The motif of restored youth remained in the transmitted folklore, but it was transferred to the end of the story.

According to Jewish sources, Seraḥ reappeared in Biblical history during David's reign. She is identified with the wise woman who saves the town of Abel-beth-maacah by surrendering up the head of Sheba, the son of Bichri, to Joab (II Samuel 20:14–22).[54] Why the aggadists assigned Seraḥ this role is not clear, though it is true that an unnamed Biblical personage virtually cries out to be named, and that Seraḥ would seem an appropriate choice. Granted immortality she is available for the role, a role similar to the one that she plays in the Joseph tales. In both incidences she "saves the day;" in Egypt through her memory of how and where Joseph was buried and her mastery of magic and incantations; in Abel-beth-maacah through her mastery of diplomacy and her eloquence. When the wise woman addresses Joab her speech has an incantatory quality: "Then she spoke saying: They were wont to speak in old times, saying: they shall surely ask council at Abel; and so they ended the matter." (II Samuel 20:18). While Joab's response is recorded in prose, the wise woman's words are in poetry. She is not only a woman of eloquence but also a woman of action. She goes to the people and has them throw Sheba's head to Joab, thus ending the siege and saving "a mother city" in Israel.[55]

Though Serah is granted immortality in both the Jewish and Islamic traditions this did not prevent her from being assigned a tomb. For the immortal saint cannot be venerated if a site of pilgrimage isn't provided. Her tomb was said to be in the Persian city of Isfahan.

> Isfahan is also the seat of one of the most revered Jewish "holy sites" and a place of pilgrimage and prayer for all the Persian Jews. It has in its vicinity, in Pir Bakran, the alleged tomb and sanctuary of Serah bat Asher ben Yaqub...visiting holy places and tombs was widespread also among the Jews in Persia, who used to make the pilgrimages to the alleged tomb of Mordechai and Esther in Hamadam, to the tomb of Daniel in Susa, and to the burial places of other Biblical heroes alleged to be on Persian soil.[56]

This predilection for visiting the tombs of holy personages is characteristic of the folkways of Shi'ite Islam. It also typifies, to a lesser degree, habits of pilgrimage among Sunni Muslims and the Jews of the Muslim world. Each town in the sphere of Persian Islam competed for the distinction of being the final resting place of a saint. Supplication at one of these tombs was believed to be efficacious in fulfilling specific requests, *e.g.*, curing an illness, conceiving children, safeguarding the welfare of the family. For both Jews and Muslims, a visit to the tomb of Serah was seen as assuring longevity, as well as granting supplicants the renewal of beauty and the restoration of youthful vigor.

The legends that surround the figure of Serah—stories of immortality, magical power, the sanctity and power of the saint's remains—are familiar elements in popular religious folklore. Serah, though mentioned twice in the Bible, and then only in passing, becomes a fully developed literary character through the accretion of detail about her very long life. Like both Enoch and Elijah, she is a character who appears at times when Jews are in peril. And like Elijah, whose cave on Mt. Carmel is a site of pilgrimage and supplication, her burial place has taken on an aura of sanctity and power.

Seraḥ's portrayal in Midrash, a portrayal that mixes the heroic and the pietistic—she is both a great beauty and one who can "awaken the holy spirit" in her grandfather Jacob—serves to remind us that Joseph, too, will be remembered in death as he was celebrated, and elevated, in life. The other women of the narratives, Rachel, Tamar, Asenath, and Potiphar's wife, are fully drawn in the Biblical saga. In the hands of the storytellers the edges of these characters are softened somewhat. Their power and agency is diminished and their behavior is valorized as pietistic rather than heroic. Seraḥ, brought up in Jacob's house, "walked in the way of pious children," and Asenath is dubbed "the perfect one, on account of her pious, perfect deeds." But not all of their heroic characteristics are obscured; the aggadists saw fit to assign Seraḥ to the role of the wise woman who saves the city of Abel-beth-maacah by surrendering the head of the rebel Sheba to Joab, the commander of David's army.

In constructing an inclusive and cogent narrative of Biblical history some aggadists found it necessary to include all of the women of the tales within the people of Israel. In the cases of Tamar and Asenath, both of whom are described in Genesis as daughters of foreigners, their inclusion in the people Israel is rendered more plausible by attributing to them an Israelite genealogy. Parallel Islamic legends tell of Potiphar's wife, repenting of her sins, and living out her life as a pious Muslim.[57]

But it was not only in the bloom of youth that Joseph exerted a fascination on the women and men who encountered him. Later in life, when he ruled over Egypt, one Midrash relates that the daughters of Egypt "crawled over the walls" to get a glimpse of him. Most intriguing is the singular fact that even after telling of his death and burial, storytellers concerned themselves with the fate of the *physical* Joseph. In a development that is unique in Jewish lore, Joseph's bones become, for a time, sacred relics in a culture that discouraged the reverence for the reliquary. In our final chapter, I will examine and analyze three aspects of this unique body of lore: the reverence accorded Joseph's remains, the development of his tomb as a locus of pilgrimage, and the notion that Joseph's descendants are immune to the effects of the "evil eye." In a strikingly similar manner, each of these links to Joseph are centered on the Potiphar's Wife motif.

A Repentant Zuleikha Meets Joseph

6

Joseph's Bones:
Linking Canaan and Egypt

In the desert Israel carried two shrines with them, one the
coffin containing the bones of the dead man Joseph, the
other the ark containing the covenant of the living God.
Mekilta de Rabbi Ishmael
(c. 500 C.E.)

Joseph's Bones

Genesis ends with Joseph's announcement to his brothers
of his impending death. He then puts them under oath that
they will carry his bones to Canaan when they are delivered
from Egypt (Genesis 50:24–25). Joseph's interment, and the
text's concern for the fate of his remains, occupies a pivotal
point in Biblical narrative, for it represents the culmination of
the Patriarchal period in Hebrew tradition. The eventual deposi-
tion of Joseph's remains is the subject of two additional Biblical
references (one in Exodus and one in the Book of Joshua), both
of which occur at structurally significant points in the text.
Joseph's resistance to Potiphar's wife is not alluded to in these
short posthumous references to Joseph's remains. But this did
not deter the authors and compilers of Midrash and Qiṣaṣ from
placing that fateful incident in center stage when they came to
explain the extraordinary attention payed to Joseph's bones.

The three Biblical references which speak of Joseph's remains
are:

1) The closing verse of Genesis, which reflects the Egyptian
setting of the tale:

Joseph died at the age of 110 years. He was embalmed and laid to rest in a coffin in Egypt.

(Genesis 50:26)

As we noted in chapter 1, 110 years was considered by
the Egyptians to be the ideal life span, and this notion
parallels the Hebrew ideal of 120 years, an ideal based
on Genesis 6, and on Moses' death at that age.[1] The
Talmud and the classical Jewish commentaries seem
unaware of the Egyptian background of the age of 110 as
an ideal life span. They viewed Joseph's demise as a *premature one.* For, compared to Abraham, Isaac, and Jacob
he died at a relatively "early age." The rabbis attributed
this "punishment" it to a number of causes. The Talmud
states:

Why did Joseph die before his brethren? Because he
assumed airs of authority.[2]

Elsewhere, the Talmud views Joseph's early death as
the result of the burdens of public office. This is in keeping
with the dictum that, "Dominion buries him that exercises
it,"[3] and is an intriguing example of the recognition in
antiquity of the effects of work-related stress.

The Bible's terse description of the burial and em-
balming of Joseph is in sharp contrast to the more elaborate rites conducted for Jacob (Genesis 50:1-13). While
Jacob insisted on immediate burial in Canaan, Joseph did
not. His speech to his brothers has a prophetic quality to
it:

When God has taken notice of you, be sure to take
up my bones from here.

(Genesis 50:25)

That is to say, when you are delivered...then you shall
bring my bones.[4]

Most Islamic sources, not influenced by the Biblical
reference to 110 years, state that Joseph was 120 years
old when he died.[5] This divergence from the Biblical
statement is consistent with the fact that Sūrat Yūsuf

does not concern itself with Joseph's later years or with his death. Rather, it focuses on his rise to power, his relationship with his master's wife and his reunion with his brothers. This was the material that held the greatest import for Muḥammad and the community of believers, other events in Joseph's life are omitted or glossed over. Though these "omitted" aspects of the Joseph story may later be taken up in Islamic legends, they do not merit attention in the Qur'ān's narrative. And when these aspects are discussed in Islamic texts, it is not necessarily the Biblical chronology that dominates the choice of detail. Some Muslim historians were familiar with the Biblical verses on the death of Joseph and offered the Biblical details as another version of the story. After citing the tradition that Joseph died at the age of 120, Ṭabari notes that "in the Torah it is said that he lived one hundred and ten years, and that Ephraim and Manasseh were born to him."[6]

Let us continue our analysis of the Bible's treatment of Joseph's bones. As we have seen Genesis 50:25 links two events, the promised deliverance from Egypt and the removal of Joseph's bones. This link is later confirmed and strengthened by the two other Biblical references to Joseph's remains.

2) In Exodus 13:19, "And Moses took the bones of Joseph with him," we read of the fulfillment of Joseph's wish. Structurally, this verse serves as the end of the Egyptian bondage narrative; the removal of the bones is Moses' last act on Egyptian soil.

3) The final Biblical mention of the bones also appears at a critical juncture in Biblical narrative. At the end of the book of Joshua we are told of the burial of the bones, "And the bones of Joseph, which the children of Israel brought up out of Egypt, they buried in Shechem" (Joshua 24:32).

This description of the final interment of Joseph closes the conquest and settlement narratives. Joseph's bones thus link the period of the patriarchs, with its roots in Mesopotamia, the Hebrew bondage in the land of Egypt, and the conquest and settlement of Canaan. As G. W. Coats noted, "The death report about Joseph, with

its bond concerning Joseph's bones as part of the move
back to Canaan, expands the Joseph tradition into the
future stages of Israel's life on the land."[7]

This link is implied by the placement of the verses cited, and
it was elaborated upon in post-Biblical legend. Though the
classical Jewish commentaries do not draw our attention to the
Bible's placement of the three references to the bones, they do
recognize the symbolic function of Joseph's remains, and they
do so by imputing to the bones magical properties. The bones
are treated as relics, though this is antithetical in spirit to
Deuteronomy 34:6 where Moses' burial place is concealed, as
many Jewish commentators understood, in order to prevent his
bones from becoming relics.

Genesis Rabbah links Moses treatment at the hands of God
with his own treatment of Joseph's remains: "The Holy One,
blessed be he, said to Moses: In thee is fulfilled the verse: 'The
wise in heart will receive commandments.' (Proverbs 10:8)
Joseph was in duty bound to bury his father, being a son, but
thou, though neither his son nor his grandson, has occupied
thyself with his burial. So will I too occupy myself with thy
burial, though I am not obliged to do so for anyone."

As we shall see in our discussions of magic in the Joseph
legends, much of the supernatural material concerning Joseph's
life stems from the legends concerning his death and burial.
Appropriately, it is the magic of the Egyptians, in Rabbinic
literature the magicians *par excellence*, that is invoked in these
stories.

> For three days and three nights preceding the exodus
> Moses hunted up and down through the land of Egypt
> for Joseph's coffin, because he knew that Israel could
> not leave Egypt without heeding the oath given to
> Joseph. But his trouble was in vain; the coffin was
> nowhere to be found. Serah, the daughter of Asher, met
> Moses, tired and exhausted, and in answer to her
> question about the cause of his weariness, he told her of
> his fruitless search. Serah took him to the Nile river, and
> told him that the leaden coffin made for Joseph by the
> Egyptians had been sunk there after having been sealed

up on all sides. The Egyptians had done this at the instigation and with the help of the magicians, who, knowing that Israel could not leave the country without the coffin, had used their arts to put it in a place whence it could not be removed.

Another early Midrash adds, "The Egyptians had sunk the coffin in the Nile, so that its waters should be abundant."[8] Through magic this would ensure the "abundance" of the river, the periodic inundation of the Nile. And a third aggadaic source tells us that Joseph's brothers, and not the Egyptian, "sank the coffin in the Nile to prevent the Egyptians from worshipping it."[9]

The use of Joseph's coffin to ensure Egypt's fertility also appears in Islamic folklore. Al-Bayḍāwī, in his commentary on Sūrat Yūsuf, tells us that:

...the Egyptians disputed about Yūsuf's burial place until they were on the verge of fighting, so they decided to place him in a marble sarcophagus and bury him in the Nile in such a way that the water would pass over him and thereafter reach all of Egypt. Then the Egyptians would all be on an equal footing in regard to him.[10]

(That is, they would all benefit from the blessings associated with his remains.)

As the coffin had magical qualities, it could be recovered only by a person who was a master of the magical *praxis*. For the Jewish aggadist, Seraḥ, daughter of Asher, was an appropriate choice as magician. As we have seen in the previous chapter, she was deemed immortal, and at the time of the Exodus she was hundreds of year old but still retained her youthful beauty. As the sole survivor of the entourage that entered Egypt with Jacob (Genesis 46:5–7), she was the only one who knew the whereabouts of Joseph's coffin and how to go about recovering it. Seraḥ gives Moses explicit instructions on the correct praxis to be employed. It includes 1) a physical act: Moses is to cut up Joseph's silver cup (the cup hidden in Benjamin's sack mentioned in Genesis 43:2) and throw each of the pieces of it into the Nile. This is to be followed by 2) an incantation specific to the occasion: "Joseph, Joseph, the hour for the redemption has arrived." The formula was successful and Moses joyfully carries off the coffin.[11] E. Goodenough has argued that this magical recovery motif is related to a tendency within Hellenistic Judaism and early Christianity to equate Joseph with Osiris, the Egyptian god who is identified with both death and the forces of renewal in the universe. The identification of Joseph with Osiris situates the legends of the bones in an Hellenistic Egyptian cultural context. Belief in the efficacy of magic, and in the power of sacred relics, permeates these later Joseph legends. Later in this chapter we shall have the opportunity to trace the identification of Joseph with Osiris, the Egyptian god of the dead, as well as with the composite deity Serapis.

Israel's fulfillment of the oath to return Joseph's remains to Canaan was to become a paradigm of the fulfilled promise. A thirteenth century "Jews Oath in Mamluk Egypt," which opens with a testimony of faith in God and the Law of Moses, is made up of a list of "historical" examples that serve as warnings to the unfaithful: "If what I say is not true, then may I be enslaved to Pharoah and Haman." Among these imprecations is "may I be the one who advised leaving Joseph's coffin in Egypt."[12]

The Two Shrines

After their recovery by Serah Joseph's bones become an object of veneration: In the desert Israel carried two shrines with them, one the coffin containing the bones of the dead man Joseph, the other the ark containing the covenant of the living God.

> Mekilta de Rabbi Ishmael

The Mekilta goes on to list the Ten Commandments and link each commandment to Joseph's life. Here, too, the Potiphar's Wife story takes center stage. "Here it is written, thou shalt not kill, and he refrained from murdering Potiphar when Potiphar's wife urged him to do it. Here it is written, thou shalt not commit adultery, and he scorned the adulterous proposals of Potiphar's wife."

The Midrash Hadar is extravagant in depicting the bone's magical qualities, and it blurs the distinction made above between the two shrines, that of the living and that of the dead. According to this source, Moses took Joseph's bones and wrapped them up in a sheep's skin upon which he wrote the name of God; the dead bones and the skin then came to life, and assuming the form of a sheep, it followed the camp of Israel during their wanderings through the wilderness.[13]

This vivid image of the bones resurrected through magic hearkens back to the methods used to recover the coffin: the physical act and the appropriate incantation that caused the coffin to come to the surface of the Nile are here replicated in order to bring the bones to life. This is accomplished by wrapping the bones and writing the Tetragrammaton, the ineffable name of God. The usual magical practice would be to *recite* a magic formula, in the case of the Tetragrammaton this would be forbidden; therefore, the name was *written* on the sheepskin. The Tetragrammaton could be written for sacred purposes, but on no condition could it be pronounced, even if one knew how to pronounce it.

An aura of magic and mystery surrounds the tales of Joseph's remains. Pilgrims to his tomb in Shechem were eager to experience the benefits of this magic. In a pattern familiar from medieval and modern accounts of pilgrimage to the tombs of Jewish and Muslim "saints," Joseph's tomb was the locus of pilgrimage and a site where popular religious practices flourished.

Joseph's Tomb

The bones of Joseph, which the people of Israel brought up from Egypt, were buried in Shechem, in the parcel of ground which Jacob brought from the sons of Hamor, the father of Shechem, for a hundred pieces of silver; it became an inheritance of the descendants of Joseph."

(Joshua 24:32)

M. Astour and other scholars have pointed to affinities between Shechem and other oracular-cultic centers in the Mediterranean world. Characteristic of such centers were a spring, a sacred tree, and the grave of a revered ancestor.[14]

Relying on this analysis, some scholars have attempted to link the veneration of Joseph with the Dionysus cult of Greece, and they equate the burial of Joseph's bones at Shechem with the disposition of Dionysus' bones at Delphi. Proponents of this theory see Joseph, "...not as a type, but as an archetype...In short we have to do here with no man but with the young 'Dying God.'" This interpretation is firmly grounded in Frazer's treatment of the Tammuz myth.[15] The widespread and facile application of that material to Biblical narrative has been questioned in a number of publications by U. Cassuto, C. H. Gordon, and others.[16] Their work is at odds with the "dying God" interpretation of Biblical heroes in general and of Joseph in particular. In their view, Joseph is a figure whose description is grounded in historical reality. This is attested to by the fidelity of the narrative to its Egyptian background, as indicated by the linguistic, geographic, and sociological detail of Genesis 37–50. Joseph, a heroic and pivotal figure in the life of his people, is venerated in death. Speculation that this veneration is related to the cult of Tammuz, the harvest god of the Assyrian and Babylonian pantheons, is not, according to these scholars, supported by the primary texts. Today, many scholars would agree.

Beyond the cultic associations with the shrine of Shechem, Joseph's association with the city of Shechem allowed for the development of more creative storytelling. For the associative and symbolic power of the city of Shechem was considerable. In the Biblical accounts of the conquest and settlement of Canaan, Shechem was granted to Joseph's descendants. Here, too, a Midrash forges a link to the Potiphar's Wife incident. Shechem, according to Genesis, was a gift to Joseph from Jacob. A Midrash explains why: "Shechem was his reward, because with his chastity, he stemmed the tide of immorality that burst loose in Shechem first of all." Not content with this link between two strands of the Patriarchal narratives—the rape of Dinah by Shechem in Genesis 34 and the Potiphar's Wife episode of Genesis 39, another Midrash goes on to tie both strands to a third story in Genesis, Joseph's marriage to Asenath.

> Joseph had a prior claim upon the city. Shechem, son of Hamor, the master of the city, had given it to Dinah as a present, and the wife of Joseph, Asenath, being the daughter of Dinah, the city belonged to him by right."[17]

Why was Joseph buried in Shechem? The text in Genesis 50:25 does not indicate that Joseph expressed a wish as to *where* he should be buried, only that his bones should be taken to the land of his fathers. In this he stands in marked contradistinction to Jacob, who is very specific about his burial site. In Genesis 49:29–32, Jacob states that he wishes to be buried with his fathers. He names the chosen burial site (the cave of the Machpelah), its locale (the east of Mamre), and the land in which it is situated (Canaan). Such precise identification underscores the importance of that site, and no other. Our question then is twofold: Why didn't Joseph choose Hebron if his father attached such importance to it? And if not Hebron, then why Shechem? The Talmud anticipated these questions when it had God address the tribes in this fashion, "From Shechem did you steal him, and unto Shechem you shall return him."[18] This is an interesting homiletic solution to our two questions, though not a totally satisfying one. That the Rabbis themselves were puzzled by the choice of Shechem over Hebron is indicated in a legend where we find Joseph himself expressing a wish to be buried in Hebron, a wish that was to be denied.[19] We have seen in our discussion of the women of the Joseph story that according to one legend Jacob's request to bury Rachel in Hebron was also denied.

These two conflicting elements in Jewish lore, the unequivocal, textual reference to Shechem as Joseph's burial place, and the aggadic material about Hebron as a wished for burial site, may account for the unusual treatment of the topic in Islamic tradition. The Qur'ān itself makes no mention of Joseph's death or burial; these details are beyond the scope of the Sura. Islamic tradition cites Shechem-Nablus as the primary site of Joseph's tomb, though the site of Joseph's tomb is later identified as being in the "Ḥaram al-Khalīl" in Hebron. Its location there is very specifically identified by some early Muslim geographers, and at the present time, a Mosque of Joseph is situated in the precincts of Hebron Haram.[20]

The Islamic tradition that Joseph was buried in Hebron may be the result of 1) the persistence of an aggadic tradition that Joseph wished to be buried in Hebron and the logical assumption that as a "nabī" (prophet), his wish would be fulfilled. 2) Islamic reaction to the Samaritan claims concerning Joseph's tomb. As the Samaritans claimed descent from Joseph, they elevated Joseph's tomb in their holy city of Shechem to a position of great sanctity. The Samaritan chronicles, as quoted by James A. Montgomery in his pioneering work on the sect, records a series of conflicts with Christians over possession of the site:

"The Christians came and attempted to carry off Joseph's bones in order to transport them to their own cities. This undertaking was frustrated by miracles, including a wondrous light and cloud and finally they contented themselves with building a church over the spot. This was destroyed by the Samaritans, and the community bought itself off from the punishment only through payment of a fine. Thereupon, they made the tomb inaccessible for all time."[21]

The historical validity of this chronicle is not relevant to our discussion, but Samaritan reverence for the shrine is. This reverence may have influenced the early Islamic tradition that *rejected* this notion and in turn claimed that the tomb had to be a site other than Nablus-Shechem. The implication is that the Samaritans could not be correct in their choice of Nablus as its site, and Joseph's tomb is no doubt found with those of his ancestors in Hebron.

That the Qur'ān and the early *ḥadīth* may have influenced by Samaritan material has been suggested by M. Gaster, who cited examples of possible Samaritan influence on Qur'ān and Hadith.[22] And we have seen in our discussion of Joseph's marriage to Asenath that Islamic and Samaritan sources, united in their common opposition to uncle-niece marriages, both rejected one Jewish claim that Asenath was the daughter of Dinah and Shechem.

But on other issues, such as the location of Joseph's tomb, Islamic sources take exception to Samaritan claims. J. Finkel has pointed out that some enigmatic references in the Qur'ān may be understood as *reactions against Samaritan claims.* Finkel explains Sura 2:95 and its commentaries, that imply that Solomon was *not* an evil magician, as Muḥammad's response to Samaritan anti-Solomonic propaganda.[23] In a similar fashion, I would explain early Islamic insistence on Hebron as the site of Joseph's tomb as a reaction against the Samaritan tradition. If the Samaritans insist that Joseph's tomb is in *their* cultic center, Schechem, the "authentic" tomb must be elsewhere. Had not the Rabbis expressed "misgivings" about the choice of Shechem when they had Joseph request burial in Hebron?

The classical Muslim geographers describe Joseph's purported burial site in the Ḥaram al-Khalil of Hebron with great detail. 'Ali of Herat visited the site in 1119 A.D. and described the opening of the tomb by one of the Fatimid Caliphs:

> Joseph's tomb is situated on the west...over which they have built a beautiful dome. On this site, where the ground is level, that is, beyond the sepulchre of Joseph, lies a great cemetery, wither they bring the dead from many parts to be buried.[24]

As was often the case with the tombs of saints, great merit accrued from interment near Joseph's sepulchre.

Yāqūt (d. 1229), writing a century later, first quotes 'Ali of Herat and other earlier travelers, and then goes on to add the embellishment that the Ḥaram was built by Solomon:

> In the cave is the tomb of Adam, and behind the enclosure is that of Joseph. Joseph's body was brought hither by Moses, having at first been buried in the middle of the Nile. The cave is under the earth, the enclosure is above and around it, most strongly built.[25]

In Yāqūt's report, we have a combination of two folkloric elements: the attribution of the structure to Solomon and the reference to the Biblical (and later Islamic) tales of the recovery of Joseph's bones.

Ibn Battuta (d. 1369), the most famed of Muslim geographers, visited Hebron in the mid-fourteenth century, and his account adds a charming detail to Yāqūt's report. "The Ḥaram at Hebron is built of hewn stone...it is said to have been built by Solomon, aided by the Jinn."[26] This Ḥaram was only one of many monumental sites attributed to the Jinn. In al-Tha'labī's *Tale of Bilqis*, the Jinn are ordered by Solomon to build castles in the Yemen for Bilqis, the Biblical Queen of Sheba. "The height and beauty of these structures awed all who saw them."[27] Similarly, some peasants in nineteenth century Egypt were convinced that the ancient Egyptian monuments had been built by the Jinn.[28] Though it may seem inconsistent to the modern reader, the same geographers quoted earlier also cite traditions that place Joseph's tomb in Nablus. 'Ali of Herat writes, "There is also near Nablus the spring of Al Khidr (Elijah) and the field of Yūsuf; further, Yūsuf is buried at the foot of the tree at this place, and this is the true story." And again, later, Yāqūt says, "Yūsuf is buried in Balatah (near Nablus)...and his tomb is well known, lying under the tree."[29]

These inconsistencies did not seem to bother the geographers or their readers. It is a known phenomenon in popular Middle Eastern religion that a holy man or woman can have more than one tomb. In the case of Joseph, a third site, near Beit Ijaza, is also mentioned by later geographers.[30] These competing sites all claim to be authentic; they are not to be confused with the cenotaphs of the Greco-Roman world, which were monuments to illustrious people who were buried elsewhere.

A point on which all of the reports concur is that Joseph's tomb was a place of pilgrimage, a desirable place to be buried near, and the focus of magical practices. This reverence for Joseph's tomb was shared by Jews, Christians, Samaritans, and Muslims, and pilgrimage to the tomb has survived into the modern era. The practices allied with pilgrimage to the site are remarkably similar and they demonstrate a degree of cultural continuity between the late medieval world and the nineteenth and twentieth centuries. The following examples will serve to illustrate this point:

Jewish practices: A nineteenth-century British traveler, Miss M. E. Rogers, visited Joseph's tomb in Nablus in 1870 and left us a detailed description of the site. She describes plastered pillars of stone that are set up next to the tomb:

These pillars are eighteen inches in diameter, and resemble rude altars. In the shallow basins thus formed I have seen traces of fire, as if votive offerings had recently been burnt there. It is said that small objects, such as kerchiefs of embroidered muslin or silk shawls and other trifles are occasionally sacrificed at this tomb by the Jews.[31]

Samaritan practices: In his chapter on "The Modern Samaritans" (c. 1900) J. A. Montgomery discusses their treatment of the dead:

The Samaritans appear to-day to make a point of forgetting their dead, and have no subsequent commem-

orations, except their visits to the tombs of the Patriarchs...*They are said to share with the Jews the custom
of burning combustible items at Joseph's tomb.*[32]

Muslim practices: G. E. Wright (*Shechem*, 1954) describes the village of Balatah (near Nablus) as a place:

...which is supposed to house the tomb of Joseph. Here
today women with their children come once or twice a
week, sometimes from considerable distances, for an all
day picnic and song festival whenever there is something
to celebrate. Here, too, individual women not infrequently
came to pray when facing trouble of one kind or another.[33]

Joseph's tomb became a focus for the practices of "popular
religion." Practices allied to magic, such as presenting "burnt
offerings" of cloth, singing and chanting, were engaged in at this
sacred spot. It became a center for both private and public
attempts at intercession with the divine through the personage
of Joseph. For, as I demonstrated earlier, the living Joseph was
depicted in the folklore as a master magician; and one that
excelled as a magician in a land that was the "home of magic."
The living Joseph was intimately connected with magical *praxis*;
in the same fashion, his tomb was perceived as possessing
magical power. In many Jewish and Islamic legends the origins
of this spiritual and magical power lie in Joseph's resistance to
the advances of Potiphar's wife. The reverence accorded Joseph's
remains during the wandering in the desert, when his bones
were carried in a shrine, was understood to be his reward for
chastity. His burial in Shechem, and the assignment of that city
to his heirs is also linked to the Potiphar's Wife motif, for
Joseph's chastity is contrasted with the sexual abandon of
Shechem and its rulers. The city's punishment—the men of
Shechem, whose prince had raped Jacob's daughter Dinah,
were killed when they were weak from the pain of circumcision—further highlights the theme of sexual restraint.

Joseph's power to effect, and counter, magic is linked to the
concept of the "evil eye," a belief that also has a sexual aspect,
and we would do well to look for ties between Joseph and this
persistent and widespread folkloric belief.

Joseph and the Evil Eye

We have seen that both divine and human characteristics were attributed to Joseph. He was beautiful, wise, "well-favored," and an interpreter of dreams. In both life and death Joseph exerted a powerful charisma, and it was only natural that his name would be invoked in magical practice, most specifically in spells that serve to guard against the evil eye. In Jewish folklore, the people most susceptible to the evil eye are, "the young, the prominent, and the beautiful."[34] Joseph surely fits into all of these categories and would seem to be a highly susceptible subject. It is the *immunity* to the evil eye that is attributed to him in the folkloric material that makes the invocation of his name a protective charm. This theme runs through both the Jewish and Islamic sources.

Theories about the origins and meaning of the evil-eye concept abound. The secondary literature is massive, and, as Alan Dundes noted:

"One has an unmanageable number of sources available to consult for relevant information. There have been few attempts to explain the evil eye belief complex in terms of a holistic integrated theory...by far the majority of the discussions of the evil eye consist solely of anecdotal reporting of various incidents...But probably, *the most widely accepted theory of the evil eye contends that it is based upon envy.*[35]

The connection between the evil eye and envy is consonant with the cultures of the two Ancient Near Eastern traditions with which Joseph is associated, Mesopotamia and Egypt. These twin cultural associations are emphasized in the Biblical text. Joseph is the last of Jacob's children to be born in Aram, the Mesopotamian sphere of influence. In Genesis 30:25, Joseph's birth and the departure from Haran are inextricably linked:

After Rachel had borne Joseph, Jacob said to Laban, "Give me leave to go to my own homeland."

In a similar fashion, Joseph's descent into Egypt from Canaan is portrayed as preordained. This is implied in Genesis 39:1: "When Joseph was taken down to Egypt, a certain Egyptian, Potiphar, a courtier of Pharaoh and his chief steward, bought him from the Ishmaelites who had brought him there." Some commentators have noted the use of the passive voice in the opening phrase as implying inevitability.[36] Joseph is thus the divinely ordained link between Aram, Canaan, and Egypt. In each of these cultures the evil eye belief complex operates, though with differing degrees of centrality.

From third millenium B.C.E. Mesopotamia we have an early Sumerian text which contains an incantation against the evil eye:

> The eye *ad-gir*, the eye a man has. The eye afflicting man with evil, the *ad-gir*. Unto heaven it approached and the storm sent no rain; unto earth it approached and the fresh verdure sprang not forth.[37]

The text goes on to list areas of divine and human endeavor that the evil eye may effect deleteriously: "the growth of herds, the production of milk, the vigor of men, and the modesty of the maiden." That is, everything that might be envied by another is vulnerable to the malevolent force of the evil eye. Incantations of this sort are not uncommon in Sumerian and Akkadian literature. In Egypt, charms of this sort are known, but are not common. Gardiner quotes instances of evil eye belief in the Greco-Roman period, but these, of course, might be the product of outside influence and not from an indigenous Egyptian tradition. Other than these, he cites only two sources from Ancient Egypt: 1) the title of a book in the Edfu inventory containing "spells for driving out the eye," and 2) the end of the well-known hymn to Thoth in *The Third Anastasia Papyrus*, "O Thoth, thou shalt be my helper; so I shall not fear the eye."[38] This paucity of sources indicates that the Egyptian belief in the evil eye did not achieve the widespread dissemination that it did in Mesopotamia.

That envy is the central motivating factor in the fear of the evil eye is also made clear from the Incantation Bowl Texts of the fourth through eighth centuries C.E. In many Aramaic texts we find the phrase—"the evil and envious eye."[39] In the Mandaic texts the parallel phrase is "the evil eye and the envious and dim-seeing eye of poverty."[40]

In light of this Near Eastern background, we can trace the theme of envy operating in the Joseph tales, both in the scriptural sources and in the later aggadaic elaborations. Envy is the narrative engine of the tale. The brothers' envy is unabashed, and in Genesis 37:4, clearly stated:

> When his brothers saw that their father loved him more than any of his other sons they came to hate him so much that they could not say a kind word to him.

Envy is further highlighted in Genesis 37:11:

> But while his brothers were wrought up at him, his father pondered the matter.

and in Qur'ān 12:7:

> Surely Joseph and his brother are dearer to our father than we.

This is followed in the Qur'ān by:

> Our father is in manifest error.

Baiḍawi highlights the emotion of envy in his comment on the phrase "in manifest error":

> ...because of his preferring that which is inferior; or because of his unfairness in loving. There is a tradition that Joseph was dearer to Jacob because of the "signs" which Jacob saw in him, and his brothers envied him. So when Joseph had seen the vision, Jacob's love increased to such an extent that he could not bear to be parted from him, and their envy was intensified until it impelled them to make an attempt on him.[41]

Though the immediate consequences of the brothers' envy are dire—he is thrown into the pit and sold into slavery—Joseph eventually overcomes the effect of the "eye" and rises to prominence. But other eyes are later cast on him. Potiphar's wife's attraction to Joseph is described by the idiom (In Speiser's apt translation), "His master's wife fixed her eye on Joseph." (Genesis 39:7)[42]

Before his brothers express their envy, and long before Potiphar's wife fixed her eyes on him, an incident occurred in

Joseph's life which an early Midrash presents as a foreshadowing of Joseph's protective power. Chased by his angry brother Esau, Joseph's father Jacob divides his family into separate groupings, placing each of the mothers with their children. When each group presented itself to Esau, the mother of that group came forth first, followed by her children. But in Rachel's case, the text implies that Joseph walked in front of his mother. (Genesis 33.7) In doing so "he was protecting her from the lascivious eyes of Esau, for which Joseph was rewarded through the exemption of his descendants from the spell of the evil eye."[43]

Because Joseph overcomes the effect of all of these eyes, he is later perceived to be immune to the effects of the evil eye. This is a unique conflation of the idea of the eyes as sexually powerful, and the eye as symbolizing envy. Here again, as with the sanctity of his bones and the cultic significance of his tomb, his resistance to Potiphar's wife is of paramount significance in the development of the elaborations of scripture. The motif of chastity is retrojected back to his mother Rachel, with whom Joseph was so often identified. In protecting his mother from her brother-in-law's covetous gaze he is foreshadowing his own ability to resist sexual temptation.

The Babylonian Talmud (Berakhot 20a) relates that the descendants of Joseph are immune from the effects of the evil eye. The Rabbis support this contention with a scriptural reference to Jacob's blessing of Joseph in Genesis 49:22, (Joseph is a fruitful vine, a fruitful vine by a fountain):

> R. Giddal was accustomed to go and sit at the gates of the bathing place. He used to say to the women (who came to bathe): Bathe thus, or bathe thus. The rabbis said to him: Is not the Master afraid lest his passion get the better of him?—He replied: They look to me like so many white geese. R. Johanan was accustomed to go and sit at the gates of the bathing place. He said: When the daughters of Israel come up from bathing they look at me and they have children as handsome as I am. Said the Rabbis to him: Is not the Master afraid of the evil eye?—He replied: *I come from the seed of Joseph, over whom the evil eye has not power, as it is written: Joseph is a fruitful vine, a fruitful vine above the eye, and*

R. Abbahu said with regard to this, do not read 'ale 'ayin
but 'ole 'ayin. R. Judah son of R. Hanina derived it from
the text: And let them multiply like fishes [we-yidgu] in
the midst of the earth. Just as fishes [dagim] in the sea
are covered by water and the evil eye has no power over
them, so the evil eye has no power over the seed of
Joseph. Or, if you prefer, I can say: The evil eye has no
power over the eye which refused to feed itself on what
did not belong to it.[44]

In the digressions that follow this statement, the Talmud
implies that even if one is not actually a descendant of Joseph,
one can dissimulate and claim such descent to protect oneself
from the evil eye. Here, too, the same word-play on the Biblical
verse is used to make the point:

If a man on going into a town is afraid of the evil eye,
let him take the thumb of his right hand in his left hand
and the thumb of his left hand in his right hand, and
say: I, so and so, am of the seed of Joseph over which
the evil eye has no power, as it says: "Joseph is a fruitful
vine, a fruitful vine by a fountain." Do not read 'ale 'ayin
[by a fountain] but 'ole 'ayin [overcoming the evil eye]. R.
Jose b. R. Hanina derived it from here: "And let them
grow into a multitude [we-yidgu] in the midst of the
earth;" just as the fishes [dagim] in the sea are covered
by the waters, and the evil eye has no power over them,
so the evil eye has not power over the seed of Joseph. If
he is afraid of his own evil eye, he should look at the
side of his left nostril.[45]

Islamic sources echo this belief in the protective power of
Joseph's name. That "the evil eye is a reality" is a saying
attributed to Muḥammad in the canonical collections of Hadith.
Belief in the power of al-ʿayn, "the eye" was widespread in the
Islamic world and "it frequently finds expression both in
religious traditions and in popular folklore."[46] In Islamic folklore
the very text of Sūrat Yūsuf is invoked as a protection against
envy. Commenting on the last verse of the Sura: "And a direction and mercy unto people who believe," al-Bayḍāwī comments:

There is a tradition of the Prophet, "Teach your slaves the Surah of Joseph, for if any Muslim studies it and teaches it to his household and to those whom he owns, God will lighten for him the pains of death and give him the power not to envy any other Muslim."[47]

The implication is that there are those possessed of the evil eye who have no control over it, and that they need external aid to help them control the impulse to envy. This belief in the involuntary nature of the "roving" evil eye has been noted by students of medieval and modern Middle Eastern folklore.[48]

The didactic intent of Sūrat Yūsuf is quite clear. We are reminded of that intent in the verse "And a direction and mercy unto people who believe," and it is envy that is singled out as the great pitfall. We have a veiled reference to the power of the evil eye in verse 68 in which Jacob tells his sons to enter Egypt "by different gates." The commentaries attribute this to Jacob's fear that they would attract the evil eye. A saying attributed to Muḥammad is invoked to illustrate the power of the word of God to protect one from the ʿayn, the eye.

I take refuge in God's perfect words from every evil eye and from every Satan and creeping thing.[49]

The Arabic original has the formulaic, rhymed quality of an incantation; it was obviously thought to be efficacious. Also of note is the connection made between the evil eye and the demonic.

In Genesis Rabbah we find Jacob expressing a similar fear of the eye. Commenting on Genesis 42:1 (Jacob said unto his sons: Why do you look upon one another) the Midrash says, "Do not all enter through one gate for fear of the evil eye."[50]

Mystical Aspects of Joseph's Restraint

In life, Joseph was admired for his beauty and praised for his wisdom and self-restraint. From a psychological standpoint one could say that he represents the triumph of the superego over the id, of the rational over the instinctual. This understanding of Joseph's self-reserve is manifest in Jewish mysticism: In the Kabbalistic system of the sefirot, the "ten stages of emanation that form the realm of God's manifestation in his various attributes," Joseph is identified with the *sefirah* of *yesod olam*, the "foundation of the world." When the *sefirot* are mapped on to diagrams of the male body, as they are in fourteenth century Kabbalistic texts, *yesod olam* is identified with the sexual organs. In a related development, when Biblical heroes are identified with the *sefirot*, Joseph is the manifestation of *yesod*. This is an apt identification, as Gershom Scholem has noted, for it accords with "the Talmudic picture of him as Joseph "the righteous keeper of the covenant," who resists the temptations of the sexual instinct. As the *Shomer Habrit*, the guardian of the covenant, Joseph comes to symbolize all aspects of the rite of circumcision, as well as symbolizing the sexual drive and the power to bear children. The symbolism is understood to extend not only to the people Israel, but to all of humankind."[51]

Conversely, Potiphar's wife symbolizes the "evil inclination," that lack of restraint that brings punishment down upon the world. In the Zohar's extended homily on Genesis 39 we read:

> "and much as she coaxed Joseph day after day"—this is to say the accuser (Satan) ascends every day and brings ever so many evil reports and calumnies in order to destroy mankind. "He did not yield to her request to lie beside her"—because He has compassion on the world. "To be with her"—that is, to permit the accuser to exercise dominion over the world."[52]

In the Zohar's reading we are no longer in the domain of personal passion and court intrigue. Zuleikha is here demonized, and the seduction attempt symbolizes and foreshadows a cosmic drama, one in which Satan threatens to gain dominion over mankind.

In death, with the temptations of this world behind him, Joseph is identified with the Tablets of the Law carried in the Ark, with those institutions that impose restraint on the instinctual. The image conjured up in the *Mekilta*, that of the children of Israel carrying two shrines with them, one with Joseph's bones and the other with the Tablets of the Law, reinforces this identification. As we noted earlier, the Mekilta further emphasizes this point when it links each of the Ten Commandments to episodes in Joseph's relationship with his master's wife.

In Islamic tradition, Yūsuf's restraint also takes on a mystical aspect. In the great Persian poet Jāmī's epic work *Yūsuf and Zuleikha* (written in the 1480s) Yūsuf represents divine beauty and Zuleikha the yearning human soul. Zuleikha is told by her nurse that "passion for your beauty will arise in his heart, from all his soul he will long to be united with you." To kindle that passion Zuleikha is advised to cover the walls of her bed chamber with pictures of herself and Yūsuf "sitting together like lover and beloved and embracing each other with the love of heart and soul. Here she kissed his lips; there he opened her bodice."[53] Despite the great skill with which the pictures are painted, and despite Zuleikha's attempts to bring the story told in the pictures to life, her plans are thwarted. Yūsuf remains chaste. The soul yearns for the divine; its ultimate goal, union with the divine, is elusive.

In both Judaism and Islam, the call for restraint on the model of Joseph is a call to moderate the sexual drive, not a call for its suppression. For Joseph is also the symbol of fertility and plenitude. The children of his marriage to Asenath, Ephraim and Manasseh, are the progenitors of "thousands and tens of thousands." (Deuteronomy 33:17) In Jewish and Muslim folk practice, a visit to Joseph's tomb and the invocation of his name are depicted as powerful charms for barren women who pray for children.

The amuletic use of Joseph's name persisted into the sixteenth century, when magical charms were preserved and disseminated in early printed editions of Kabbalistic manuscripts. In a copy of *Sefer Raziel* there is an illustration of an amulet[54] that invokes the name and power of Joseph in order to gain kindness and power for the person it is meant to serve. This is not only an amulet designed to protect the owner against evil, but also, to attract to him positive attributes and gain. The Biblical quote used in support of this wish is Genesis 39:21:

> God remained with Joseph; he extended kindness to
> him and disposed the chief jailer favorably toward him.

In the text of the amulet the second part of the verse is misquoted to read:

> And disposed all who see him, favorably toward him.

This extends the power of Joseph's magic. The full text of the charm reads:

> An amulet for grace and favor; write upon deer skin: "By Thy universal name of grace and favor YHVH, set They grace YHVH upon N, son of N, as it rested upon Joseph, the righteous one, as it is said, God remained with Joseph; he extended kindness to him, and disposed all who see him, favorably towards him." In the name of Michael, Gabriel, Raphael, Uriel, Kabshiel, Yah (repeated eight times), Ehyeh, Ahah (four times), Yehu (nine times).[55]

Another medieval Jewish magical practice, the use of semi-precious stones as amulets, makes reference to Joseph. In keeping with the Biblical description of the priestly breastplate, "The stones shall be according to the names of the children of Israel, twelve, according to their names," (Exodus 28:21) the Jewish commentaries assigned each stone to the eponymous anccstor of cach tribe. The first stone mentioned, 'odem, is assigned to Reuben; the remaining eleven stones are matched with the remaining eleven sons. Joseph is identified with the stone shoham, which is a protective charm.

> Shoham (onyx) This is the stone called nikli (nichilus, an agate). It is Joseph's stone and it begets grace...And it is called "shoham" these being the letters of Hashem [the divine name], in reference to the verse and "Hashem was with Joseph"...One who wears it at a gathering of people will find it useful.[56]

As was the case with the amulet reproduced in *Sefer Raziel*, the power of the stone is perceived as a positive one, one that will bring gain and respect. The user is encouraged to wear it when speaking in public or performing administrative duties.

In a form of word-play common in magical practice, *shoham* is viewed as an allusion to *hashem* "the name," the name of God. (Genesis 39:21) The verse used in the above-mentioned amulet is cited again in the gem text before us.

The use of Joseph's name in amulets may have its origins in a practice known during the Hellenistic period. The Babylonian

Talmud states that, "All pagan images should be cast into the Dead Sea." This is attributed to Rabbi Judah, who goes on to say:

This also included the picture of a woman giving suck, and to Serapis. A woman giving suck alludes to Eve, who suckled the whole world; Serapis alludes to Joseph who became prince [sar] and appeased [hefis] the whole world.[57]

E. Goodenough has pointed out that, "Under a general rule that a prohibition indicates a practice, it is reasonable to conclude that some Jews did make amulets or use figures of the sort described."[58]

Serapis, whose representations combined the characteristics of Osiris, god of the dead, and Apis, the sacred bull, was a composite god introduced into Egypt under the rule of Ptolemy I (304–282 B.C.E.) the Greek general who served under Alexander the Great and later ruled Egypt. Both of these gods lent themselves to identification with Joseph. Osiris was worshipped as the father of organized agriculture and it was only natural that the Jews of Hellenistic Egypt should identify him with Joseph, the provider who saved Egypt from famine by organizing the production and storage of grain. (Genesis 41:47–49)[59] Another link between Osiris and Joseph lies in the tale of the recovery of Joseph's coffin. As noted earlier, this tale reverberates with elements of the Osiris myth: the disappearance of the body in the Nile, the determined search, and the successful conclusion of that search. The Hellenistic Egyptian composite deity, Serapis, was a supplier of corn, like Joseph, and, "He was practically identified with the Nile, the cause of the annual irrigation and thus fertility itself." The suggestion has also been made that, "...the bull as the symbol of the Joseph tribe (see Deuteronomy 33:17)...could be a reminder of Apis."[60] Apis was worshipped in the form of the sacred bull of Memphis. Known in Egyptian as Hapi ("Apis" to the Greeks) this god was associated with both Ptah, god of creation, and Osiris, god of the underworld. In Ptolomaic Egypt Apis and Osiris were joined in the composite deity, Serapis, whose cult spread throughout the Greco-Roman world, and in some Jewish circles Serapis was associated with the Biblical Joseph.

Louis Feldman has suggested that the identification of Joseph with Serapis is explained by the fact that in the cult of the Hellenistic Egyptian god "the interpretation of dreams was developed into a fixed technique." As Joseph was identified by first century B.C.E. authors as a "prophet" of dreams, the identification with Serapis was a natural one.[61]

Though the Talmud explicitly prohibits the magical use of Joseph's *image*, subsequent developments in the Jewish magical tradition indicate that the magical use of Joseph's power in other forms did persist. Use of the image may have been forbidden; the magical use of Joseph's name remained within the realm of the permissible. The form may have changed (from Hellenistic amulets to medieval *segulot*), but the concept remained the same: Joseph's name would both protect one from the evil eye *and* ensure success and prosperity. The idea that Joseph was a protective "sign," had its origins in the Biblical descriptions of the Hebrew experience in Ancient Egypt. It later resurfaced in Midrashic, Hellenistic, early Islamic, and Medieval Jewish sources.

In all of these traditions, Joseph's chastity and his control over his own "eye," is the attribute that empowers him. He in turn is impervious to the effects of the eye. This power was transmitted to his descendants and to all who invoke his name. As the thirteenth century Midrash Hagadol relates:

> The woman and the maidens of the nobility looked out of the windows to gaze upon Joseph's beauty, and they poured down chains upon him, and rings and jewels, that he might but direct his eyes toward them. Yet he did not look up, and as a reward God made him proof against the evil eye, nor has it ever the power of inflicting harm on any of his descendants.[62]

Thus the figure of Joseph, the object of sibling rivalry and sexual attention in his youth, and the wielder of great political and administrative power in his maturity, was transformed after his death into a symbol of magical and apotropaic power. And though the Bible and later Jewish sources consistently rejected the "magic of Egypt" (as the Talmud notes "nine parts of the magic came from Egypt"), magic of a more acceptable sort persisted.

The ancient dead and their sacred tombs are not exempt from the exigencies of contemporary Middle East politics. One of the serious stumbling blocks to an Israeli-Palestinian political settlement is the question of the fate of the holy places common to Jews and Muslims. There are four major sites under dispute. Two of them are the tombs of Rachel and Joseph. The others are the cave of the Machpelah at Hebron, where legend tells us that Jacob wished Rachel to be buried and where Joseph himself asked to be interred, and the most famous of disputed Middle Eastern holy sites, Jerusalem's Temple Mount, sacred to Jews as the site of the First and Second Temples, and sacred to Muslims as the *haram al-sharif*, the Noble Sanctuary.[63]

Joseph, pivotal in the historical unfolding of the scriptural narrative, also occupied center stage in the development of folklore and popular religious practices. Though forbidden in its more extreme Hellenizing form, "Joseph magic" and worship at his tomb(s) persisted in a religiously acceptable form for a remarkable length of time, and in some Middle Eastern circles, persists to this day.

Jacob Blessing the Sons of Joseph

Summary and Conclusions

Our survey of medieval and modern Biblical commentary demonstrated that the Joseph story of Genesis 37–50 was viewed throughout Jewish history as the central narrative in Genesis and as the most artfully constructed tale in the Pentateuch.

In the Qur'ān, Sūrat Yūsuf was perceived by the classical commentaries and modern Islamicists as a superior narrative, "the best of all stories," as well as a teaching parable, "a guidance, and a mercy to a people who believe" (Qur'ān 12:4, 112).

The Joseph story's exalted status ensured it a place in religious polemic. In its entirety, and in its component parts, it figured prominently in the Jewish-Islamic polemic and in sectarian polemics within Islam. These polemics represent the intellectual expression of the Joseph figure's popularity. In more popular modes of religious expression, those of local religious practice, Joseph emerges as a holy man and magician. Both Jewish and Islamic legends focus on Joseph's power as a magician in the "land of magic," Egypt of the Pharaohs.

Joseph's power was seen to derive from his resistance to the advances of Potiphar's wife. In chapter 2 the account of Genesis 39:1–23 was contrasted with parallel, but not identical, accounts in Ancient Egyptian and Homeric literature. The argument that there is continuity between these ancient versions and the Qur'ānic retelling of Joseph's story was affirmed and refined in this chapter. We noted that both the Jewish and Islamic elaborations of the tale are more didactic in nature than their Ancient Near Eastern precursors. They are "teaching parables" about chastity and temptation, rather than myths of national or religious origin. In some Jewish legends Potiphar's wife comes to symbolize "the strange woman, the alien woman that maketh smooth her words" of Proverbs 7:5. Islamic legend and poetic epic tell of a repentant Zuleikha, a woman who confesses the sins of her youth to a saintly Joseph.

In Chapter 3 our study then moved to examine the actual and alleged Ancient Egyptian background of the Joseph story of scripture and legend. While some scholars see anachronizing details scattered throughout in the story, others see the Biblical tale as permeated with authentic Egyptian realia. Ancient Egyptian place names and character names, descriptions of geography and agricultural life, and reflections of the social mores of the Egyptians are woven into the text. Attitudes of the Egyptians toward foreigners, and of the Hebrews towards the Egyptians, were examined through a close reading of the relevant Biblical verses and commentaries. We demonstrated that the Jewish exegetes saw fit to embellish and reinforce the sense of Egyptian *separateness* conveyed in the Biblical text. This is less so in the Islamic legends that touch on the same themes. Jewish scholars were eager to distance themselves and their co-religionists from Egyptian ways; for Islam, this was less of an issue; Egypt as a threatening pagan civilization was long dead. In analyzing the relationship of Jewish and Islamic folklore and the question of whether stories were borrowed from tradition to tradition, the evidence points to the fact that *legalistic* considerations were often the determining ones. One tradition will not adapt a story from another if the point of the story works against a known legal principle or injunction. For despite their great popularity, the primary function of the corpus of legends were to act as a "handmaiden of the Law." Outside of that function, the study of legends was a secondary, if not suspect, endeavor within the worlds of traditional Jewish and Muslim scholarship and piety.

The catalyst for Potiphar's Wife's folly is Joseph's charm and beauty. Chapter 4 developed a portrait of Joseph—his beauty is extolled in all of our texts—but not without an accompanying awareness that such beauty can bring its possessor great trouble and sorrow. In Islamic art, Joseph figures prominently; a medieval Central Asian portrait is described in the presentation of the pictorial evidence. The "origins" of Joseph's beauty—his ancestors, and its nature—provocative, with an element of the androgynous—were then elaborated upon.

The characters in the story that are portrayed as most affected by his charms, the women in the tales, were discussed at length in Chapter 5. In Genesis, the women's role is an active, assertive one. In the later pietistic texts of both Judaism and Islam, women's status as protagonists is diminished. Analyses of the role of the five women (and one group of women) in our story indicates that *kayd* (intrigue, malice, deceit) emerges as a dominant theme in explanations of women's behavior. Other literary expressions of *kayd* were explored, with emphasis on the stories of *The Thousand and One Nights*. Despite cultural prejudices that tend to denigrate women, these tales do not exonerate the male characters of the tales. Women may have their wiles, but so do men. In the storyteller's world treachery and deceit are qualities shared by both men and women, and not always in equal measure. In the *Nights*, where the motif of *kayd* abounds, Joseph is cited as a paradigm of beauty, and the *Nights*, both in its structure and content, has strong links to the Potiphar's Wife motif.

With Joseph's death at the close of Genesis narratives, we come to the end of the tale of the *living Joseph*. Chapter 6 provides a survey of legends that indicates that in the popular imagination Joseph assumed great importance in death. His remains and tomb were objects of veneration. Joseph's tomb at Shechem-Nablus became a site of pilgrimage to Jews, Samaritans, and Muslims. Cultic practices common to these religious groups were found to have some shared characteristics, but on closer examination were seen to be quite distinct in both form and meaning. Joseph's name was invoked in magical incantations of the three religions and in medieval Jewish folklore "ben porat yosef" becomes a popular apotropaic charm. It remains in use to this day. As the anthropologist Harvey Goldberg has noted, this "is one of the most frequent phrases on the lips of traditional North African Jews." Throughout our discussion, Joseph's resistance to his master's wife is identified as the source of his apotropaic power.

Among some Jews of the Hellenistic Near East, Joseph was identified with the figure of Serapis. This conflation, which links the Ancient Egyptian, Greek, and Jewish cultural spheres, illustrates the remarkable continuity of folkloric themes among the peoples of the Near East. Expressions of the impulse to glorify and invoke Joseph later appeared in the Aramaic Magic Bowls, Arabic legends, and medieval Jewish legends. As with our study of the Potiphar's Wife motif, the picture that emerges from a comparative study of the "Joseph as Serapis" material indicates that the cultures of the Near East actively borrowed motifs and narrative detail one from the other. In Judaism and Islam it was the legal and social implication of any one tale that determined whether it became "normative" within that tradition. But for all of the cultures under discussion here, the story of Joseph, that "best of all tales," exerted a fascination that continues undiminished to this day.

Notes

Introduction

1. S. Thompson, *The Motif Index of Folk-Literature* (Bloomington: Indiana University, 1955–1958), V:5.

2. John D. Yohannan, *Joseph and Potiphar's Wife in World Literature* (New Directions, 1968). For a recent survey of the literature on the Ancient Egyptian treatment of the motif, see Susan Hollis, "The Woman in Ancient Examples of the Potiphar's Wife Motif" in P. Day (ed.), *Gender and Difference in Ancient Israel* (Fortress Press, 1989), 28–43. Two recent works which examine aspects of the Joseph Narratives are M. Niehoff, *The Figure of Joseph in Post-Biblical Jewish Literature* (Leiden: Brill, 1992) and J. Kugel, *In Potiphar's House: The Interpretive Life of Biblical Text*. (San Francisco: Harpers, 1990).

3. "Midrash Hagadol," *Encyclopedia Judaica*, 16 vols. (Jerusalem: Keter, 1972), 11:1515. This work was chosen as the *latest* Midrashic compendium to be discussed in this study. This is because of its: 1) contemporaneity with the Islamic texts cited in this book and 2) "Its multitude of extracts...from ancient tannaitic Midrashim either unknown, or only partially known, from other sources. In addition, it is valuable for the accuracy of its quotations from known sources, such as the Talmud and the Midrashim."

4. Abū Isḥāq Aḥmad b. Muḥammad al-Tha'labī, *Qiṣaṣ al-anbiyā'* (also known as 'Arā'is al-majālis) appears in many editions, but there is no standard critical edition. al-Kisā'ī's work of the same name was published in a critical edition edited by Isaac Eisenberg (Leiden, 1922). It has been translated by Wheeler Thackston, *The Tales of the Prophets of al-Kisā'i* (Boston, 1978).

5. G. D. Newby, *A History of the Jews of Arabia: From Ancient Times to Their Eclipse Under Islam* (Columbia: 1988), 13.

6. R. Firestone, "Prophethood, Marriageable Consanguinity and Text," *Jewish Quarterly Review*, 83 (1993): 331. For a vindication of Goitein's statement in *Jews and Arabs*, see the article by D. Halperin and G. Newby cited in note 17.

7. S. D. Goitein, *Jews and Arabs* (New York, 1965). For an exhaustive survey of these legends, see H. Schwarzbaum, *Biblical and Extra Biblical Legends in Islamic Folk Literature* (1982). For an early formulation of Goitein's ideas on this topic see his paper in *Tarbiz*, 6, 1934–35, 89–101.

8. W. B. Brinner, "Prophets and Prophecy in the Islamic Jewish Traditions" in W. B. Brinner and S. D. Ricks, *Studies in Islamic and Jewish Traditions II*, Brown Judaic Series (Scholars Press, 1988), 178.

9. *Ibid.*

10. S. Spiegel, Introduction to Ginzberg's *Legends of the Bible* (JPS, 1975).

11. On the elusive definition of "folklore", see A. Dundes, "Texture, Text, and Context," *Interpreting Folklore* (Indiana, 1980), 20–32. On the application of the methodology of folklore studies to Biblical tales, see J. M. Sasson, *Ruth: A*

New Translation (Baltimore, 1979), 197–202, and the recent work by S. Niditch, *Folklore and the Hebrew Bible* (Fortress Press, 1993).

12. In the wake of the September 1993 Israeli-P.L.O. accords, many opponents of that pact have couched their opposition to the accords in terms that are scripturally referenced. On the Palestinian side, the leaders of the Hamas movement called on their followers to resist the implementation of the accords. Their manifestoes were structured around quotations from the Qur'ān, and in these manifestoes there were specific reference to Muslim holy places in the West Bank. In early 1994, Jewish settlers attempted to establish a Yeshiva at the site of Joseph's Tomb outside of Nablus. The Israeli military command objected, and, at a ceremony in which a Torah Scroll was to be brought into the Yeshiva, there was a violent clash between settlers and soldiers. The Hebron massacre of late February 1994, in which a Jewish settler from Kiryat Arba killed worshippers in the mosque at the Tomb of the Patriarchs, reinforced the Biblical associations of this political-military conflict.

13. Alan Dundes in R. Segal (ed.), *In Quest of the Hero* (New York, 1988), 179. This essay was originally published in A. Dundes, *Interpreting Folklore* (Bloomington: Indiana University Press, 1980).

14. G. Newby has warned us against "privileging" the Bible, regarding it as the ur-version. "If one assumes with Muslims that the Qur'ān represents the correct version of God's word (or actually God's word) then it is the privileged version, despite the appearance of the Qur'ān historically later than the Bible" (*The Last Prophet*, 30, note 92). For a survey of western scholarship on Qur'ānic "sources," see F. Rahman, *Major Themes of the Qur'ān* (Chicago, 1980), 150–61. Rahman, who was Professor of Islamic thought at the University of Chicago, makes the trenchant observation that Western scholars "are so preoccupied by the problems of the relationship of the Qur'ān to the Judaeo-Christian religious documents and traditions, that they hardly ever discuss the presence of these ideas among the Meccan-Arab population before Islam."

15. On the status of women in early Islam and the cultural underpinnings of that status, see the survey in L. Ahmed, *Women and Gender in Islam: Historical Roots of a Modern Debate* (New Haven, 1992), 25–35.

16. H. Lazarus-Yafeh in *Intertwined Worlds* (1992). As mentioned above (note 2), two recent works that examine the Joseph story in the light of comparative study are Maren Niehoff, *The Figure of Joseph in Post-Biblical Jewish Literature* (Leiden: Brill, 1992) and James Kugel, *In Potiphar's House: The Interpretive Life of Biblical Text* (San Francisco: Harpers, 1990). Niehoff, working in the tradition of classical studies, examines the portrayal of Joseph in the works of Philo and Josephus. As both of these first-century authors wrote in Greek for a Jewish audience whose literary and cultural referents were a fusion of the Judaic and Greco-Roman, their portrayals of Biblical figures were often "tainted" with narrative motifs borrowed from Greek myth and religion. Of special interest to Niehoff is the Greek-language text "Joseph and Asenath" which I will discuss in the section on Asenath in our chapter on "The Women of the Joseph Story."

Kugel's essays on the Joseph Narratives and the Potiphar's Wife episode is the title piece in a book of essays on the interpretation of biblical texts. For Kugel's earlier work on another aspect of the Joseph Narratives see his essay in Wayne Meek's volume on *Early Biblical Interpretation* (Philadelphia, The Westminster Press, 1986). While Kugel's main concern in his 1990 essay is with the history and biography of "Mrs. Potiphar" (an infelicitious locution which I have tried to avoid), he does make reference to the many Islamic legends that sprung up about Joseph's fateful encounter with the wife of his master. For further references to Kugel's essay on Potiphar's Wife see my notes in Chapter 2, note 13, Chapter 4, note 26, and Chapter 6, note 9.

17. "Creative Borrowing: Greece in the Arabian Nights," *Medieval Islam* (1946). For notes towards a methodology with which we can explore links between Islam and Ancient Near Eastern cultures, see Ilse Lichtenstadter, "Origin and Interpretation of Some Koranic Symbols" in G. Makdisi, *Arabic and Islamic Studies* (1965), 426–36, W. F. Albright, "Islam and the Religions of the Ancient Orient," *Journal of the American Oriental Society* 60 (1940): 283–91 and the discussion and extensive bibliography in D. Halperin and G. Newby, Two Castrated Bulls: A Study in the Haggadah of Ka'b al-Ahbar," *Journal of the American Oriental Society* 102 (1982):4, 631–38.

18. D. Redford, *A Study*, 94.

19. Thompson, op. cit. Susan Hollis in *The Tale of Two Brothers* (1990), noted that there are eleven discernible folk motifs in the Biblical Joseph narratives.

Chapter 1 The Centrality and Significance of the Joseph Narratives

1. W. F. Albright, "Historical and Mythical Elements in the Story of Joseph," *The Journal of Biblical Literature* 37 (1918), 111.

2. Eric I. Lowenthal, *The Joseph Narrative in Genesis* (New York, 1973), 1.

3. On the use of "toledot" in the construction of the Patriarchal narratives, see U. Cassuto, *A Commentary on the Book of Genesis: From Adam to Noah* (Jerusalem, 1961).

4. Donald Redford, *A Study of the Biblical Story of Joseph* (Leiden: E. J. Brill, 1970), 66.

5. Redford, *ibid*. For recent critical opinion, see G. W. Coats, "Joseph, Son of Jacob," in *The Anchor Bible Dictionary* (ed.) by D. N. Freedman, 3 (1992): 976–81.

6. N. Sarna, "Joseph," *Encyclopedia Judaica* 10 (1972 ed.): 209.

7. Gordon, *Ancient Near East*, 64.

8. N. Sarna, "Joseph," 208–10.

9. E. A. Speiser, *Genesis: A New Translation, The Anchor Bible* (New York: Doubleday and Co., 1964), 292.

10. Speiser, *ibid*.

11. G. Von Rad, *Genesis: A Commentary*, trans. by John H. Marks (Philadelphia: The Westminster Press, 1961), 342–43. John Van Seters has noted that "Since the time of Wellhausen, the various doublets and tensions within the story have made it a prime example of the division of sources into parallel J and E versions." *Prologue to History: The Yahwist as Historian in Genesis* (Westminster, 1992).

12. Speiser, *Genesis*, 291. For a sustained argument against "higher criticism," see U. Cassuto, *The Documentary Hypothesis* (Jerusalem, 1952). In his notes to each book of the Pentateuch, Rabbi J. Hertz, Chief Rabbi of the British Empire, brings evidence to bear against the findings of the Higher

Criticism. See J. H. Hertz, *The Pentateuch and Haftorahs: Hebrew Text, English Translation, and Commentary* (Soncino: London, 1968).

13. O. S. Wintermute, "Joseph," *The Interpreter's Dictionary of the Bible* (New York: The Abingdon Press, 1962): 2:983. For a review of "J and E in the Story of Joseph," see Redford, *A Study*, 251–53.

14. Coats, "Joseph," *The Anchor Bible Dictionary* (1992), 979.

15. G. Rendsburg, *The Redaction of Genesis* (Indiana: Eisenbrauns, 1986), 79. In *The Literary Guide to the Bible*, J. P. Fokelman quotes Northrop Frye's observation that "higher" criticism is actually a kind of lower criticism. This is reminiscent of Max Margolis' remark that "the higher criticism is a higher form of anti-Semitism."

16. Lowenstein, *The Joseph Narrative*, 1.

17. H. Freedman and M. Simon (eds.), *Midrash Rabbah*, II (London: Soncino, 1939): 772–73.

18. That there is a genealogical, as well as spiritual link, between Joseph and Joshua is also emphasized by the fact that they are both described as having identical life spans—110 years.

19. S. M. Stern, "Muhammad and Joseph: A Study of Koranic Narrative," *Journal of Near Eastern Studies* 44, 3 (1985): 193.

20. On the question of the reliability of the genealogical data in the Bible in the context of the wider Ancient Near Eastern historiography, see T. Thompson, "Israelite Historiography" in *The Anchor Bible Dictionary* (1992), 207–8.

21. M. G. S. Hodgson, *The Venture of Islam* (Chicago: University of Chicago Press, 1974), 184. On the significance and originality of Hodgson's work, see A. Hourani, "Patterns of the Past," in *Paths to the Middle East*, (ed.) T. Naff (New York, 1992), 46–47.

22. Abdullah Yusuf Ali, *The Holy Qur'ān: Text, Translation and Commentary* (Washington, DC: The Islamic Center, 1946), 550.

23. Montgomery Watt, *W. Bell's Introduction to the Qur'ān* (Edinburgh: The University Press, 1970), 81.

24. M. R. Waldman, "New Approaches to 'Biblical' material in the Qur'ān," *The Muslim World* I, 1 (January 1985): 5.

25. "Yūsuf," *The Encyclopedia of Islam*, 3: 1178–79.

26. M. Asad, *The Meaning of the Quran* (Gibraltar: Dar al Andalus, 1980), 357 (emphasis is my own).

27. Stern, "Muhammad and Joseph," 212.

28. *Ibid.* Surat Yūsuf is thought to belong to the late Meccan period. It should also be pointed out that Muhammad's *primary* identification was with Moses. This is richly developed in the *Sirah* literature. See G. D. Newby, *The Making of the Last Prophet*, 24.

29. M. J. Kister, "Legends in tafsir and hadith literature: The Creation of Adam and Related Stories," in *Approaches to the History of the Interpretation of the Qur'ān* (ed.) A. Rippin (Oxford, 1988).

30. *Ibid.*

31. A. F. L. Beeston, "Notes on a Middle-Arabic Joseph Poem," *Bulletin of the School of Oriental and African Studies* 40, 2 (1977): 287. On the use of "qassas," see N. Abbot, *Arabic Literary Papyri*.

32. R. Y. Ebied and M. J. L. Young, (eds.), "The Story of Joseph in Arabic Verse" (The Leeds Arabic Manuscript 347). Supplement #3 to, *Annual of Leeds University Oriental Society* (Leiden: E. J. Brill, 1975), 6-7.

33. *Ibid.*, 48. A parallel use of an "Egyptianized" text to ascribe a Jewish legend to Egyptian Jewish sources may be found in J. Heinemann, *Aggadah and its Development* (Jerusalem: Keter, 1974), 56.

34. Both Joseph and Daniel function in their respective tales as dream interpreters for foreigner rulers. See C. H. Gordon, *Ancient Near East*, 77, note 10. On the affinities between the Joseph narratives and the tale of Daniel, see Sandra B. Berg, The Book of Esther, S. B. L. Dissertation Series, Number 44 (Missoula: Montana Scholars Press, 1979), 143.

35. Ebied and Young, "The Story of Joseph," 48.

36. "Tawrāt," *The Encyclopedia of Islam*, 1st ed., 4: 706. On Jewish-Islamic polemics see N. Stillman, *The Jews of Arab Lands: A History and Source Book* (Philadelphia: Jewish Publication Society, 1979), 11–13, 150–51, 259–60.

37. "Tahrif," *op. cit.*, 618–19. Similar arguments were presented by Christian polemicists. Moshe Pearlmann has pointed out that "Syriac Christian theologians accused the Jews of having tampered with the Scriptures with the result that differences arose between the Hebrew text and the Septuagint." M. Pearlmann, "Polemics Between Islam and Judaism," in S. D. Goitein (ed.), *Religion in a Religious Age* (Princeton, 1965).

38. Al-Tabari, *The Commentary on the Qur'ān Vol. I*, with introduction and notes by J. Cooper (Oxford: Oxford University Press, 1987), 450.

39. A. F. L. Beeston, *Baidawi's Commentary on Surah 12 of the Qur'ān* (Oxford: Oxford University Press, 1963), 1.

40. Hodgson, *The Venture of Islam*, 177.

41. Beeston, "Notes," 3.

42. Abū Isḥāq al-Tha'labī, *Qiṣaṣ al-Anbiyā'*. On the significance of narrative detail in the Jewish-Muslim polemic, see the introduction to M. Pearlmann (ed. and trans.), *Ifham al-Yahud* (Silencing the Jews), Proceedings of the Academy for Jewish Research, 23. (New York, 1964).

43. C. H. Gordon, "The Patriarchal Age," *Journal of Bible and Religion* (1953), 21:242. "The idea conveyed by Joseph's dream—that stars symbolize individual people, is a well known one in the Ancient Near East. When Joseph (Genesis 37:9) dreams of heavenly bodies symbolizing people, his imagery is that duplicated in the Babylonian Gilgamesh Epic (I:v:26–27); (II:I:1–23), where Gilgamesh dreams of a star symbolizing Enkidu."

44. al-Tha'labī, *Qisas*, 236–37. On the semantic range of the Arabic word *tawrat*, see R. Firestone, *Journeys in Holy Lands*, 189, note 26. On the early Muslim view of history and the Torah as an historical document, a seminal work if Franz Rosenthal's "The Influence of the Biblical Tradition on Muslim Historiography," in B. Lewis and P. M. Holt, *Historians of the Middle East* (Oxford: Oxford University Press, 1962).

45. "Salman al-Farisi," *Encyclopedia of Islam*, 4, 16–17.

46. On Ka'b, see the article in *Encyclopedia of Islam*, 2nd ed., and Firestone, *Journeys in Holy Lands*, 113. On Wahb, see B. Lewis, *The Jews of Islam*, 97. For an example of Islamic legends transmitted in the names of both Ka'b al-aḥbar and Wahb ibn Munabbih, see G. Newby, *The Making of the Last Prophet*, 227–28.

47. I. Friedlander, *The Heterodoxies of the Shiites According to ibn Hazm* (New Haven, 1909), 33. On Ibn Hazm, see also B. Lewis, *The Jews of Islam* (Princeton, 1984), 87. On Ibn Hazm's views on the Biblical narratives, see H. Lazarus-Yafeh, *Intertwined Worlds* (Princeton, 1992). The description of the

Kharijites is from J. A. Williams, "Kharijis," *The Encyclopedia of Religion* (New York, 1987), 8: 288.

48. T. Noldeke and F. Schwally, *Geschichte des Qorans* (Leipzig, 1909–38), II, 94. On Kharijite ideology, see G. Levi Della Vita, "Karidjites," *Encyclopedia of Islam*, 2nd ed. (1978), IV: 1076–77.

49. J. Burton, *The Collection of the Qur'ān* (Cambridge: Cambridge University Press, 1977), 83.

50. D. Grossberg, "Number Harmony and Life Spans in the Bible," *Semitics* (1984), 9:54. On the distinction between *avot* and *shevatim*, see N. Leibowitz, *Studies in Bereshit* (Jerusalem: The Jewish Agency, 1974), 430.

51. B. Mandelbaum (ed.), *Pesikta de Rav Kahana: With Commentary and Introduction* (New York: Jewish Theological Seminary, 1962), 61–62. As the three names were thought to be obscure and foreign to the reader of the Bible, the Midrash provides a clue to their identity.

52. For a detailed analysis of this "successor" theme in Sūrat Yūsuf, see S. M. Stern, "Joseph and Muhammad," 196–97. On the concept of *nabi* in Islam, see W. Brinner, "Prophets and Prophecy in the Islamic and Jewish Traditions" in Brinner and Ricks, *Studies in Islamic and Judaic Tradition*, II, 63–82.

53. S. D. Goitein, *Jews and Arabs* (New York: Schocken Books, 1965), 55–56.

54. W. M. Thackston, *The Tales of the Prophets of al-Kisa'i*, 208–9.

55. G. Newby, *The Making of the Last Prophet*, 143. On p. 115, Newby provides an ingenious explanation of the origins of the "Moses Son of Manasseh" legend.

56. *Babylonian Talmud*, Kiddushin 49:b.

57. Freeman and Simon, *Midrash Rabbah*, II:804.

58. *Ḥarshin*, both by itself and modified by *bishin*, appears in the Aramaic bowls. For examples, see Charles Isbell, *Corpus of the Aramaic Incantation Bowls*, Society of Biblical Literature, Dissertation Series No. 17 (Missoula: Scholar's Press, 1975), 166, #318. On the use of *ḥarshin* as a magical term in Ugaritic, see C. H. Gordon, *Ugaritic Textbook* (Rome: Pontifical Biblical Institute, 1965), Glossary, item #903, where it is cited as appearing in text 126:6. On the use of *ḥarshin* in Mandaic magical literature, see E. M. Yamauchi, *Mandaic Incantation Texts* (New Haven: American Oriental Society, 1967), 324. For Neusner's analysis of this Midrash, see J. Neusner, E. Frerichs, and P. Flesher (eds.), *Religion, Science, and Magic In Concert and In Conflict* (Oxford, 1989), 75–76.

59. A. S. Yahuda, *The Language of the Pentateuch in its Relation to Egyptian* (Oxford: Oxford University Press, 1933), 11. For a current bibliography on the origin of '*abrek*, see D. Redford, *A Study*, 226–28. Midrash Rabbah interprets *abrek* as a contraction "*av* (father) in widsom, rakh (young) in years." (90:3)

60. R. H. Charles, *The Book of Jubilees: Translated From the Editor's Ethiopic Text* (London: A. and C. Black, 1902), 226. On the difficulty of assigning a precise date to the composition of *Jubilees* see Lou H. Silberman's remarks in "Jubilees, Book of," *Encyclopedia Brittanica*, 1971, 13:101.

61. Brinner, Tha'labi, *Qissas*, 249.

62. *Ibid.*, 289.

63. *Ibid.*

64. "Gematria," *Encyclopedia Judaica* 7:367.

65. "Abdjad," *Encyclopedia of Islam* (new edition) 1:97.

66. S. Gevirtz, "The Life Spans of Joseph and Enoch and the Parallelism sib'tayim-sib'im wesib'ah," *Journal of Biblical Literature* (1977), 96:570.

67. J. Vergote, *Joseph en Egypte* (Louvain: Universite, 1959). For a survey of the literature, see D. Spanel, *Through Ancient Eyes: Egyptian Portraiture* (Birmingham, 1988), 25.

68. Gevirtz, "Life Spans," 96:570.

69. J. G. Williams, "Number symbolism and Joseph as Symbol of Completion," *Journal of Biblical Literature* (1979), 98:87.

70. *Ibid.*, 98:86. (Emphasis is my own.)

71. Grossberg, "Number Harmony," 9:55–56.

72. *Ibid.*, 9:64.

73. On Tolstoy's Hebrew studies, see H. Troyat, *Tolstoy* (New York, 1967), 430.

74. On Manns' Joseph novels, see M. Yourcenar, "Humanism and Occultism in Thomas Mann," in *The Dark Brain of Piranesi, and Other Essays*, 199–231. For a less laudatory view of the Joseph novels, see L. Fiedler's remarks in "Master of Dreams: The Jew in a Gentile World" in *To The Gentiles*, where Fiedler characterizes Mann's work as a "true but tedious retelling of the tale."

75. For speculation on the historical and thematic relationship between Greek epic and Near Eastern literature see the extensive bibliography in Richard Y. Hathorn, *Greek Mythology* (Beirut, American University of Beirut Press, 1977), 35–36. On the "sociology of knowledge" aspect of this question, see M. Bernal, *Black Athena*, 400–38. For a discussion of the Church Fathers' views on Joseph and Bellerophon, see Doniger/Bonnefoy II 656. Some scholars also consider the "Hippolytus Triangle" and its many retellings an expression of the Potiphar's Wife mofit. See D. Keene, "The Hippolytus Triangle East and West," *Yearbook of Comparative and General Literature II*, 1962, 162–71. As the attempted seduction and accusation of rape in the Phaedra genre is directed by a *stepmother* towards her stepson, I have excluded it from this discussion.

Chapter 2 The Spurned Woman: Potiphar's Wife in Scripture and Folklore

1. Stith Thompson, *Motif Index of Folk Literature* (Bloomington: The University of Indiana Press, 1955), V, Motif K 2111.

2. M. Bloomfield, "Joseph and Potiphar in Hindu Fiction," *Transactions and Proceedings of the American Philological Association*, 54 (1923), 142. Noting that "the tradition of the Prophet Yūsuf is one of the most popular of all the countries of Islam," Jan Knippert cites textual traditions in Berber, Javanese, and Swahili, which refashion much of the Tales of the Prophet literature. See his *Islamic Legends: Histories of the Heroes, Saints, and Prophets of Islam* (Leiden: Brill, 1985), 85–86.

3. This was first noted by E. Meyer, *Geschichte des Altertums*, 2 vols. (Stuttgart: J. G. Cottasche, 1931), II, 301.

4. Cyrus H. Gordon, *The Common Background of Greek and Hebrew Civilizations* (New York: W. W. Norton and Co., 1965), 119–20. For other Classical versions on our motif, see R. Graves and R. Patai, *Hebrew Myths* (New York, 1964), 264. For a survey of the Bellerophon story in Greek sources,

see T. Gantz, *Early Greek Myth: A Guide to Literary and Artistic Sources* (Baltimore, 1993), 314–16. For a parallel Iranian myth, see V. S. Curtis, *Persian Myths* (London, 1993), 43. For a survey of the Bellerophon myth, see Y. Bonnefoy's *Mythologies*, (ed.) by W. Doniger (Chicago: University of Chicago Press, 1991), 1:401–3. On the genealogy of Bellerophon, as described in Greek sources, see F. and J. Boswell, *What Men or Gods Are These?: A Genealogical Approach to Classical Mythology* (London, 1980), 106–9. On the stylistic differences between Biblical epic and Homeric epic, see E. Auerbach's magisterial essay, "Odysseus Scar" in *Mimesis: The Representation of Reality in Western Literature*. There are very striking contrasts between the texts that Auerbach examines, Book 19 of the Odyssey and Genesis 22, the "Binding of Isaac." Less striking are the differences between the two versions of Potiphar's wife under discussion here.

5. The recent study referred to is that of S. Hollis, *The Tale of Two Brothers* (1990). For a discussion of the comparative material on Joseph and divine figures, see G. Mussies, "The Interpretario Judaica of Serapis," in *Studies in Hellenistic Religions* (ed.) M. J. Vermasern (Leiden: E. J. Brill, 1979). On Joseph as hero, see Lord Raglan's *The Hero: A Study in Tradition*, Part II. For a recent discussion, see J. R. King, "The Joseph Story and Divine Politics," *Journal of Biblical Literature* (1987), 577–94. Despite the similarities between the classical and biblical "Joseph" stories there are profound differences between them. As Graves and Patai point out, "No moral conclusions were drawn from the deeds of Greek heroes...Famous warriors of an earlier generation, such as Theseus and Bellerophon, had been destined to end miserably, victims of divine nemesis, yet Abraham, Isaac, and Joseph died in peaceful old age and were honorably gathered to their fathers." R. Graves and R. Patai, *Hebrew Myths: The Book of Genesis* (New York, 1964), 16–17.

6. References are to the following editions: R. Lattimore, *The Iliad* (Chicago: University of Chicago Press, 1962); J. Wilson in Pritchard, A.N.E.T. All Biblical quotations are from the 1985 JPS translation unless otherwise noted.

7. Ruth Rabbah 6:1.

8. This type of behavior among the gods is exemplified in the Ancient Egyptian tale of, "The Contendings of Horus and Seth." For a discussion of this text see Gordon, *The Common Background of Greek and Hebrew Civilizations*, 125–26.

9. See M. Astour, *Hellenosemitica*, 2nd ed. (Leiden: E. J. Brill, 1962), 258–61.

10. T. Gantz, *Early Greek Myth*, 315.

11. For a comprehensive survey of the literature, see Susan T. Hollis, *The Ancient Egyptian "Tale of Two Brothers": The Oldest Fairy Tale in the World* (London: University of Oklahoma Press, 1990), 1–48, 97–102.

12. Genesis Rabbah 87, 1. For a more detailed reading of Joseph as wisdom literature figure, and for a feminist critique of the Potiphar's Wife motif, see S. Niditch in *The Woman's Bible Commentary* (London, 1992).

13. Genesis Rabbah, 87, 3. Rashi (39–6) quotes a variation of this Midrash in which Joseph is chastised for preening himself while his father is in mourning for him. For other indications of Joseph's complicity in the seduction attempt see J. Kugel, *In Potiphar's House: The Interpretive Life of Biblical Texts* (1990), 94–98.

14. In similar fashion the Greek sources differ as to the woman's name. Homer calls her Anteia, other writers (Apollodorus, Pindar) name her

Notes 157

Stheneboea. For a discussion of the names that the Jewish sources give to
Potiphar's wife, see Ginzberg, *The Legends of the Jews* V (Philadelphia: Jewish
Publication Society, 1909–946), 339, #111. On the predictions of the court
astrologers see Genesis Rabbah, 85:2.

15. *Babylonian Talmud*, Yoma 35b, cited and translated in Ginzberg. In
the *Tale of Two Brothers* the "master's wife" also offers new clothes to the young
man.

16. *Loc. cit.*

17. *Sefer ha-Zohar* (Leghorn, 1866), III, 213b.

18. Thackston/Al-Kisa'i.

19. Sotah 36b. Other legends in this same Talmudic passage link the
addition of the letter *heh* to his name to his ability to resist temptation. See
Leviticus Rabbah 23, 10.

20. On the place of the scribe in Ancient Egyptian society, see Gordon, *The
Ancient Near East*, 58. On Solomon, see Tabari, Sura 2, 190 and many other
Jewish and Muslim legends.

21. Genesis Rabbah 87.7; Midrash Hagadol, Vayeshev, 686. These
Midrashim have been adapted and translated in Ginzberg, *Legends*, II, 53.

22. Quoting Sotah 36b. Rashi's comments are translated and cited in
Nehama Leibowitz, *Studies in Bereshit* (Jerusalem, 1974), 415. The Yalkut
Shimonei quote and other similar legends are cited in "Joseph," *The Jewish
Encyclopedia*, 249.

23. Mann/Joseph.

24. Midrash Rabbah, 87.7, Sotah 36b.

25. Midrash Rabbah 87.7, Sotah 36b.

26. R. L. Rubenstein, *The Religious Imagination* (Brown Classics in
Judaica, NY, 1985), 77–78.

27. Midrash Hagadol, I:665.

28. Ginzberg, *Legends*, II, 59.

29. al-Tha'labī, *Qisas al-Anbiya*.

30. For the pictorial evidence, see M. Sequy, *The Miraculous Journey of
Mahomet: Miraj Nameh* (Paris: Bibliotheque Nationale), Manuscript Supplement
Turc 190 (New York: Braziller, 1977), Plate XVI.

31. Martin Lings, *Muhammad: His Life Based on the Earliest Sources*
(London, 1986), 17–18. Lings' translation here is based on Ibn Hishām.

32. The Rabbinic, Christian, and Moslem sources are cited in I. Schapiro,
Die haggadischen Elemente in erzahlenden Teil des Korans (Berlin: Itzkowski,
1907). The issue of Potiphar's sexual orientation and his adoption of Joseph
will be discussed in chapter 4, "A Portrait of Joseph." The name Qitfir was
based on an alternative reading of Potiphar.

33. It is beyond the scope of this chapter to review the voluminous
literature on the question of predestination and free will in Islam. For a review
of the topic, see "Al-Kada' Wa-l-Kadr," *Encyclopedia of Islam*, new ed. (1978), 4,
365–67.

34. Thackston/Kisai', 175.

35. al-Tabarī, *History*, vol. II, 156.

36. A. F. L. Beeston, *Baidawi's Commentary on Sura 12 of the Qur'an*
(Oxford: Oxford University Press, 1963), 17.

37. P. Sanders, "Gendering the Ungendered Body: Hermaphodites in
Medieval Islamic Law," in N. Keddie and B. Baron, *Women in Middle Eastern*

158   Notes

History: Shifting Boundaries in Sex and Gender (New Haven, 1991), 75. G. Newby, *The Making of the Last Prophet*, 103.

38. M. Lings, *Muhammad: His Life Based on the Earliest Sources*, 339.

39. H. E. Kassis, *A Concordance of the Qur'ān* (Berkeley, University of California Press, 1983), 675–76.

40. All references to the Qur'ān in translation are to Alfred Arberry, *The Koran Interpreted* (Toronto: Macmillan, 1969).

41. On *teraphim*, see C. H. Gordon, "Erebu Marriage," Studies on the Civilization and Culture of Nuzi and the Hurrians (Winona Lake: Eisenbrauns, 1981), 155–60. For references to other readings of the *teraphim* incident, see T. Frymer-Kensky, *In the Wake of the Goddesses* (New York, 1992), 268.

42. For a feminist reading of the trickster motif in Genesis, see S. Niditch, *The Women's Bible Commentary* (London, 1992), 18–24.

43. R. Khawam (ed. and trans.), *The Subtle Ruse: The Book of Arabic Wisdom and Guile*, Bibliotheque Nationale, Manuscript #3548 (London: East West Books, 1980).

44. John Payne, trans., *The Book of the Thousand Nights and One Night*, 9 vols. (London: 1882–1894). All citations are from Payne's translation unless otherwise indicated. I have also consulted Burton's translation, H. Haddawy's 1990 English translation and J. J. Rivlin's Hebrew translation, *'Elef Layla wa-Layla* (Tel Aviv: Kiryat Sefer, 1947). My comments on the *kayd* motif in *The Thousand and One Nights* refer to the early *Nights* material and the larger corpus of tales that were translated into French and English in the eighteenth and nineteenth centuries. As both M. Mahdi and H. Haddawy point out, much of what was translated and anthologized in Payne, Lane, and Burton, is of questionable authenticity, for "the mania for collecting more stories and 'completing' the work led some copyists to resort even to forgery." For the history of these additions and their effect on the various translations see the introduction to H. Haddawy's recent translation of *The Arabian Nights* (New York, 1990).

45. On the jinn, see J. B. Long, "Demons," *The Encyclopedia of Religion* (New York, 1987), 4:286. On the *Sindibadnama* see S. Belcher, "The Diffusion of the Book of Sindbad," Fabula, 28, 1987, 34–58.

46. Payne, *Arabian Nights*, III, 7. For a feminist reading of the *kayd* motif in the *Nights* see F. Malti-Douglas, *Woman's Body, Woman's Word: Gender and Discourse in Arabo-Islamic Writing* (Princeton, 1991).

47. *Ibid.*, III, 8. For the suggestion that this frame devise is related to the content and structure of the Book of Esther, see J. Jacobs, "Arabian Nights," *The Jewish Encyclopedia* (New York, 1904).

48. On the trickster in Middle Eastern folklore see Haim Schwartzbaum, *Studies in Jewish and World Folklore* (Berlin: De Gryter, 1968), 176–77. On the theme in Biblical literature see S. Niditch, *The Women's Bible Commentary* (London, 1992), 18–24.

49. Payne, *Arabian Nights*, V, 260. In a footnote to his translation of the "Malice of Women" section, Sir Richard Burton argued that these tales "belong to a certain stage when the sexes are at war with each other; and they characterize chivalrous Europe as well as misogynous Asia." (Burton, 6, 129).

50. R. Irwin, *The Arabian Nights: A Companion* (London: 1994), 75.

51. Payne, *Arabian Nights*, V, 345.

52. D. Pinault, *Story-Telling Techniques in the Arabian Nights* (Leiaen, 1992), 58-59. As Pinault notes "Sura 12:28 is echoed elsewhere in the *Nights*."

53. On this motif in *Genji*, see D. J. Enright, *"The Tale of Genji and Two Women Diarists," A Mania for Sentences* (London, 1983), 87.

54. H. Haddawy, (trans.) *The Arabian Nights* (New York, 1990).

55. G. von Grunebaum, *Medieval Islam* (New York, 1946), 319.

56. S. D. Goiten, "The Oldest Documentary Evidence for the Title *Alf-Laila wa-Laila,*" *Journal of the American Oriental Society*, 78, 1958, 301–2.

57. M. Epstein, *Tales of Sendebar: An Edition and Translation of the Hebrew Version of the Seven Sages*. Philadelphia: The Jewish Publication Society, 1967.

Chapter 3 The Egyptian Background of the Joseph Story

1. D. Redford, *A Study of the Biblical Story of Joseph*, Supplements to Vetus Testamentum, Vol. XX (Leiden: E. J. Brill, 1970), 189. For a recent survey of the literature, see Susan Hollis, *The Ancient Egyptian "Tale of Two Brothers": The Oldest Fairy Tale in the World* (University of Oklahoma Press, 1990).

2. J. M. A. Janssen, "Egyptological Remarks on the Story of Joseph in Genesis" (Ex Oriente Lux, 1955–56) 14:63.

3. C. H. Gordon, *The Ancient Near East* (New York: W. W. Norton and Company, 1965), 138–39.

4. G. Coats, "Joseph, Son of Jacob" in *The Anchor Bible Dictionary* (New York, 1992), III:980. On the social history of archaeology as a discipline, see Neil Asher Silberman, *Between Past and Present: Archaeology, Ideology, and Nationalism in the Modern Middle East* (New York, 1989).

5. "Egypt," *The Encyclopedia Brittanica*, 15th edition, 18, 146.

6. The description of *Sinuhe* is that of C. H. Gordon, *The Ancient Near East*, 63–64. For a translation of *Sinuhe* and notes on the history of the text, see M. Lichtheim, *Ancient Egyptian Literature*, vol. I (University of California Press, 1976). The suggestion that Joseph is based on *Sinuhe* is that of A. Meinhold as quoted in J. R. King, *Journal of Biblical Literature* 106/4, 1987, 578.

7. All citations from Genesis are from the new JPS translation.

8. A. S. Yahuda, *The Accuracy of the Bible* (London: Heinemann, 1934), 8. On opposition to Yahuda's views see *Encyclopedia Judaica* 16:703, where the controversy concerning his theories is mentioned.

9. G. Steindorff and K. C. Steele, *When Egypt Ruled the East* (Chicago: University of Chicago Press, 1957), 48.

10. R. O. Faulkner, *A Concise Dictionary of Middle Egyptian* (Oxford: Griffith Institute, 1981), 128.

11. C. F. Burney, *The Book of Judges* (London: Rivington, 1930), reprinted with Prolegomenon by W. F. Albright (New York: Ktav, 1970), 107.

12. C. H. Gordon, "Homer and the Bible," *Hebrew Union College Annual* (1955), 26:84–85, #99.

13. C. M. Doughty, *Travels in Arabia Deserta*, 2 vols. (London: Jonathan Cape, 1930), I, 516.

14. C. H. Gordon, *Ancient Near East*, 64.

15. *Ibid.*, 139.

16. This observation is made by D. Redford, *A Study*, 50.

17. A. S. Yahuda, *The Language of the Pentateuch in its Relation to Egyptian* (Oxford: Oxford University Press, 1933), 51.

18. "Egypt," *Encyclopedia Brittanica*, 18, 146.

19. C. H. Gordon, *The Ancient Near East*, 88. On current views on the date of the Joseph narratives see Coats, *Anchor Bible Dictionary*, III:980.

20. For citations and classifications, see F. Brown, S. R. Driver, C. A. Briggs, *A Hebrew and English Lexicon of the Old Testament* (Oxford: Oxford University Press, 1907), 1072–73.

21. *Loc. Cit.*

22. Herodotus, Book II:98 (G. Rawlinson translation).

23. *Book II:95*

24. Redford, 235.

25. Yahuda, *Language*, 95, italics added.

26. W. L. Humphreys, "Novella," in G. W. Coats, (ed.), *Saga, Legend, Tale, Novella, Fable: Narrative Forms in Old Testament Literature* (*Journal for the Study of the Old Testament*, Supplement Series 35, 1985).

27. Gordon, *The Ancient Near East*, 173.

28. *Loc. Cit.*, note #9.

29. C. H. Gordon, "Fratriarchy in the Old Testament," *Journal of Biblical Literature* (1935), 54:226.

30. For a comprehensive survey of this topic, see K. Spanier, "Aspects of Fratriarchy in the Old Testament," Ph.D. Dissertation, New York University, 1989.

31. Redford, *A Study*, 71.

32. See chapter 5 for a full treatment of the Asenath legends.

33. L. Ginzberg, *On Jewish Law and Legend*, 77–124. On Ginzberg's oevre, see "Ginzberg, Louis" in the *Encyclopedia Judaica* (7:584) and S. Spiegel's introduction to the one volume work *The Legends of the Bible*.

34. L. Ginzberg, *The Legends of the Jews* (Philadelphia: The Jewish Publication Society, 1928), II:68

35. Redford, *A Study*, 76. A similar series of "converted imperfects" appears in Genesis 25:34.

36. *Babylonian Talmud*, Rosh Hashanah 11a. Also see the parallel legend, mentioned in the Book of Jubilees, that Jacob heard of Joseph's "death" on Yom Kippur.

37. This tradition is cited in Rashi, Genesis 42:23.

38. Both sources are quoted and translated in Ginzberg, *Legends*, II:96.

39. Rashi, Genesis 43:32.

40. Author's translation. For a review of Ibn Ezra's critical methodology and of the views expressed in his commentaries see, "Ibn Ezra as Commentator on the Bible," *Encyclopedia Judaica*, 8, 1166–68.

41. M. Asad, *The Meaning of the Qur'an* (Gibraltar: Dar Al Andalus, 1980).

42. Qur'ān, Sura 10:91, Sura 11:98.

43. al-Tha'labī's *Qisas al-Anbiya'*, 227.

44. Al-Maqrizi, *al-khitat wa'lāthār* 1:207.

45. On the Jewish parallels to these legends, see Ginzberg.

46. al-Tha'labī, *Qisas*, 283-4.

47. *Ibid.*, 278–79.

48. On the ecumene of the Ancient Near East, see C. H. Gordon, *The Ancient Near East*. On the application of this model to the Muslim world, see the introduction to Hodgson's *The Venture of Islam*. In his last published paper the late A. Hourani affirmed the validity and relevance of Hodgson's views on

the Islamic *oikoumene*. See A. Hourani, "Patterns of the Past" in T. Naff, *Paths to the Middle East* (SUNY, 1992), 46, 55.

Chapter 4 A Portrait of Joseph

1. The JPS translation. E. A. Speiser's translation in *The Anchor Bible: Genesis* (New York: Doubleday, 1964), 301, is that "Joseph was handsome of figure and features."

2. Though not all translations interpret the verse in this way. See the *Authorized Version's*, "And Joseph was a goodly person and well favoured."

3. For a review of the literature see, "Yusuf," *Encyclopedia of Islam* (Leiden: E. J. Brill, 1960), 4, 1178–79. In Tabari's *History* the chapter on Joseph opens in this way. "Jacob's son Joseph had, like his mother, more beauty than any other human being. W. Brinner, trans., *The History of Al-Tabari*, vol. II, 148.

4. Personal communication, C. H. Gordon, New York University, February 7, 1986. In *The Fairytale*, Max Lüthi notes that "In many instances beauty sets the entire plot in motion....Often it also operates as *movens* within a story that is already underway, as it advances of the plot."

5. J. B. Trotti, "Beauty in the Old Testament," Ph.D. Dissertation, Yale University, 1964.

6. M. Pope, in his Commentary to *The Anchor Bible: Song of Songs* (New York: Doubleday, 1977), 355–56.

7. See Chapter 2, section I.

8. E. A. Speiser, *Genesis*, 303. Gilgamesh dreams of his encounter with Enkidu and later helps interpret Enkidu's dream. For a discussion see F. Guirand , "Assyro-Babylonian Mythology," in *New Larrousse Encyclopedia of Mythology* N.Y., 1968, 66–68.

9. For a discussion of these statements on Joseph's beauty, see *Encyclopedia of Islam*, "Yusuf."

10. al-Tha'labi's *Qisas al-Anbiya'* and other sources. Franz Rosenthal suggests that this legend "is no doubt connected with the Talmudic statement that Jerusalem possessed nine-tenths of all existing beauty, but how the transference of the motif from Jerusalem to Yūsuf took place is hard to explain." "The Influence of the Biblical Tradition on Muslim Historiography" in B. Lewis and P. M. Holt, *Historians of the Middle East* (London: Oxford University Press, 1962).

11. Genesis Rabbah, 86.6.

12. For legends that emphasize Joseph's resemblance to his father, see "Joseph," *The Jewish Encyclopedia.*

13. Bouhdiba, p. 26.

14. al-Tha'labi, *op. cit.* For an unflattering picture of Sarah's beauty as compared to Eve's, see Babylonian Talmud: Baba Bathra 58a.

15. *Sefer Hayashar* (Livorno: Bilforti, 1870).

16. Genesis Rabbah 85, quoted in H. N. Bialik and Y. H. Rabinitsky, (eds.), *Sefer Ha-aggadah* (Tel Aviv: Dvir, 1960).

17. al-Tha'labi, *op. cit.*, 238. Ibn Ishaq, *The Life of Muhammad*, translated by Guillaume (Oxford, 1955).

18. R. Y. Ebied and M. J. L. Young, (eds.), *The Story of Joseph in Arabic Verse: The Leeds Arabic Manuscript 347*, (Leiden: E. J. Brill, 1975) 27.

19. M. Seguy, *The Miraculous Journey of Mahomet: Miraj Nameh* (Paris: Bibliotheque Nationale, Manuscript Supplement Turc 190, plate #16) (New York: Braziller, 1977).

20. Ginzberg, *Legends*, II, 7.

21. *Ibid.*

22. Pirkei De Rabbi Eliezer, quoted in Ginzberg, *Legends*, vol. II, 17. "Pirkei De Rabbi Eliezer...follows the model of the Arabic collections of biblical legends, in which narrative received more emphasis than exegesis...It was composed in Eretz Israel during the first half of the eighth century, just prior to the fall of the Omayyad dynasty, but before the rise of the Abbasid dynasty."; "Pirkei De Rabbi Eliezer," *Encyclopedia Judaica*, 16 vols. (Keter: Jerusalem), 13, 559.

23. Thackston, al-Kisāʾī, 172.

24. W. F. Albright, "Historical and Mythical Elements in the Story of Joseph."

25. *Babylonian Talmud*, Sotah 13b; (quoted in Rashi on Genesis 41:45) Jerome on Genesis 37:36. See also I. Schapiro, *Die haggadischen Elemente im erzählenden Teils des Korans* (Berlin: Itzkowski, 1907). For an earlier review of the literature, see Albright, *op. cit.*

26. On the question of the appropriateness of translating *saris* as eunuch, see G. Kadish, "Eunuchs in Ancient Egypt?" in *Studies in Honor of John A Wilson* (Studies in Ancient Oriental Civilization, no. 35) (Chicago, 1969), 56. For other possible readings of *Saris* see J. Kugel, *In Potiphar's House: The Interpretive Life of Biblical Texts* (1990), 74–75, 90–91.

27. "Yūsuf B. Yaʻqub" and "Kitfir," *Encyclopedia of Islam* (Leiden: E. J. Brill, 1934), quote a number of opinions on Qitfir's preferences. Tabari's historical account of Joseph appears in W. M. Brinner, trans., *The History of Tabari*, vol. III., 148–86.

28. For a review of the various names, see Encyclopedia if Islam articles cited above.

29. Thackston, al-Kisāʾī, 173.

30. Genesis Rabbah 87.9. The editors note: "The comment is based on the (Biblical) words, "After this manner did they servant unto me." For an ingenious attempt to reconcile Potiphar's physical state and his feelings towards his wife see the comments in the *Siftei Hakhamim*, (the seventeenth century commentary on Rashi) on Genesis 41:45.

31. Brinner, al-Thaʻlabī, *op. cit.* Newby, *The Making of the Last Prophet*, 108.

32. A. F. L. Beeston, *Baidawi's Commentary on Surah 12 of the Qur'an* (Oxford: Oxford University Press, 1963), 50.

33. al-Thaʻlabī, *op. cit.* On Wahb ibn Munabbih, see Kister, "Legends in Tafsir," 82.

34. *Joseph in Egypt*, 802–3.

35. Targum Yerushalmi on Genesis 39:21.

36. al-Thaʻlabī, *op. cit.*, 269.

37. Quoted in Ginzberg, *Legends*, II, 74.

38. See D. Redford, *Akhenaten*, (Princeton: Princeton University Press, 1984) 165–66 for a description and discussion of these representations.

39. Genesis Rabbah 82.8, II, 759. For a discussion of the implications of this legend, see Rashi's comment on Genesis 46:26 and Nachmanides' comments on Genesis 46:15.

40. Genesis Rabbah, *op. cit.*, quoted in Ginzberg, II, 37–39. For a different interpretation of this legend, see Graves and Patai, *Hebrew Myths*, 217–19.

41. E. W. Lane, *The Thousand and One Nights: The Arabian Nights Entertainments*, 3 vols. (London: Chatto and Windus, 1883), II, 59.

42. *Ibid.*, I, 519.

43. Ginsberg, *Legends*, V, 369.

44. al-Tabari, *Tafsir*, 7:213.

45. See the account in al-Tabari's History (Brinner trans.), II, 148. As Brinner notes, this account of Joseph's childhood explains the Qur'ānic reference to Joseph having stolen something (12:77).

Chapter 5 The Women of the Joseph Story

1. For the opposing view, that women are treated as fundamentally inferior and singled out as tricksters, see E. Fuch's suggestion that "gender is a *primary* factor which determines the literary presentation of deception in the biblical narrative." *Semeia*, 42 (1988), 68. My analysis in this chapter is informed by T. Frymer-Kensky's *In the Wake of the Goddesses* (New York, 1992). On the issue of "woman as trickster," see the items cited in Frymer-Kensky, 255, and the articles in J. Cheryl Exum and J. W. H. Bos, "Reasoning with the Foxes: Female Wit in a World of Male Power," *Semeia*, 42 (1988).

2. S. Niditch in *The Women's Bible Commentary* (London, 1992), 24.

3. Whether this Biblical portrait is an accurate portrayal of the social reality of Ancient Israel is another matter. As Frymer-Kensky points out, the Bible provides us with "a portrait of biblical, not ancient Israelite, women," 256, note 19. See S. D. Goitein, "Women as Authors in the Bible," in I. Zemorah, *Women of the Bible* (Hebrew) (Tel Aviv: Davar, 1964). On the status of women in the heroic period of Biblical history, cf. C. H. Gordon, "Homer and the Bible," *Hebrew Union College Annual* (1955) 26, 78–80.

4. Zohar, I, 216 B.

5. "Rahil," *The Encyclopedia of Islam* (Leiden: E. J. Brill, 1913–1942), 4, 1103–4.

6. On the use and origins of this phrase, see E. Ben Yehuda, *Dictionary and Thesaurus of the Hebrew Language* (New York, 1960), V: 416.

7. Baidawi quoted in J. Macdonald, "Joseph in the Qur'ān and Muslim Commentary," *The Muslim World* (1956) 46:113–31, 207–24.

8. Genesis Rabbah, 74.9.

9. Rashi is quoting the *Babylonian Talmud*, Sotah 13b. See also Genesis Rabbah, 85:3.

10. Genesis Rabbah, 82:10.

11. For the Islamic sources, see G. Le Strange, *Palestine Under the Muslims*, Beirut, 1965, 314. For the Jewish legend, see Ginzberg, *Legends*, V, 377.

12. "Rachel," *Jewish Encyclopedia*, 10, 305-7.

13. *Ibid.*

14. Speiser, *Genesis*, 299. That this evaluation is still current in some circles is confirmed in John Van Seters recent comment, "There seems to be little dispute among Biblical exegetes that this chapter represents such an awkward digression within the Joseph story that it cannot have been original to it." J. Van Seters, *Prologue to History* (1992). For a discussion of Abrabanel's

comment see Y. Zakovitch and A. Shinan, *The Tale of Judah and Tamar* (Jerusalem, The Hebrew University, 1991), 14–15.

15. C. H. Gordon, *The Ancient Near East*, 135.

16. Rashi on Genesis 38:1.

17. Genesis Rabbah 85:2 and Rashi on Genesis 39:1.

18. Niditch, *op. cit.*, 21.

19. Robert Alter, *The Art of Biblical Narrative* (New York: Harper and Row, 1982), 6.

20. For bibliography and discussion, see J. Goldin, "The Youngest Son, or Where Does Genesis 38 Belong?," *Journal of Biblical Literature* (1977), 96 and N. Furman, "His Story Versus Her Story: Male Genealogy and Female Strategy in the Jacob Cycle," *Semeia* 46 (1989).

21. Genesis Rabbah 85.2 and Midrash Hagadol, I, 596.

22. Nachmanides on Genesis 38:2 provides a survey of opinions on Tamar's ancestors. Also, see, Ginzberg, *Legends*, V, 333, note 79.

23. Midrash Rabbah 85:9.

24. E. Meyer, Geschichte des Altertums, II, 301. On the history and reception of this theory, see S. Hollis, *The Tale of Two Brothers* (1990).

25. Ginzberg, *Legends*, V, 339–40, note 118.

26. *Loc. cit.*

27. S. D. Goitein, *Jews and Arabs* (New York: Shocken Books, 1954), 194–95. Italics added.

28. On the fruit of the Tree of Knowledge, see Genesis Rabbah 15, 7. On the natural and cultural history of the *etrog*, see the articles of that title in the *Encyclopedia Judaica* and the *Jewish Encyclopedia*. On modern Arabic words for the tangerine see E. Badawi and M. Hinds, *A Dictionary of Egyptian Arabic* (Beirut, 1986).

29. On "build up and climax," see C. H. Gordon, "Poetic Legends and Myths from Ugarit," *Berytus* (1977), 25:64.

30. A. Bouhdiba, *Sexuality in Islam* (London, 1985), 25.

31. Beeston, *Baiḍawi*, 17. Razi, quoting Al-Azhari, also translates the phrase in this way.

32. W. M. Brinner (trans.), *The History of al-Ṭabari* (Albany: State University of New York Press, 1987), II, 159–60.

33. *Ibid.*, 18–19; note 64.

34. Bouhdiba, *op. cit.*, 26.

35. J. Vergote, *Joseph en Egypte* (Louvain, 1959), 149 and D. Redford, *A Study of the Biblical Story of Joseph* (Leiden, 1970), 229–30. Galetee, in the *Anchor Bible Dictionary* 1:476 notes that "this is a common name of the middle kingdom and the first intermediate, 2000–1500 b.c."

36. Quoted in V. Aptowitzer, "Asenath, the Wife of Joseph: An Haggadic Literary-historical Study," *Hebrew Union College Annual* (1924), I:244.

37. C. H. Gordon, *Homer and Bible*, 78.

38. Aptowitzer, "Asenath," 246–47. Kauffman Kohler has suggested that "the view of Asenath having been a proselyte was superseded by the theory that she was the daughter of Dinah." "Ascnath" *The Jewish Encyclopedia*, 2:175.

39. Midrash Aggada, Genesis 41:45, quoted in Ginzberg II:76. For a similar legend about Joseph's Egyptian name, Genesis Rabbah, 90:4.

40. Rabbi Joshua ben Levi in Genesis Rabbah 85.2.

41. Quoted in I. Goldziher, "Proben muhammadanisher Polemik gegen der Talmud," *Jeschurun* (1872), VIII. English translation is by Aptowitzer, "Asenath," 251–52. On Ibn Hazm see R. Arnaldez, "Ibn Hazm," *Encyclopedia of Islam* 2nd ed. My conclusion about Ibn Hazm's views on Dinah confirms Arnaldez's observation that "In discussing the non-Muslim religions, Ibn Hazm does not attempt to understand them in themselves; he is interested in them only in relation to dogmas or problems which enable him to compare them with Islam." (Vol. III:796).

42. V. Aptowitzer, "Asenath," 253, note 37. On the Islamic prohibition against marrying a niece and its relationship to similar question in Jewish law, cf. A. Katsh, *Judaism in Islam* (New York: New York University Press, 1954), 154, note 3. On the relevance of legal strictures to the development of Islamic legend, see R. Firestone, "Prophethood, Marriageable Consanguinity, and Text" *Jewish Quarterly Review*, 83/3–4, 1993, 331–347, where this analysis is applied to the Abraham and Sarah stories.

43. Quoted in M. Buber, *Midrash Aggadah*; English translation is my own.

44. Aptowitzer, *op. cit.*, 253, note 37.

45. Ginzberg, II:77–78.

46. Brinner/al-Tabari, 157.

47. Quoted in Ginzberg II, 175. On the Greek Asenath text, see now R. Kraemer "Jewish Women in the Diaspora World of Late Antiquity," J. R. Baskin (ed.) *Jewish Women in Historical Perspective* (Detroit: Wayne State University Press, 1991), 53–66.

48. See Graves and Patai, *Hebrew Myths*, 278, for the sources of this legend.

49. Translated by Ginzberg from *Sefer Hayashar*. The idea that Serah was immortal, "is very likely presupposed in such old sources as Genesis Rabbah." Ginzberg, *Legends*, II, 39. C. Kerenyi's observation about Greek myth is relevant to the Serah legends: "Legends of heroes trouble themselves but seldom with the age of their characters, and almost everlasting youth was characteristic of heroines." *The Heroes of the Greeks*, London, 1959, 81.

50. "Serah," *The Jewish Encyclopedia*, 1904 ed., 2, 200–201.

51. The translation is that of Ginzberg, *Legends*, II, 39.

52. Midrash Avot as quoted in "Serah," *The Jewish Encyclopedia*, 1904 ed., 2, 200.

53. Quoted in Ginzberg, *op. cit.*, II, 115.

54. According to Ecclesistes Rabbah VII:11. See also, Midrash Hagadol, Vayigash, 780.

55. This Midrash places Serah squarely in the heroic tradition of Biblical Israel. "The Hebrew 'wise woman' was a highly valued member of society, whose services were required in the highest circles...A town could entrust its leadership to a wise woman at the most critical moment in the community's history (II Samuel 20:16 ff). C. H. Gordon, *Homer and Bible*, 76.

56. W. Fischel, "Isfahan," *The Joshua Starr Memorial Volume* (New York, Conference on Jewish Relations, 1953). As to why Serah would be buried in Isfahan, Ernest Herzfeld suggests that, "The only explanation might be that the colony [of Isfahan] belonged to the tribe Asher." Quoted in V. Moreen, "Persecution of Iranian Jews During the Reign of Shah 'Abbas II," *Hebrew*

Union College Annual (1981), 299. Moreen provides an updated bibliography on the Serah's tomb legends.

57. The question of Asenath's origins was discussed earlier. On Tamar's "Canaanite" or Israelite origins see the sources collected in Y. Zakovitch and A. Shinan, *The Tale of Judah and Tamar* (Jerusalem: The Hebrew University, 1991), 22.

Chapter 6 Joseph's Bones: Linking Canaan and Egypt

1. Noted by C. H. Gordon, *The Ancient Near East*, 3rd ed. (New York: Norton and Co., 1965), 116, note 4. For the Egyptian sources on the ideal age span, see D. Spanel, *Through Egyptian Eyes: Egyptian Portraiture* (Seattle, 1988), 25. Of note here is the observation that the word *bashagam* in Genesis 6 is the numerical equivalent (*gematria*) of *Moshe*, Moses.

2. *Babylonian Talmud*, Berakhot 55a.

3. Pesahim 87a.

4. E. A. Speiser, *The Anchor Bible: Genesis* (New York: Doubleday, 1964). The standard translations do not convey this "prophetic" sense. See the *Authorized Version*'s "God will surely visit you, and ye shall carry up my bones from hence."

5. *E.g.*, al-Baydāwī, see A. F. L. Beeston, *al-Baydāwī's Commentary on Sura 12 of the Qur'an* (Oxford: Oxford University Press, 1963), 51. al-Tha'labī also puts Yūsuf's age at his death as 120.

6. al-Ṭabari/Tarikh, 185. Newby, *Making of the Last Prophet*, 112.

7. G. W. Coats, "Joseph, son of Jacob," *The Anchor Bible Dictionary* 3:981, 1992.

8. *Mekilta de-Rabbi Ishmael: a Critical Edition*, (ed.) J. Lauterbach (Philadelphia: Jewish Publication Society, 1946), 176.

9. Midrash Tanhuma, Beshallah. For a survey of the historical development of these midrashim see J. Kugel, *In Potiphar's House*, 125–55.

10. Al-Baydāwī, *Commentary*, 51, verse 102.

11. Midrash Hagadol, Veyehi, 886–87. Babylonian Talmud, Sotah 13 a, b.

12. N. A. Stillman, *The Jews of Arab Lands: A History and Source Book*, 267–68 and references there.

13. Midrash Hadar on Exodus 13:9, for related sources see Ginzberg, *op. cit.*, V, 376.

14. M. Astour, *Hellenosemitica*, 2nd ed. (Leiden: E. J. Brill, 1962), 75.

15. J. Frazer, *The Golden Bough* vol. 6 (London: Macmillan, 1900). A modern application of this approach to the Joseph narrative is in G. R. Wright's, "Joseph's Grave," *Vetus Testamentum* (1972), Vol. XXII. On the application of the Tammuz myth to Biblical epic, see W. F. Albright, *From Stone Age to Christianity* (New York: Doubleday Anchor, 1934), and R. H. Pfeiffer, *Introduction to the Old Testament* (New York: Harper Brothers, 1941), 461, 715. On Frazer and Biblical Studies see now S. Niditch, *Folklore and the Hebrew Bible* (Minneapolis, Fortress Press, 1993), 14–15.

16. *E.g.*, the introduction to *Ugaritic Literature* (Rome: Pontifical Biblical Institute, 1949). For the history of the application of the Tammuz model see L. K. Hardy, "Tammuz," *The Anchor Bible Dictionary*, VI, (New York, 1992), 318.

17. Ginzberg II: 139.

18. *Babylonian Talmud*, Sotah 13b. Joseph was sold near Dothan, where he finds his brothers after seeking them in Shechem. Genesis 37:12, 17.

Notes 167

19. Quoted in Ginzberg, *op. cit.*, V, 377.
20. 'Ali of Herat (c. 1173), Yaqut (1225), quoted in G. Le Strange, *Palestine Under the Muslims* (Beirut, 1890), reprint 1965, 512, 416.
21. J. A. Montgomery, *The Samaritans* (Philadelphia: J. C. Winston, 1907), 107.
22. "Samaritans," *The Encyclopedia of Islam*, 4, 125.
23. J. Finkel, "Jewish, Christian, and Samaritan Influences on Arabia," *Macdonald Presentation Volume* (Princeton, 1933).
24. Quoted in Le Strange, *Palestine Under the Moslems*, 314.
25. Quoted in Le Strange, *Palestine Under the Moslems*, 314.
26. *Loc. cit.* This allusion to magic and folklore is typical of Ibn Battuta, arguably the greatest of all Moslem travelers and geographers. His work is, "A marvellous compendium of antecdote, folklore, and descriptions of myth, miracles, and magic, many of which derive from the author's infatuation with the Sufi orders and holy men of the day"; Ian Netton, "Miracle and Magic in the Rihla of Ibn Battuta," *Journal of Semitic Studies* (Spring 1984), 24:133–34. For a more sober view and an investigation of the chronology of Ibn Battuta's *Rihla*, see Adel Allouche, "A Study of Ibn Battutah's Account of His 726/1126 Journey Through Syria and Arabia," *Journal of Semitic Studies* (August, 1990), 35/2:283–299.
27. See my *The Tale of Bilqis in Al-Tha'labi's Qisas Al-Anbiyā'*, M. A. thesis, Columbia University, 1980. A new translation of this tale has been published in J. Lassner, *Demonizing the Queen of Sheba* (Chicago, 1993).
28. E. Lane, *An Account of the Manners and Customs of the Modern Egyptians* (London: John Murray, 1836), 226. "Many of the Arabs ascribe the erection of the pyramids and all the most stupendous remains of antiquity in Egypt, to Gann Ibn Gann and his servants the ginn."
29. Le Strange, *Palestine Under the Moslems*, 512.
30. T. Canaan, *Muhammaden Shrines in Palestine* (Jerusalem, 1927).
31. C. Wilson, (ed.), Samaria and the Plain of Esdraelon," *Picturesque Palestine, Sinai and Egypt* (New York: Appelton, 1881), 240–41.
32. J. A. Montgomery, *The Samaritans*, 44. Emphasis added.
33. G. E. Wright, *Shechem* (New York: McGraw-Hill, 1965), 3.
34. "Evil Eye," *Encyclopedia Judaica*, 6, 998–1000.
35. A. Dundes, *The Evil Eye: A Folklore Casebook* (New York: Garland Publishers, 1981), 262. Emphasis is my own.
36. See the classical Jewish commentaries, especially Rashi.
37. Translated by S. Langdon in *Babylonian Liturgies* (Paris: Libraire Paul Geuthner, 1913), 11–12.
38. A Gardiner, "A Shawabati-Figure With Interesting Names: The Evil Eye in Egypt," *The Proceedings of the Society of Biblical Archaeology* (May 1916), 129–30.
39. Charles Isbell, *Corpus of the Aramaic Incantation Bowls*, Society of Biblical Literature Dissertation Series no. 17 (Missoula: Scholar's Press, 1975), text 42:9, 180.
40. E. M. Yamauchi, *Mandaic Incantation Texts* (New Haven: American Oriental Society, 1967), text 21:19, 228. For the early secondary literature on the magic bowls, see J. A. Montgomery, *Aramaic Bowls From Nippur*. For a more recent review of the literature, see C. H. Gordon, "Magic Bowls in the Moriah Collection," *Orientalia* (1984), 2:220–41.

41. Beeston, al-Bayḍāwī, *Commentary*, 6.
42. E. A. Speiser, *The Anchor Bible: Genesis*, 301.
43. Joseph," *The Jewish Encyclopedia*, quoting Genesis Rabbah, 78.13. Rashi quotes this Midrash with slight variation.
44. *Babylonian Talmud*, Berakhot 55a. Translation in Soncino ed., emphasis is my own.
45. *Ibid.*, emphasis added.
46. P. Marcais, "'ayn" EI 2, 1, 786.
47. Beeston, al-Bayḍāwī, *Commentary*, 68, emphasis added.
48. D. B. Macdonald, *The Religious Attitude and Life in Islam* (Chicago, 1909), 119. Macdonald quotes Ibn Khaldun to the effect that, "The evil eye differs from all other magic, in that it needs not the will of him who has it. It works automatically and he cannot control it."
49. Quoted by al-Bayḍāwī, *Commentary*, Arabic text, 90; English translation by Beeston, 46.
50. Genesis Rabbah 96.1. The anthropologist Harvey Goldberg has noted that "one of the most frequent phrases on the lips of traditional North African Jews is "ben porat yosef." (personal communication, May, 1995).
51. G. Scholem, "Kabbalah," *Encyclopedia Judaica* and "Yosef" *Encyclopedia Hebraica*.
52. *Zohar*, Vayeshev, 190b. On the problematic question of the relationship between Jewish mystical ideas and the Biblical text see E. R. Wolfson, "Beautiful Maidens without Eyes: Peshat and Sod in Zoharic Hermeneutics" in M. Fishbane (ed.) *The Midrashic Imagination; Jewish Exegesis, Thought, and History.* (SUNY Press, 1993), 155–197.
53. The translation of Jāmī's verses is by J. C. Burgel, *The Feather of Simurgh: The "Licit Magic" of the Arts in Medieval Islam* (New York, 1988), 132.
54. Sefer Raziel, 1812 (Jewish Theological Seminary, Rare Book Collection). Also see "Raziel, Book of," *Encyclopedia Judaica* 13:1392.
55. Trachtenberg, *Jewish Magic and Superstition*, 142.
56. *Loc cit.*
57. *Babylonian Talmud*, Avodah Zarah 43a, Soncino translation.
58. Goodenough, *Jewish Symbols*, II, 282.
59. For a discussion of the relevant material, see G. Mussies, "The Interpretation Judaica of Serapis," *Studies in Hellenistic Religions*, (ed.) M. J. Vermasern (Leiden: E. J. Brill, 1979), 205–14.
60. *Ibid.*, 214.
61. L. H. Feldman, *Jew and Gentile in the Ancient World* (Princeton: Princeton University Press, 1993), 526–27.
62. Ginzberg, II:74.
63. On the political and religious aspects of these disputes, see R. Friedland and R. Hecht, "The Politics of Sacred Place: Jerusalem's Temple Mount/al-haram al-sharif" in J. Scott and P. Simpson-Housley, *Sacred Places and Profane Spaces* (1991), 21–63.

Bibliography

Judaica

Bible

Tanakh: A New Translation of the Holy Scriptures According to the Traditional Hebrew Text. Philadelphia: The Jewish Publication Society of America, 1985.
The Holy Scriptures According to the Masoretic Text. Philadelphia: The Jewish Publication Society of America, 1917.
The Anchor Bible: Genesis. Introduction, Translation and Notes by E. A. Speiser. New York: Doubleday and Company, 1964.

Mishnah

Mishnah. Edited and translated by H. Danby. London: Oxford University Press, 1933.

Talmud

The Babylonian Talmud. Edited by I. Epstein. 34 vols. London: Soncino, 1935.

Targum

Sperber, A., (ed.) *The Bible in Aramaic.* 5 vols. Leiden: E. J. Brill, 1959.

Midrash

Mekilta de Rabbi Ishmael. Edited by J. Z. Lauterbach. Philadelphia: Jewish Publication Society, 1949.
Midrash Rabbah. 10 vols. Edited by H. Freedman and M. Simon. London: Soncino, 1939.
Pesikta de Rab Kahana: With Commentary and Introduction by B. Mandelbaum. New York: Jewish Theological Seminar, 1962, 61–62.
Pirke De Rabbi Eliezer. Edited by G. Friedlander. London: Hermon, 1916.

Zohar

The Zohar. Edited and translated by H. Sperling and M. Simon. London: Soncino Press, 1932.

Islamica

Qur'ān

Ali, Abdullah Yusuf. *The Holy Qur'ān: Text, Translation and Commentary.*
Washington, D.C.: The Islamic Center, 1946.
Arberry, A. J. *The Koran Interpreted.* Toronto: Macmillan, 1969.
Asad, M. *The Meaning of the Qur'ān.* Gibraltar: Dar al Andalus, 1980.
Pickthall, M. *The Meaning of the Glorious Koran, an Explanatory Translation.*
London, 1930.

Tafsīr

al-Bayḍāwī. *Anwār al-tanzil wa-asrar al-ta'wīl.* Cairo: Bulaq.
al-Ṭabari. *Tafsīr al-Ṭabari.* Cairo.

Hadith

Wensinck, A. J. *A Handbook of Early Muhammadan Tradition.* Leiden: E. J.
Brill, 1927.

Qiṣaṣ

al-Kisā'ī, Muhammad. *Qisas al-Anbiya.* 2 vols. Edited by I. Eisenberg. Leiden:
E. J. Brill, 1923.
al-Kisā'ī. *The Tales of the Prophets of al-Kisa'i.* Translated by W. M. Thackson.
Boston, Twayne Publishers, 1978.
al-Tha'labī. *Qiṣaṣ al-Anbiyā.* ('Arāis al-majālis.) Cairo: Bulaq, 1869.

Ta'rikh

al-Maqrizi. *Ighāthah al-ummah bi-kashf al-ghummah.* Cairo, 1974.
———. (*Muslim Economics.*) Translated by A. Allouche. Salt Lake City: University of Utah Press, 1994.
al-Musabbihi. *Akhbār miṣr fī-sanatay 414-15 H.* (*The History of Egypt in the
Years 414-415 A.H.*). Edited by W. J. Milward. Cairo, 1980.
al-Ṭabari. *Ta'rihk al-rusul wa'l-mūlūk.* (*The History of al-Ṭabari.*) Translated in 38
volumes, SUNY Series in Near Eastern Studies.

General Works

Ahmed, L. *Women and Gender in Islam: Historical Roots of a Modern Debate.*
New Haven, Yale University Press, 1992.
Albright, W. F. "Islam and the Religions of the Ancient Orient," *Journal of the
American Oriental Society,* vol. 60 (1940).
———. "Historical and Mythical Elements in the Story of Joseph," *The Journal
of Biblical Literature,* 37 (1918).
Alter, R. *The Art of Biblical Narrative.* New York: Harper & Row, 1982.
Alter, R. and Kermode, F. *The Literary Guide to the Bible.* Cambridge, Mass.:
Harvard University Press, 1987.

Aptowitzer, V. "Asenath, the Wife of Joseph: An Haggadic Literary Historical Study," *Hebrew Union College Annual*, 1924 (I).

Astour, M. *Hellenosemitica*. 2nd edition. Leiden: E. J. Brill, 1962.

Auerbach, E. *Mimesis: The Representation of Reality in Western Literature.* Princeton: Princeton University Press, 1953.

Baron, S. *A Social and Religious History of the Jews.* New York: Columbia University Press, 1952.

Beeston, A. F. L. *Baidawi's Commentary on Surah 12 of the Qur'ān.* Oxford: Oxford University Press, 1963.

———. "Notes on a Middle-Arabic Joseph Poem," *Bulletin of the School of Oriental and African Studies*, Vol. 40, pt. 2. 1977.

Hell, R. Bell's *Introduction to the Qur'ān.* Revised and Enlarged by W. Montgomery Watt. Edinburgh: The Edinburgh University Press, 1970.

Berg, Sandra B. *The Book of Esther.* S. B. L. Dissertation Series, Number 44. Missoula, Montana: Scholar's Press, 1979, 143.

Bernal, M. *Black Athena: The Afroasiatic Roots of Classical Civilization.* Vol. I New Brunswick, NJ: Rutgers University Press, 1987.

Bialik, H. N. and Rabinitsky, Y. H. *Sefer Ha-aggadah.* Tel Aviv: Dvir, 1960.

Bonnefoy, U. and Doniger, W. *Mythologies.* Chicago: University of Chicago Press, 1991.

Boswell, F. and J. *What Men or Gods Are These? A Genealogical Approach to Classical Mythology.* London, 1980.

Bouhdiba, Abdelwahab. *Sexuality in Islam.* Translated by Alan Sheridan. London: Routledge & Kegan Paul, 1985.

Brinner, William M., trans. *The History of al-Tabari. Volume II: Prophets and Patriarchs.* Albany: State University of New York Press, 1987.

Brinner, William M., trans. *The History of al-Tabari. Volume III: The Children of Israel.* Albany: State University of New York Press, 1991.

Brinner, W. and Ricks, S. *Studies in Islamic and Judaic Traditions II* (Brown Judaic Series 178) Scholars Press, 1988.

Brown, F., Driver, S. R., Briggs, C. A. *A Hebrew and English Lexicon of the Old Testament.* Oxford: Oxford University Press, 1907.

Buhl, F. "Tahrif," *Encyclopedia of Islam*, 4 vols., Leiden: E. J. Brill, 1913–1942, 4, 618–19.

Burgel, J. C. *The Feather of Simurgh: The "Licit Magic" of the Arts in Medieval Islam.* New York: New York University Press, 1988.

Burney, C. F. *The Book of Judges.* London: Rivingtons, 1930; reprinted with Prolegomenon by W. F. Albright. New York: Ktav, 1970.

Burton, J. *The Collection of the Qur'ān.* Cmabridge: Cambridge University Press, 1977.

Campbell, J. *The Portable Arabian Nights.* New York: Viking, 1952.

Canaan, T. *Mohammedan Saints and Sanctuaries in Palestine.* London: Ariel Publishers, 1927.

Carter, Jimmy. *The Blood of Abraham.* Boston: Houghton Mifflin Company, 1985.

Cassuto, U. *A Commentary on the Book of Genesis: From Adam to Noah.* Translated by I. Abrams. (Jerusalem: Magnes Press, 1961).

Cassuto, U. *The Documentary Hypothesis.* Translated by Israel Abrahams. Jerusalem: The Magnes Press, The Hebrew University, 1961.

Charles, R. H. *The Book of Jubilees: Translated from the Editor's Ethiopic Text.* London: A. and C. Black, 1912.

Doughty, C. M. *Travels in Arabia Deserta.* London: Jonathan Cape, 1930.

Dundes, A. *The Evil Eye: A Folklore Casebook.* New York: Garland Publishers, 1981.

Ebied, R. Y. and Young, M. J. L., (eds.) *The Story of Joseph in Arabic Verse: The Leeds Arabic Manuscript 347.* Leiden: E. J. Brill, 1975.

Enright, D. J. *A Mania for Sentences.* Boston: David R. Godine, 1985.

Epstein, M. (ed. and trans.) *Tales of Sendebar.* Philadelphia: The Jewish Publication Society, 1967.

Exum, J. Cheryl and Johanna W. H. Bos, ed. *Reasoning with the Foxes: Female Wit in a World of Male Power.* Semeia 42 (Atlanta: 1988): 1–132.

Faulkner, R. O. *A Concise Dictionary of Middle Egyptian.* Oxford: Griffith Institute, 1981.

Fiedler, L. *To the Gentiles.* New York: Stein and Day, 1972.

Finkel, J. "Jewish, Christian and Samartian Influences on Arabia," *The Macdonald Presentation Volume.* Princeton, 1933.

Firestone, R. *Journeys in the Holy Lands: The Evolution of the Abraham-Ishmael Legends in Islamic Exegesis.* Albany: SUNY, 1990.

Fischel, W. "Isfahan." *The Joshua Starr Memorial Volume.* New York: Conference on Jewish Relations, 1953.

Frazer, J. G. *The Golden Bough: A Study in Magic and Religion.* 2nd ed. London and New York: Macmillan, 1900.

Friedlander, I. *The Heterodoxies of the Shiites According to Ibn Hazam.* New Haven: n. n., 1909, 33.

Frymer-Kensky, Tikva. *In The Wake of the Goddess.* New York: The Free Press, 1992.

Ganz, T. *Early Greek Myth: A Guide to Literary and Artistic Sources.* Baltimore: Johns Hopkins University Press, 1993.

Gardet, L. "Al-Kada wa-'l-Kadr," *Encyclopedia of Islam.* Leiden: Brill. New edition, 1978, 4.

Gardiner, A. "A Shawabti-Figure With Interesting Names: The Evil Eye in Egypt," *The Proceedings of the Society of Biblical Archaeology.* May 1916.

———. *Egyptian Grammar.* 3rd ed. London: Oxford University Press, 1973.

Gaster, M. "Samaritans," *Encyclopedia of Islam.* Vol. IV. Leiden: E. J. Brill, 1934.

Gevirtz, S. "The Life Spans of Joseph and Enoch and the Parallelism sib'tayim-sib'im wesib'ah," *Journal of Biblical Literature,* vol. 96, 1977.

Ginzberg, L. *The Legends of the Jews.* 7 vols. Translated by H. Szold. Philadelphia: The Jewish Publication Society, 1913–38.

———. *On Jewish Law and Lore.* Philadelphia: The Jewish Publication Society, 1955.

Goitein, S. D. *Jews and Arabs.* New York: Schocken Books, 1965.

———. "Who Were Mohammad's Chief Teachers" (in Hebrew), *Weil Jubilee Volume.* Jerusalem: Magnes Press, 1952.

———. "Women as Authors in the Bible," in Zemorah, I. *Women of the Bible* (in Hebrew). Tel Aviv: Davar, 1964.

Goiten, S. D., ed. *Religion in a Religious Age.* Cambridge, MA: Association for Jewish Studies, 1974.

Goldin, J. "The Youngest Son, or Where Does Genesis 38 Belong?," *Journal of Biblical Literature,* 96, 1977.

Goldman, S. L. *The Joseph Story in Jewish and Islamic Lore.* Ph.D. Dissertation, New York University, 1986.

Goldziher, I. "Proben muhammadanischer Polemik gegen der Talmud," *Jeschurun*, vol. 8, 1982.
Goodenough, E. *Jewish Symbols in the Greco-Roman Period.* 13 vols. Princeton: Princeton University Press, 1953–1968.
Gordon, C. H. *The Ancient Near East.* 3rd edition. New York: W. W. Norton and Co., 1965.
———. *The Common Background of Greek and Hebrew Civilizations.* New York: W. W. Norton and Co., 1965.
———. "The Daughter of Baal and Allah," *The Muslim World*, vol. 33, no. 1, Jan. 1943.
———. "Erebu Marriage," *Studies on the Civilization and Culture of Nuzi and the Hurrians: In Honor of Ernest R. Lacheman.* Winona Lake Illinois: Eisenbrauns, 1981.
———. "Fratriarchy in the Old Testament." *Journal of Biblical Literature*, vol. 54, 1935.
———. "Homer and the Bible," *Hebrew Union College Annual*, vol. 26, 1955.
———. "Paternity at Two Levels," *Journal of Biblical Literature*, vol. 96, 1977.
———. "The Patriarchal Age," *Journal of Bible and Religion*, vol. 21, 1953.
———. *Ugaritic Literature.* Rome: Pontifical Biblical Institute, 1949.
———. *Ugaritic Textbook.* Rome: Pontifical Biblical Institute, 1965.
Graves, R. and Patai, R. *Hebrew Myths: The Book of Genesis.* New York: Doubleday, 1964.
Grossberg, D. "Number Harmony and Life Spans in the Bible," *Semitics*, vol. 9, 1984.
Guirand, F. *New Larrousse Encyclopedia of Mythology.* New York: Crown Publishers, 1968.
Haddawy, H. (trans.). *The Arabian Nights.* New York: W. W. Norton, 1990.
Heinemann, J. *Aggadah and its Development.* Jerusalem: Keter, 1974.
Heller, B. "Rahil," *Encyclopedia of Islam*, Leiden: E. J. Brill, vol. IV, 1913–1942.
———. "Yusuf," *Encyclopedia of Islam*, 1st ed., Leiden: E. J. Brill, 1960.
Hodgson, M. G. S. *The Venture of Islam.* 3 vols. Chicago: The University of Chicago Press, 1974.
Hollis, S. *The Tale of Two Brothers.* Norman: University of Oklahoma Press, 1990.
Horovitz, J. "Tawrat," *Encyclopedia of Islam*, 1st ed., Leiden: E. J. Brill, 1913–1942, vol. IV, 706.
Humphreys, W. L. "Novella," G. W. Coats (ed.), *Saga, Legend, Tale, Novella, Fable: Narrative Forms in Old Testament Literature. Journal for the Study of the Old Testament*, Supplement Series 35, 1985.
Irwin, R. *The Arabian Nights: A Companion.* London: Penguin, 1994.
Isbell, C. *Corpus of the Aramaic Incantation Bowls.* Society of Biblical Literature Dissertation Series no. 17, Missoula: Scholar's Press, 1975.
Israelit-Groll, Sarah, (ed.). *Pharaonic Egypt: The Bible and Christianity.* Jerusalem: The Magnes Press, The Hebrew University, 1985.
James T. G. H. "Egypt," *The Encyclopedia Brittanica*, 15th ed., vol. 18, 146.
Janssen, J. M. A., "Egyptological Remarks on the Story of Joseph in Genesis," *Ex Oriente Lux*, vol. 13, 1955.
Kadish, Gerald, E. "Eunichs in Ancient Egype." *Studies in Ancient Oriental Civilization* no. 35 (1969): 55–62.
Kasher, M. M. *Encyclopedia of Biblical Interpretation: Genesis*, New York: American Biblical Encyclopedia Society, 1953.

Katsh, A. *Judaism in Islam.* New York: New York University Press, 1954.

Keddie, Nikki R., and Beth Baron, (ed.). *Women in Middle Eastern History: Shifting Boundaries in Sex and Gender.* New Haven: Yale University Press, 1991.

Khawan, R., (ed. and trans.). *The Subtle Ruse: The Book of Arabic Wisdom and Guile.* Paris: Bibliotheque Nationale, Manuscript 3548. London: East West Books, 1980.

Kister, M. J. (ed.). *Jerusalem Studies in Arabic and Islam,* vol. 7. Jerusalem, Magnes Press, 1986.

Knappert, J. *Islamic Legends: Histories of the Heroes, Saints, and Prophets of Islam.* Leiden: Brill, 1985.

Kugel, J. *In Potiphar's House: The Interpretive Life of Biblical Text.* San Francisco, Harpers, 1990.

Lane, E. W. *An Account of the Manners and Customs of the Modern Egyptians.* London: John Murray, 1836.

———, trans. *The Thousand and One Nights: Or Arabian Nights' Entertainments.* 4 vols. London: George Bell and Sons, 1906.

Langdon, S. *Tammuz and Ishtar.* Oxford: Clarendon Press, 1914.

Lassner, J. *Demonizing the Queen of Sheba: Boundaries of Gender and Culture in Postbiblical Judaism and Medieval Islam.* Chicago: University of Chicago Press, 1993.

Lattimore, R., trans. *The Iliad.* Chicago: University of Chicago Press, 1962.

Lazarus-Yafeh, Hava. *Intertwined Worlds: Medieval Islam and Bible Criticism.* Princeton: Princeton University Press, 1992.

Lazarus-Yafeh, Hava. "Some Religious Aspects of Islam," *Judaism and Islam: Some Aspects of Mutual Cultural Influences,* Leiden: E. J. Brill, 1982.

Le Strange, F. *Palestine Under the Moslems.* Beirut: Khayats, 1965.

Leibowitz, N. *Studies in Bereshit.* Jerusalem: The World Zionist Organization, 1974.

Lewis, B. *The Jews of Islam.* Princeton: Princeton University Press, 1984.

Lichtenstadter, I. "Origin and Interpretation of Some Koranic Symbols," G. Makdisi (ed.), *H. A. R. Gibb. Volume (Arabic and Islamic Studies),* Harvard University Press, 1965, 426–436.

Lichtheim, M. *Ancient Egyptian Literature.* 3 vols. Berkeley: University of California Press, 1976.

Lings, M. *Muhammad: His Life Based on the Earliest Sources.* New York: Inner Traditions International, 1983.

Lowenstein, Eric I. *The Joseph Narrative in Genesis.* New York: Ktav Publishing House, 1973.

Luthi, Max. *The Fairytale as Art Form and Portrait of Man.* Bloomington: Indiana University Press, 1987.

Macdonald D. B. *The Religious Attitude and Life in Islam.* Chicago: The University of Chicago Press, 1909.

Macdonald, J. "Joseph in the Koran and Muslim Commentary," *The Muslim World,* 1956, 4:113–31, 207–24.

Makdisi, George, (ed.). *Arabic and Islamic Studies in Honor of Hamilton A. R. Gibb.* Cambridge: Harvard University Press, 1965.

Malti-Douglas, F. *Woman's Body, Woman's Word: Gender and Discourse in Arabo-Islamic Writing.* Princeton: Princeton University Press, 1991.

Martin, Richard C. *Structural Analysis and the Qur'ān: Newer Approaches to Islamic Texts*, Journal of the American Academy of Religion Thematic Issue, vol. XLVII, no. 4 S (Chico, California: December, 1979), 649–64.

Meyer, E. *Geschichte des Altertums*. Stuttgart: J. G. Cottasche, 1934.

Montgomery, J. A. *Aramaic Incantation Texts from Nippur*. Philadelphia: University Museum, 1913.

——. *The Samaritans*. Philadelphia: J. C. Winston, 1907.

Montgomery, Watt, W. *Bell's Introduction to the Qur'ān*. Edinburgh: The University Press, 1970.

Moreen, Vera. "Persecution of Iranian Jews During the Reign of Shah Abbas II," *Hebrew Union College Annual*, 1984.

Mussies, G. "The Interpretatio Judaica of Serapis," *Studies in Hellenic Religions*, M. J. Vermasern (ed.), Leiden: E. J. Brill, 1979.

Netton, N. "Miracle and Magic in the Rihla of Ibn Battuta," *Journal of Semitic Studies*, Spring 1984, 29.

Neusner, J., Frerichs, E., and Flesher, P. (eds.). *Religion, Science, and Magic: in Concert and in Conflict*. Oxford: Oxford University Press, 1989.

Newby, G. D. *The Development of Qur'ān Commentary in Early Islam in its Relationship to Judaeo-Christian Traditions of Scriptural Commentary*, Journal of the American Academy of Religion Thematic Issue, vol. XLVII, no. 4 S (Chico, California: December, 1980), 697–97.

——. *A History of the Jews of Arabia: From Ancient Times to Their Eclipse Under Islam*. Columbia: University of South Carolina Press, 1988.

——. *The Making of the Last Prophet*. Columbia: University of South Carolina Press, 1989.

Nicholson, Reynold A. *The Mystics of Islam*. London and Boston: Routledge and Kegan Paul, 1965.

Niditch, S. *Folklore and the Hebrew Bible*. Minneapolis, Fortress Press, 1993.

Niehoff, M. *The Figure of Joseph in Post-Biblical Jewish Literature*. Leiden: Brill, 1992.

Noldeke, T. and Schwally F. *Geschichte des Qorans*. Leipzig: Dietrichschen Buchhandlung, 1909–1938.

Noy, D. "Evil Eye," *Encyclopedia Judaic*, 1972 ed., 6, 998–1000.

——. "Folklore, " *Encyclopedia Judaica*, 1972 ed., 6, 1377–79.

——. "Motif-Index of Talmudic-Midrashic Literature," unpublished dissertation for the Ph.D., Indiana University, 1954.

Payne, John. *The Book of the Thousand Nights and One Night*. 9 vols. New York: R. Worthington, 1884–1885.

Perlmann, Moshe. *Ibn Kammuna's Examination of the Three Faiths*. Berkeley: University of California Press, 1971.

Peters, F. E. *Judaism, Christianity and Islam: The Classical Texts and their Interpretation*. Princeton: Princeton University Press, 1990.

Pfeiffer, R. *Introduction to the Old Testament*. New York: Harper Brothers, 1941.

Pinault, D. *Story-Telling Techniques in the Arabian Nights*. Leiden: E. J. Brill, 1992.

Pope, M. trans. *The Anchor Bible: Song of Songs*. New York: Doubleday, 1977.

Preschel, T. "Ibn Ezra as Commentator of the Bible," *Encyclopedia Judaica*, 1972 ed., 8, 1166–68.

Pritchard, J. (ed.). *Ancient Near Eastern Texts Relating to the Old Testament*. Princeton: Princeton University Press, 1950.

Rahman, F. *Major Themes in the Qur'ān.* Chicago: Bibliotheca Islamica, 1980.

Rank, Otto, Lord Raglan, and Alan Dundes. *In Quest of the Hero.* Princeton: Princeton University Press, 1990.

Redford, D. *Akhenaten.* Princeton: Princeton University Press, 1984.

———. *A Study of the Biblical Story of Joseph.* Supplements to Vetus Testamentum, Vol. XX, Leiden: E. J. Brill, 1970.

Rendsburg, Gary A. *The Redaction of Genesis.* Winona Lake, Indiana: Eisenbrauns, 1986.

Rippin, Andrew, (ed.). *Approaches to the History of the Interpretation of the Qur'ān.* Oxford: Clarendon Press, 1988.

Rosenthal, Franz, trans. *The History of al-Tabari Volume I: General Introduction and from the Creation to the Flood.* Albany: State University of New York Press, 1989.

Rubenstein, R. *The Religious Imagination: A Study in Psychoanalysis and Jewish Theology.* Brown Classics in Judaica: New York, 1985.

Sarna, N. M. "Joseph," *Encyclopedia Judaica,* 1972 ed., 10, 210–18.

———. *Understanding Genesis.* New York: The Jewish Theological Seminary of America, 1966.

Sasson, J. M. *Ruth, A New Translation with a Philological Commentary and a Formalist-Folklorist Interpretation.* Baltimore: Johns Hopkins University Press, 1979.

Schapiro, I. *Die haggadischen Elemente im erzahlenden Teil des Korans.* Berlin: Itzkowski, 1907.

Schwarzbaum, H. *Biblical and Extra-Biblical Legends in Islamic Folk Literature.* Waldorf-Hessen: Verlagtur Orientkunde, 1982.

———. *Studies in Jewish and World Folklore.* Berlin: De Gruyter, 1968.

———. "Jewish, Christian, and Moslem Legends of the Death of Aaron the High Priest," *Fabula,* V.

Scott, J. and P. Simpson-Housley (eds.), *Sacred Places and Profane Spaces: Essays in the Geographics of Judaism, Christianity, and Islam.* New York: Greenwood Press, 1991.

Seguy, M. *The Miraculous Journey of Mohamet: Miraj Nameh.* Paris: Bibliotheque Nationale. Manuscript Supplement Turc 190, plate #16; New York: Braziller, 1977.

Seligsogn, Max. "Joseph," *The Jewish Encyclopedia,* 1904 ed., 7, 250.

Silberman, Neil Asher. *Between Past and Present: Archaeology, Ideology, and Nationalism in the Modern Middle East.* New York: Holt, 1989.

Spanel, D. *Through Egyptian Eyes: Egyptian Portraiture.* Seattle: University of Washington, 1988.

Spanier, K. "Aspects of Fratriarchy in the Old Testament," Ph.D. dissertation, New York University, 1989.

Speiser, E. A., trans. *The Anchor Bible: Genesis.* New York: Doubleday and Co., 1964.

Steindorff G. and Seele, K. C. *When Egypt Ruled the East.* Chicago: The University of Chicago Press, 1957.

Stern, S. M. "Muhammad and Joseph: A Study of Koranic Narrative," *Journal of Near Eastern Studies,* 1985, 44:3, 193.

Stillman, N. *The Jews of Arab Lands: A History and Source Book.* Philadelphia: Jewish Publication Society, 1979.

Swartz, Merlin L., trans. *Studies on Islam.* New York: Oxford University Press, 1981.

Thackston, W. M., Jr. *The Tales of the Prophets of al-Kisa'i.* Boston: Twayne Publishers, 1978.

Thompson, Stith. *Motif-Index of Folk Literature.* Bloomington: The University of Indiana Press, 1955.

Trachenberg, J. *Jewish Magic and Superstition: A Study in Folk Religion.* New York: Antheneum, 1979.

Trotti, J. B. *Beauty in the Old Testament.* Ph.D. dissertation, Yale University, 1964.

Van Seters, J. *Prologue to History: The Yahwist as Historian in Genesis.* Louisville, Westminster: John Knox Press, 1992.

Vergote, J. *Joseph en Egypte.* Louvain: Universite Catholique, 1959.

Von Rad, G. *Genesis: A Commentary.* Philadelphia: The Westminster Press, 1961.

von Gruenbaum, Gustave E. *Medieval Islam: A Study in Cultural Orientation.* Chicago: The University of Chicago Press, 1956.

Waldman, Marilyn Robinson. *New Approaches to "Biblical" Materials in the Qur'ān.* The Muslim World, vol. LXXV. no. 1 (The Duncan Black Macdonald Center at Hartford Seminary, Hartford, Conn.: January, 1985), 1–16.

Watt, W. Montgomery. *Bell's Introduction to the Qur'ān.* Edinburgh: Edinburgh University Press, 1970.

——. *Conversion in Islam at the Time of the Prophet,* Journal of the American Academy of Religion Thematic Issue, vol. XLVII, no. 4 S (Chico, California: December, 1980), 721–731.

——. *What is Islam?* New York: Frederick A. Praeger, 1968.

Williams, J. G. "Number Symbolism and Joseph as Symbol of Completion," *Journal of Biblical Literature,* 1979.

Wintermute, O. S. "Joseph," *The Interpreter's Dictionary of the Bible,* New York: Abingdom Press, 1962.

Wright, G. E. *Shechem.* New York: McGraw-Hill, 1965.

Wright, G. R. "Joseph's Grave," *Vetus Testamentum,* 1972, XXII.

Yahuda, A. S. *The Accuracy of the Bible.* London: Heinemann, 1934.

——. *The Language of the Pentateuch in its Relation to Egyptian.* Oxford: Oxford University Press, 1933.

Yamauchi, E. M. *Mandaic Incantation Texts.* New Haven: American Oriental Society, 1967.

Yohannan, John D. *Joseph and Potiphar's Wife in World Literature.* Norfolk: New Directions, 1968.

Yourcenar, M. *The Dark Brain of Piranesi, and Other Essays.* Trans. Richard Howard. New York: Farrar, Straus, Girous, 1985.

Zakovitch, Y. and A. Shinan. *The Story of Judah and Tamar* (Heb.). Jerusalem: The Institute for Jewish Studies at the Hebrew University, 1991.

Index

"People of the Book," xvi, 16, 18
Pharaoh's cup, 25
Philology, comparative, xv, xvii
Pilgrimages
 Joseph's tomb as place of, 130, 147
 of Persian Jews, 115
Pirke De R. Eliezer, 106
Poetry, in Joseph story, 8
Politics
 Arab–Israeli conflict, xvi, 142
 Biblical allusions in, xvi,
  149–150n.12
 Middle East, 142
 sexual, xviii
Potiphar
 Asenath as daughter of, 107
 in Biblical text, xxiii, xxiv
 as court eunuch, 41, 84, 86
 role in Joseph narrative, ix
 sexual preference of, 84, 156n.32
Potiphar's wife, 102. *See also*
  Zuleikha
 Asenath adopted by, 107–108
 in Biblical narrative, 2
 characteristics of, 94–95
 innocence of, 100
 and Kharijite ideology, 19
 name of, 85, 156n.14
 repentance of, 86, 116, 118
 and society's norms, 76
 symbolism of, 138
 sympathy for, xix
Potiphar's Wife motif, x, xx
 Ancient Egyptian treatment of,
  149n.2
 Ancient Near Eastern background
  of, 31–37
 banishment in, 34
 comparative study of, 33
 development of, 54, 80
 feminist critique of, 156n.12
 in Islamic folklore, 53
 in Jewish midrashim, 37–42
 links to Joseph of, 116
 "Mediterranean model" of, 28
 mirmah/kayd in, 49–50
 in Qur'ān, 42–46
 in *The Thousand and One Nights*,
  51, 52, 147
 in 20th–century literature, 28

Prayer of Asenath, The, 108, 110
Primogeniture, law of, 101
Proitos, in Iliad, xxix–xxx
Prophet, Joseph as, 20
Proverbs, dominant theme of, 37

Qadr (predestination), doctrine of, 44
Qiṣaṣ al-anbiyā. See "Tales of the
  Prophets"
Qitfir, 85, 156, 161n.27. *See also*
  Potiphar
Qur'ān
 commentaries on, xi, 74
 foundation of, xi
 Joseph narrative in, x, xi, xii, xx,
  xxv–xxvi, 7–14, 46
 Joseph's beauty in, 89
 Joseph's thievery in, 96
 kayd in, 48
 literary nature of, 8
 Potiphar's wife in, 42–46
 Potiphar's Wife motif in, 31
 Samaritan influence on, 128
 Sūrat Yūsuf in, 145
 Twelfth Sura of, xi, 7 (*see also*
  Sūrat Yūsuf)
 "women of the city" in, 102
Qur'ānic narrative, validity of, 17

Rabbinic literature, xv, 70
Rachel (Joseph's mother), 49, 81, 84,
  90, 134–135
 beauty of, 95
 burial of, 97–98, 127
 characteristics of, 94–95
 premature death of, 97
 teraphim stolen by, 93, 96
 tomb of, 142
Ra'il, 38, 81, 85, 95. *See also*
  Potiphar's wife
Rashi, 40, 66, 72, 97, 99
Ravnitsky, Y. H., 86
Razi, 10
Rebecca, 93
Redaction of Genesis, The
  (Rendsburg), 5
Redford, Donald, 2, 57, 71
Red Sea, splitting of, 6